THE ORIGIN OF HUMANITY AND EVOLUTION

THE ORIGIN OF HUMANITY AND EVOLUTION

Science and Scripture in Conversation

Andrew Ter Ern Loke

LONDON • NEW YORK • OXFORD • NEW DELHI • SYDNEY

T&T CLARK
Bloomsbury Publishing Plc
50 Bedford Square, London, WC1B 3DP, UK
1385 Broadway, New York, NY 10018, USA
29 Earlsfort Terrace, Dublin 2, Ireland

BLOOMSBURY, T&T CLARK and the T&T Clark logo are trademarks of Bloomsbury Publishing Plc

First published in Great Britain 2022
Paperback edition published 2024

Copyright © Andrew Ter Ern Loke, 2022

Andrew Ter Ern Loke has asserted his right under the Copyright, Designs and Patents Act, 1988, to be identified as Author of this work.

For legal purposes the Acknowledgements on p. viii constitute an extension of this copyright page.

Cover images: Science Picture Co (above) and Wavebreak Media Ltd (below) / Alamy Stock Photo

All rights reserved. No part of this publication may be reproduced or transmitted in any form or by any means, electronic or mechanical, including photocopying, recording, or any information storage or retrieval system, without prior permission in writing from the publishers.

Bloomsbury Publishing Plc does not have any control over, or responsibility for, any third-party websites referred to or in this book. All internet addresses given in this book were correct at the time of going to press. The author and publisher regret any inconvenience caused if addresses have changed or sites have ceased to exist, but can accept no responsibility for any such changes.

A catalogue record for this book is available from the British Library.

Library of Congress Cataloging-in-Publication Data

Names: Loke, Andrew Ter Ern, author.
Title: The origin of humanity and evolution : science and scripture in conversation / Andrew Ter Ern Loke.
Description: London ; New York : T&T Clark, 2022. | Includes bibliographical references and index. |
Identifiers: LCCN 2021060956 (print) | LCCN 2021060957 (ebook) | ISBN 9780567706355 (hb) | ISBN 9780567706409 (paperback) | ISBN 9780567706362 (epdf) | ISBN 9780567706393 (epub)
Subjects: LCSH: Bible and evolution. | Evolution (Biology)–Religious aspects–Christianity. | Religion and science–Methodology.
Classification: LCC BS659 .L65 2022 (print) | LCC BS659 (ebook) | DDC 231.7/652–dc23/eng/20220506
LC record available at https://lccn.loc.gov/2021060956
LC ebook record available at https://lccn.loc.gov/2021060957

ISBN: HB: 978-0-5677-0635-5
PB: 978-0-5677-0640-9
ePDF: 978-0-5677-0636-2
ePUB: 978-0-5677-0639-3

Typeset by Deanta Global Publishing Services, Chennai, India

To find out more about our authors and books visit www.bloomsbury.com and sign up for our newsletters.

For Joshua Swamidass

CONTENTS

Acknowledgements	viii
Chapter 1 A TRANSDISCIPLINARY APPROACH CONCERNING HUMAN ORIGINS	1
Chapter 2 DIVINE ACCOMMODATION AND ITS IMPLICATIONS FOR BIBLICAL ANTHROPOLOGY	19
Chapter 3 THE TIME SPAN OF CREATION	33
Chapter 4 THE PROCESS OF EVOLUTIONARY CREATIONISM	67
Chapter 5 HUMAN EVOLUTION AND THE QUESTION OF ADAM	85
Chapter 6 THE TIME FRAME OF OUR COMMON ANCESTOR	129
Chapter 7 CONCLUSIONS AND IMPLICATIONS	153
Bibliography	159
Scripture Index	178
Subject Index	182

ACKNOWLEDGEMENTS

This book is transdisciplinary in nature, and I am grateful for the opportunity to interact with scholars from various disciplines. In particular, I would like to thank scientists Francis Collins, Denis Alexander, Mark Harris, Denis Lamoureux, philosophers William Lane Craig, Michael Ruse, Kwan Kai Man, historian of science Clinton Ohlers, biblical scholars John Walton, John Collins, Greg Beale, Richard Averbeck, and theologians Alister McGrath, Bethany Sollereder, Matthew Levering, Kenneth Keathley, Ray Yeo and Jonathan Johnson for helpful discussions on various aspects of my argument. I would also like to thank my research assistants Zhu Weida and Vincent Chan for their help with the Bibliography.

This book is dedicated to computational biologist Joshua Swamidass, who took the initiative to write to me in 2018 after discovering that I have been working on the origin of humanity and evolution (see p.112), and who has since helped me greatly in my work.

Hong Kong
October 2021

Chapter 1

A TRANSDISCIPLINARY APPROACH CONCERNING HUMAN ORIGINS

1.1 A defence of a transdisciplinary approach concerning human origins

1.1.1 Significance of the topic

The question of our origins has fascinated us from time immemorial. From ancient myths, philosophical writings, religious texts to modern science, many theories have been proposed to explain where we come from. There is no evidence that other species ever wrestled with this question as we do.

In our contemporary world, science and religion are two of the most significant influences shaping people's opinions concerning human origins. Modern science has undoubtedly helped us gain a better understanding of the natural world. On the other hand, religion has provided for billions of people worldwide their views concerning humanity's biggest questions, including the question of our origins and how this is related to vital issues such as the value and meaning of life. An understanding of the relationship between science and religion is therefore of great importance for understanding our world and the deep existential issues that concern our human race.

In recent years, there has been intense debate in science and religion in light of evolutionary population genetics, which indicates that the genetic diversity of the current *Homo sapiens* population requires that *Homo sapiens* descended from a large population (polygenism) (Yang 2002), rather than from a single pair (monogenism) as traditionally held by Christians, Judaists and Muslims. Polygenism had been brought into theological discussions earlier by Isaac La Peyrère in the seventeenth century following the 'discovery' of the New World with people living on the other side of the globe (antipodeans) (Livingstone 2008). It was rejected by the Roman Catholic Church because it denied the universal descent of humankind from Adam and Eve (*Humani Generis*, 1950). However, as a result of the findings of population genetics, many contemporary theologians, philosophers and scientists have called for a re-evaluation of the Scriptural account of human origins (e.g. Cole-Turner 2016, 2020; Ruse 2017; Venema and McKnight 2016). Many others have resisted their call on exegetical and theological grounds

(Riches 2017; Halton ed. 2015), but offered no good response to the objections. Among Christians, those who resisted include not only American Evangelicals and Fundamentalists but also Christians of other stripes (e.g. Roman Catholics and Eastern Orthodox Christians) around the world (see Chapter 2). The debate has generated significant global public interest, with well-known atheist biologist Jerry Coyne (2011) calling it 'the ultimate standoff between science and faith'.

This book fills a gap in the literature by addressing the above-mentioned issues using a transdisciplinary approach, that is, one which integrates different disciplines (in this case, involving philosophy of religion, natural sciences, social sciences, historical-critical biblical studies and theology) to create a new methodology that moves beyond discipline-specific approaches to address a problem. The difference between Multidisciplinary, Interdisciplinary and Transdisciplinary is as follows: 'Multidisciplinarity draws on knowledge from different disciplines but stays within their boundaries. Interdisciplinarity analyzes, synthesizes and harmonizes links between disciplines into a coordinated and coherent whole. Transdisciplinarity integrates the natural, social and health sciences in a humanities context, and transcends their traditional boundaries.'[1] My work fits the last category. It engages with contemporary science while it also advances theological conclusions that are rooted in classical Christian traditions. Specifically, my work utilizes ancient and biblically grounded theological views to formulate a new model of human origins which addresses the apparent conflict between the historicity of Adam and the theory of evolution (including evolutionary population genetics).[2] This model shows that all humans today could have a common ancestor (Adam) even though they descended from a large population of anatomical *Homo* as indicated by population genetics.

To elaborate, I reply to the objections to monogenesis using a unique variant of the Genealogical Adam and Eve (GAE) model which responds to more recent criticisms against the model (e.g. Houck 2020). My model draws on the important recent work on this model by Joshua Swamidass (2018; 2019; though my variation of the model differs from his in some respects; see Loke 2020b),[3]

---

1. https://pubmed.ncbi.nlm.nih.gov/17330451/#:~:text=The%20terms%20multi disciplinary%2C%20interdisciplinary%20and,ambiguously%20defined%20and %20interchangeably%20used.&text=Interdisciplinarity%20analyzes%2C%20synthesizes %20and%20harmonizes,a%20coordinated%20and%20coherent%20whole.

2. In this book, 'evolution' is used to refer to the process, involving the mechanisms of genetic mutation and natural selection, by which the present diversity of plant and animal life arose from a common ancestor. Such a definition does not exclude the possibility that God used this process to create various life forms (whether this view is compatible with Christian Scripture will be discussed in the rest of this book). Compare with Naturalistic Evolution (= atheistic evolution), which denies that there is a God who used this process to create various life forms.

3. Another important recent contribution is Craig (2021). I engage with Craig's work in Loke (Forthcoming).

the biblical exegetical work of Walton (2009, 2015) and Collins (2018) and recent philosophical theological literature on humans as embodied souls (e.g. Visala 2014; Farris 2016b; Loose ed. 2018). It also builds on an earlier paper in which I distinguish between Task (A) 'interpreting the Bible', Task (B) 'showing that the Biblical account is true' and Task (C) 'showing that there is no incompatibility between human evolution and Bible' (Loke 2016). For (A), one would ask for evidences for what the human biblical authors had in mind, but for (C) it is perfectly legitimate to suggest a possible model which the biblical authors may not have thought of, as long as the possibility is not contradictory to what they stated. I develop such a possible model which distinguishes between 'anatomical *Homo* which possessed the image of God' (God's-Image-Bearer, Adam being the first of these) and anatomical *Homo* which did not possess the image of God. By associating the image of God with Divine election for royal function (Moritz 2011b) and the associated capacities, I propose that God could have chosen a preexisting anatomical *Homo* and made that organism a human being (i.e. a God's-Image-Bearer) in a localized environment (the Garden of Eden). After the Fall, the image of God was passed down from this person (Adam) to his descendants some of whom procreated with non-imago-Dei-*Homo* outside the Garden. Their descendants were fully human, while non-imago-Dei-*Homo* contributed to the genetic diversity. In this way, all humans today could have a common ancestor even though this ancestor is not our sole ancestor. This conclusion is consistent with evolutionary population genetics, and with scientific studies published in the pre-eminent science journal *Nature* which have shown that all human beings today are very likely to have had a very recent common ancestor even if substantial forms of population subdivision existed with a very low rate of migration (Rohde, Olson and Chang 2004; Hein 2004). By tying various strands of arguments in recent discussions with this model, this book makes an original and significant contribution to scholarly debates on the origin of humanity which is important to both secular and religious scholars.

In addition, this book provides a comprehensive assessment of alternative proposals and engages with the arguments of scholars from a wide variety of world views, including

- Atheists/Agnostics: for example, Michael Ruse, David Christian, Richard Dawkins, Yuval Harari, Jason Rosenhouse, Jerry Coyne, Othmar Keel.
- Judaists: for example, Nahum Sarna.
- Roman Catholics: for example, John Haught, Gerald O'Collins, Pierre Teilhard de Chardin, Aaron Riches, Pope Pius XII.
- Mainline Protestants: for example, Rowan Williams, Ian McFarland, J. Wentzel van Huyssteen, Christopher Southgate, David Clough, Joshua Moritz, Cole-Turner, John Day, Daniel Harlow, Claus Westermann.
- Eastern Orthodox Christians: for example, David Bentley Hart, George Nicozisin.
- Evangelical Christians.

The last group deserves special mention. Despite the enormous efforts of science educators, the resistance of many (though not all) Evangelical Christians[4] towards mainstream scientific theories such as evolution has spread globally (Numbers 2006). One reason is that many academic writings have failed to adequately understand and engage with the detailed Scriptural reasoning and motivation that undergird their view. Given that the Bible is of central importance to the faith of Christians worldwide, these scientific theories are unlikely to find widespread acceptance among Christians (not only Evangelicals but also many Roman Catholics and Eastern Orthodox Christians) unless their concerns with regard to the compatibility of these theories with the Bible are seriously considered and adequately addressed. This book will help the wider academic world understand the motivations for these concerns and why the enormous efforts of those science educators have failed. It will provide a better way forward by addressing these concerns regarding science and the Bible and offer a systematic response to their theological objections in an academically responsible manner. Given that this subgroup of Evangelicals are the ones who have raised the strongest objections to evolutionary science among Christian groups today and that this has been a major obstacle for conversations between Science and Christianity, the removal of an important aspect of this obstacle is another significant contribution of this book. It should, however, be emphasized that the debate concerning monogenism is of great interest not only to Evangelicals but also to Roman Catholics (e.g. Pope Pius XII, *Humani Generis* 1950; Riches 2017), Eastern Orthodox Christians (e.g. Nicozisin 2017), Mainline Protestants (e.g. Cole-Turner 2016, 2020), Atheists and Agnostics (e.g. Ruse 2017), as well as Judaists and Muslims. Much of my book engages with the views of scholars from these wide variety of religious traditions and different world views, and thus my book would be of interest and a resource for these audiences as well.

1.2 On the use of a transdisciplinary approach

With regard to my use of a transdisciplinary approach to address the Big Question concerning our origins, proponents of scientism might object by claiming that science[5] is the only way for understanding the nature of reality. On the other hand,

---

4. 'Evangelical Christians' are hard to characterize nowadays. While many hold to the inerrancy of the Bible in its entirety (as affirmed, for example, by the Evangelical Theological Society), a number of 'Evangelicals' whom I interact with in this book (e.g. Denis Lamoureux, Denis Venema, Scot McKnight) do not, in fact, think that the Bible is inerrant with respect to scientific affirmations. Many of their arguments are similar to those used by secular academics who argue that there are scientific errors in the Bible.

5. In a helpful article, Mikael Stenmark (1997) discusses various forms of scientism and observes that, while the word 'science' has a variety of meanings, 'what is characteristic of

radical postmodernists would be sceptical about what science can tell us and whether such Big Questions can in principle be answered.

Scientism, however, is susceptible to the objection that scientism cannot be proven by science itself, and that its advocates 'rely in their argument not merely on scientific but also on philosophical premises' (Stenmark 2003, pp. 783–5). Moreover, the scientific method itself requires various forms of philosophical reasoning, such as deductive and inductive reasoning, for the development of its explanations. Additionally, science itself cannot answer the question 'why scientific results should be valued'; the answer to this question is philosophical rather than scientific. With respect to the criteria for a good scientific theory, cosmologist George Ellis observes the following four areas of assessment:

1. Satisfactory structure: (a) internal consistency, (b) simplicity (Ockham's razor) and (c) aesthetic appeal ('beauty' or 'elegance');
2. Intrinsic explanatory power: (a) logical tightness, (b) scope of the theory – the ability to unify otherwise separate phenomena and (c) probability of the theory or model with respect to some well-defined measure;
3. Extrinsic explanatory power, or relatedness: (a) connectedness to the rest of science, (b) extendability – providing a basis for further development;
4. Observational and experimental support, in terms of (a) testability: the ability to make quantitative as well as qualitative predictions that can be tested and (b) confirmation: the extent to which the theory is supported by such tests as have been made.

Ellis acknowledges the importance of philosophy for these criteria, noting that

'These criteria are philosophical in nature in that they themselves cannot be proven to be correct by any experiment. Rather their choice is based on past experience combined with philosophical reflection' (Ellis 2007, Section 8.1).

On the other hand, the hyper-scepticism of radical postmodernists towards science is unwarranted. Various examples of scientific theories indicate that we can discover many details about reality, including the 'unobservable causes' of phenomena (Swinburne 2005, p. 39; for responses to radical postmodernism, see further, Loke 2017a, Chapter 1). The National Academy of Sciences (2008) notes:

Many scientific theories are so well-established that no new evidence is likely to alter them substantially. For example, no new evidence will demonstrate that the Earth does not orbit around the sun (heliocentric theory), or that living

scientism is that it works with a narrow definition of science . . . the advocates of scientism use the notion of science to cover only the natural sciences and perhaps also those areas of the social sciences that are highly similar in methodology to the natural sciences' (p. 20). Such a methodology typically involves a systematic study using observation and experimentation.

things are not made of cells (cell theory), that matter is not composed of atoms, or that the surface of the Earth is not divided into solid plates that have moved over geological timescales (the theory of plate tectonics).

Building on this, I have argued in Loke (2017a, 2022a,) that the conclusions of those philosophical arguments (e.g. the argument for a Divine First Cause) which can yield answers that are more epistemically certain than scientific discoveries should be regarded as knowledge about reality on at least the same level as scientific facts. While science is a way of knowing, philosophy is another way of knowing. Against reductionism, there is a need to bring together different disciplines that would complement one another in our attempt to gain a fuller understanding of reality, in particular the complex phenomenon concerning human origins. Professor David Christian, the pioneer of 'Big History', a popular interdisciplinary course offered by universities internationally which studies the past across physics, astronomy, geology, biology and human history, observes that there is 'a growing sense, across many scholarly disciplines, that we need to move beyond the fragmented account of reality that has dominated scholarship (and served it well) for a century' (2011, p. 3), and that

> There is also a growing need for specialization to be supplemented by integration. The reason is that no complex, nonlinear system can be adequately described by dividing it up into subsystems or into various aspects, defined beforehand. If those subsystems or those aspects, all in strong interaction with one another, are studied separately, even with great care, the results, when put together, do not give a useful picture of the whole. In that sense, there is profound truth in the old adage, 'The whole is more than the sum of its parts'. (pp. 3–4)

For a Christian who thinks that there are reasons to believe that the Bible is divinely inspired (Habermas 2003, chapter 10), he/she would argue that the issue of human origins cannot be reduced to what biology tells us (important as it is), that science and philosophy needs to be complemented by theology as well, and that the relationships (including the compatibility) between the views of these disciplines would need to be examined.

Against this, some scientists have argued for a compartmentalization between science and religion, claiming that science concerns the empirical universe while religion concerns morality (e.g. the Non-Overlapping Magisteria advocated in Stephen Jay Gould 2002). However, others have objected that the Christian doctrine of creation implies an unavoidable and significant overlap, and that science and religion should converse with each other (Collins 2006, McGrath 2016). Scholars have noted that many prominent scientists who contributed to the rise of modern science were motivated by their Christian beliefs, such as the belief that an intelligent God who inspired the Scripture also created a natural order which can be understood by intelligent human beings made in the image of God (Harrison

1998; Stump 2016, chapter 2). Many popular beliefs about how Christianity has supposedly hindered the rise of modern science which have been propagated by vociferous biologist Jerry Coyne and others are based on misconceptions (Berezow and Hannam 2013). A well-documented study (Giberson and Artigas 2007) shows that a number of atheist popularizers of science such as Richard Dawkins and Stephen Hawking have persisted in creating a widespread but false impression that science as a whole is incompatible with religion, and they have repeatedly ignored critics who have pointed out their ignorance about religion and philosophy. Large-scale surveys among contemporary scientists reveal a more nuanced picture, with a significant number of scientists being open to science-and-religion dialogue (Ecklund 2010). Cosmologist William Stoeger offers an account of how science, philosophy and theology might complement one another with regard to the issue of ultimate origins:

> Physics and cosmology as sciences are incapable of exploring or directly accounting for the ultimate source of existence and order which philosophy and theology, properly understood, provide. By the same token, philosophy and theology are not equipped to investigate and describe the processes and relationships which contributed to the expansion, cooling and subsequent structuring of the universe on macroscopic and on microscopic scales. Thus, philosophy and theology seek to provide an understanding of the origin and evolution of the universe which is complementary to that which physics and cosmology contribute. (Stoeger 2010, p. 174)

In this book, I shall offer an account of how science, philosophy and theology might complement one another with regard to the issue of human origin.

1.3 On Concordism

It may be asked whether an attempt to demonstrate the compatibility between science and theology would result in Concordism. Alexander (2017a) calls Concordism a 'dreaded accusation' because it has become somewhat pejorative in recent texts on this topic. Alexander (2017b) notes, however, that there are different definitions of Concordism, and they should be evaluated separately to see if the pejoration is justified. Ted Davis (2012) observes that, while Concordism has been used sparingly in English for more than a century, its rise to prominence came after theologian Bernard Ramm used it in his book *The Christian View of Science and Scripture* (1954). Ramm understood Concordism as an attempt to seek harmony between mainstream science and the Bible. While Young Earth Creationists (YEC) also attempt to seek harmony between science and the Bible, Ramm thinks that they do so by rejecting the well-established standard geologic record accepted by mainstream science, and thus is not regarded as Concordist. A core tenet of Concordism is that since God is the author of the 'book' of nature and the book of Scripture, they must agree when properly interpreted (Davis 2012). While the term has a fairly recent history, the tenet is by no means new; similar ideas can be found in earlier theological writings (see Chapter 2).

In a helpful article, Alexander (2017b) distinguishes between three ways of seeking harmony.

Concordism Type A seeks to extract modern scientific information from scriptural passages, such as claiming that Big Bang cosmology can be inferred from biblical verses in an attempt to prove that 'The Bible taught it first!' Alexander observes that 'such an approach is very common in the Muslim community with respect to the *Qu'ran* where it is known as *I'jaz 'ilmiy* ("miraculous scientific content") theory (Guessoum 2011). For example, it is maintained that the speed of light can be calculated from *Qu'ranic* verses, and that other passages reveal the genetic code and the second law of thermodynamics.'

Concordism Type B seeks to interpret scriptural texts in the light of modern science. Concerning Genesis 1, Alexander lists gap theories and day-age theories as attempts to 'impose a scientific understanding on the Genesis text that supposedly bring it into harmony with the geological record'.

Types A and B reflect the common understanding of the term 'Concordism' among many scholars. For example, Venema and McKnight (2017, p. 215) describe Concordism as 'a way of reading/interpreting Genesis that is in concord with science as we know it now, thereby granting to the Bible knowledge of science transcending its historical context'. Ross (2012) defines his view as Concordist; it seeks 'agreement between properly interpreted Scripture passages that describe some aspect of the natural realm and indisputably and well-established data in science'. He states that 'the Bible taught the fundamentals of big bang cosmology (cosmic beginning including a beginning of space, time, matter, and energy; cosmic expansion, and constant physical laws including a pervasive law of decay) not in a mystical or subtle way but explicitly and repeatedly'.[6]

The problem with Concordism Type A is that in every purported case either

1. 'The supposed derivation of scientific insights from religious texts occurs only after the scientific discovery in question, not before' (Alexander 2017),
2. There was a range of possible interpretations and views and the proponents merely pick and choose the one that fits our current understanding of science; the above considerations make it dubious whether the Bible or Quran really 'taught it first'; it is more likely that Type A Concordists are guilty of reading meanings into vague texts which can have alternative interpretations, or

---

6. Cf. Brown (2010, p. 56), who writes 'The theory of the Big Bang does not explain the origin of the cosmos but accounts for its evolution a fraction of a second after time zero (10^{-43} seconds), prior to which the laws of general relativity break down. Similarly, the first verse of the Bible begins not at the absolute beginning of creation'.

3. Similar scientific ideas were already previously known (e.g. to the ancient Greeks).

Wielandt (2002) observes that the scientific method of interpretation did not find general approval among Muslim scholars who object that it is lexicographically untenable as it falsely attributes modern meanings to the *qurʾānic* vocabulary, and that it neglects the contexts of words or phrases within the *qurʾānic* text.

Against Concordism Type A and B, Alexander argues that it is unhelpful to impose modern scientific meanings onto texts that were never intended to bear such a weight (Alexander 2017a). To interpret any text properly, one should follow hermeneutical principles such as considering the literary genre, literary context, meaning of words, grammatical relationship and the background and concerns of the authors (historical, cultural and theological). Now, I am not claiming that proper hermeneutical principles always lead to a singular correct interpretation of the text. On the contrary, in Chapter 3, I defend a *variety* of (rather than a singular) plausible interpretations of Genesis 1. Nevertheless, while I agree that texts are open to multiple interpretations, it is not the case that all interpretations are equally plausible. Some interpretations are more plausible than others because they are better supported by the evidences related to those hermeneutical principles (e.g. evidence of detailed word studies), and in certain cases there is only one plausible interpretation.

The applicability of the above-mentioned principles to Scripture is widely recognized not only by Protestant scholars (e.g. Klein, Blomberg and Hubbard 2017; Thiselton 2006) but others as well. For example, Pope Pius XII observes that

> What is the literal sense of a passage is not always as obvious in the speeches and writings of the ancient authors of the East, as it is in the works of our own time. For what they wished to express is not to be determined by the rules of grammar and philology alone, nor solely by the context; the interpreter must, as it were, go back wholly in spirit to those remote centuries of the East and with the aid of history, archaeology, ethnology, and other sciences, accurately determine what modes of writing, so to speak, the authors of that ancient period would be likely to use, and in fact did use. (*Divino Afflante Spiritu* 35–6)

The biblical authors obviously have to use ways of expression common to their era in order to be understandable to their audience. Against those who expect a divinely inspired Scripture to reveal modern scientific explanations ahead of time, Lennox (2011, p. 30) writes,

> Suppose, for instance, that God had intended to explain the origin of the universe and life to us in detailed scientific language. Science is constantly changing, developing. . . . If the biblical explanation were at the level, say, of twenty-second-century science, it would likely be unintelligible to everyone, including scientists today. . . . Rather than scientific language, the Bible often

uses what is called phenomenological language – the language of appearance. It describes what anyone can see.

While Lennox does not think that the Bible contains modern scientific explanations, he does argue that numerous passages in the Old and New Testaments imply certain conclusions about the physical world (e.g. the beginning of the cosmos) and that these conclusions are also well supported by scientific evidences (Lennox 2011; see also the discussion of William Brown's argument in what follows).

Alexander (2017b) advocates Concordism Type C (also known as 'soft concordism' in the literature), which affirms that the Bible should be interpreted according to proper hermeneutical principles such as taking into consideration its ancient Near East context and literary genre, rather than according to modern science. Rather, it acknowledges science and theology to have their own integrity as methods of enquiry to construct their own models of reality without mutual interference, and having completed that process, it proceeds to see what types of concord or discord there may be between these two forms of knowledge, and how both of them may inform our understanding of the past by complementing each other. Type C rejects the Non-Overlapping Magisteria model of science and religion advocated by Stephen Jay Gould (2002), and affirms the possibility that God can reveal truths in both nature and scripture which overlap but do not contradict.

Alexander notes that Concordism Type C is typical of much of the present academic discussion between science and religion. It is interesting to note that Walton, who apparently rejects Concordism which he understood as the belief that the Bible 'must agree – be in concord with – all the findings of contemporary science' (Walton 2009, p. 19), argues that there is no incompatibility between Genesis 1 and the scientifically well-established 13.8 billion-year age of the universe (2009, p. 92; see discussion in Chapter 3). There is a distinction between arguing that there is 'agreement' and arguing that there is 'compatibility'. To argue for 'agreement' is to argue that the Bible teaches that the universe is 13.8 billion years old, whereas to argue for compatibility is to argue that the Bible does not affirm a time period that is contradictory to the universe being 13.8 billion years old. Walton's argument is not Concordist Types A or B, because he argues for his interpretation of Genesis 1 on the basis of hermeneutical principles such as consideration of Ancient Near Eastern (ANE) context (see further, Chapter 3).

Likewise, saying that the Bible does not contain science beyond the culture of the biblical authors (Walton 2009, p. 19) is compatible with saying that the Bible does not indicate that God did not create through an evolutionary process (p. 168). While Walton asserts that 'through the entire Bible, there is not a single sentence in which God revealed to Israel a science beyond their own culture. No passage offers a scientific perspective that was not common to the Old World science of antiquity' (p. 19), this does not imply that the Bible's claims are completely compartmentalized from science. On the contrary, Walton and Sandy (2013, p. 54 n. 4) cite John 1.3 and Col. 1.16 and write 'we do not accept a scientific suggestion about the eternality of matter because of a theological belief that the material world is contingent on God' (see also 1 Cor. 8.6; Rom. 11.26; Rev. 4.11; I argue in Loke 2017a that the scientific and philosophical evidences are against the eternality of matter).

In a similar vein, a number of scholars have noted a remarkable convergence between the biblical view that God created through His Word (Gen. 1.3; John 1.1-3) and scientific discoveries which indicate that the laws of physics are describable with the elegant language of mathematics and that the genetic code has the characteristics of a language. With regard to the latter, William Brown (2010, pp. 68–9) explains:

> The divine word in Genesis is not only formative in the process of creation, it is also informative such that it defines the roles and activities of other agencies. Information, not coincidentally, is increasingly recognized for its formative role in biology. Coded in DNA, information exhibits a particularly active agency. Like language, DNA transmits such information, specifically a message containing four different modules or nucleotides (A, C, T, G). Like letters in a written language, different sequences of DNA modules transmit different information. The interpretation or decoding of such information lies in certain biochemical mechanisms that translate the sequence of DNA nucleotides into amino acids to form proteins. It is these proteins that ultimately determine what an organism is and does.

Note that Brown is not guilty of the problems associated with Concordism, for he is not using science to interpret the Bible (e.g. he does not claim that the Bible taught the fundamentals of genetics), nor is he using the Bible to interpret science. Rather, his interpretation of the Bible concerning the divine word in Genesis being formative and informative in defining the roles and activities of other agencies is justifiable on hermeneutical grounds (see Chapter 3 of this book). Likewise the findings of genetics he cites are arrived at via proper scientific methodology. Thus, his approach of bringing the results of biblical interpretation and science together to demonstrate a convergence is valid.

In order to demonstrate that the conclusions of biblical exegesis and science support each other in the manner Brown does, one would need to provide evidence (in accordance to methodologies proper to each discipline) that those conclusions are what the Bible and science actually tell us. On the other hand, in order to demonstrate that the scientific and the biblical models of reality are not contradictory (say) with respect to natural history, one does not need to provide an actual model of the past ('it was like this . . .'). Rather, all that is required is to provide a possible and plausible model of the past ('it could have been like this . . .') to show how the scientific and biblical models could coexist. It is evident that to show this a degree of conjecture is justified. Alexander himself engages in this kind of model construction when he writes:

> In the second type of model (my personal preference), God revealed himself to a couple, or community, of farmers in the Near East at the very beginning

of a putative proto-Jewish era, the so-called *Homo divinus*. These lived in fellowship with God, understanding their responsibility to care for God's earth, but subsequently turned their back on God in disobedience, leading to human autonomy and a broken relationship with him ('sin'). The emphasis in this type of speculation is on a single family or community – relationships built and broken over a short time-span. God's new family on earth had to begin somewhere and at some time: this was it. (Alexander 2017a)

Against Alexander's attempt, McKnight (2017) objects:

> I see Denis creating his own narrative, part biblical and part genome-theory and evolution-theory shaped. There's a nice happy narrative here held by no one in the Bible, but one that makes a scientist like Denis happier. That's concordism. The concord I prefer is one that sees Genesis 1-3 more in conversation with the Ancient Near East accounts of origins and purpose.

In reply, McKnight's objection is based on a failure to note a number of important distinctions, namely the distinction between tasks (A) 'interpreting the Bible', (B) 'showing that the Biblical account is true', and (C) 'showing that there is no incompatibility between evolution and Bible'.

For (A), one might ask for positive evidence to show that a proposal is what the human biblical author holds and expresses in the text, and this would require 'conversation with the Ancient Near East accounts of origins and purpose', as McKnight says.

Likewise, for (B), one would have to provide positive evidences (scientific, historical, etc.) to show that the biblical account is true.

However, for (C) it is sufficient to suggest a possible and plausible[7] (but not necessarily actual) model that is not contradictory with positive evidences of science nor with well-established interpretations of the Bible and then say, 'for all we know, this is how it could have happened' (note that 'positive' indicates 'evidences that we have' and not 'absence of evidence' unless there is good reason to think that the absence would not have been the case if the conclusion were otherwise). For (C), it would be perfectly legitimate to suggest a possible scenario which the biblical authors may not have thought of, as long as the possibility is not contradictory to what the biblical authors expressed.

Compare this understanding with, for example, McKnight's objection and Peter Enns (2012, xiv–xv, xvii) dismissal of all efforts to reconcile Genesis with evolution on the basis that these efforts produce a 'hybrid' Adam who is utterly foreign to the biblical portrait and to the consciousness of the biblical authors, and Russman's (2000) objection that there is no biblical mandate for the distinction between anatomical *Homo sapiens* (called 'modern humans' by scientists)

---

7. For example, the model should not include ad hoc claims such as interference by aliens. I thank Bethany Sollereder for this comment.

and *Homo divinus* (humankind made in the image of God; this distinction is discussed in Chapter 5 of this book). McKnight's and Enn's objection is based on a misunderstanding of the intention of such efforts – such efforts do not have to be perceived as attempts to understand what the biblical authors had in mind, but, rather, as attempts to show that evolution is not contradictory to what the biblical authors expressed.

It should be noted that the doctrine of Divine Inspiration of Scripture does not require the human biblical authors to be omniscient just as the Divine author is, and it does not require God to reveal to the human biblical authors an exhaustive knowledge of everything (such as an exhaustive knowledge of Adam). In particular, the doctrine recognizes that the Bible is not intended to be an encyclopaedia of science; it is not intended to tell us in detail how the stars, the earth or living things work. The main concern of the biblical authors is not to write such an encyclopaedia but to tell us (using accommodative, phenomenological and common ways of expression) that the stars, the earth, living things, etc. ultimately come from the Creator God who has revealed His redemptive plan and accomplished His salvific act in human history, in particular through the death and resurrection of Jesus Christ. Passages in the Bible itself (e.g. Ps. 111.2) encourage people to study 'the works of the Lord' (Ps. 111.2), which would include the physical world given the biblical affirmation of God as the Creator of all things. According to this understanding, God did not provide an exhaustive knowledge of the physical world in the Bible (e.g. the Bible does not mention atoms, DNA, etc.), but encouraged people to study it and find out the details themselves. The encouragement to study the physical world is in line with God's command to exercise dominion over the earth (Gen. 1:26-28). The desire to study what God has made out of love for God has been one of the motivations for many of the greatest scientists in history. (It has been observed by historians of science that 'virtually all of the most prominent figures in the historiography of the Scientific Revolution were religiously devout, and some of them extremely so' (Henry 2010, p. 39) and that the Judeo-Christian perspective has fostered the rise of modern science (Harrison 1998; Berezow and Hannam 2013).)

Given what is said earlier, it can be argued that the reason a 'hybrid Adam' does not feature in the Bible is not because the human biblical authors rejected evolution but because they did not think about evolution at all. If I were to claim (A) 'The Bible teaches the evolutionary Adam model that is described in my book', then I would be guilty of committing the error of saying that the Bible says or implies certain things when, in fact, the Bible does not say or imply those things, that is, I would be guilty of 'twisting' the verses in the Scripture (cf. Ham 2017, p. 106). However, that is not what I claim. What I claim is (C) 'There is a possible (not necessarily actual) model of reality described in my book which shows that there is no incompatibility between evolution and the Bible. This model contains details (including scientific details) not found in the Bible, but that is okay because (as explained above) God did not provide an exhaustive knowledge of reality in the Bible.'

Likewise, to object to the GAE model presented in this book by complaining that it interprets statements concerning Adam in a way that 'departs from historic Christian views' (Ross 2020), that it points 'to precisely zero Scriptures for explicit affirmation'(Ross 2020), that it 'is very different from the straightforward reading of Genesis 1-4' (Carter and Sanford 2020), that it constructs an elaborate story 'to force-fit deep time and evolution into the Bible' (Carter and Sanford 2020), and that it reworks the Bible and 'imposes things into the Bible that are simply not there'(Carter and Sanford 2020) would be to confuse Task A with Task C. To elaborate, the GAE model presented in this book is not intended to be an interpretation of Scriptural statements concerning Adam; that is why it does not require Scriptures for explicit affirmation because it is not intended to be a reading of Genesis 1–4. Rather, the GAE model is intended to show how it is possible that the Scriptural statements concerning Adam do not contradict evolutionary science. By doing so it does not 'force-fit deep time and evolution into the Bible', nor rework the Bible nor 'impose things into the Bible'. Rather, it proposes a scenario which is not excluded by the Bible (there is a distinction between claiming that 'the Bible says X' and 'the Bible does not exclude X'; the model concerns the latter).

In summary, we have to be careful about what the Bible does and does not say, and in this book it will be argued that evolution is not contradictory to what the Bible does say about creation and other matters. While the evolutionary Adam suggested by such efforts may, indeed, not be what the biblical authors had in mind nor what the biblical authors mandated, 'not being what the Biblical authors had in mind nor what the Biblical authors mandated' is not the same as 'contradictory to what the Biblical authors expressed'.

It should be noted that arguing that there is no incompatibility between evolution and biblical affirmations is independent of whether evolution occurred. Indeed, some scholars who have affirmed that evolution is compatible with biblical doctrines, such as William Lane Craig (2008), have nevertheless expressed their scepticism concerning this theory on *scientific* grounds. Regardless of whether one believes the theory of evolution, one must be careful not to rule out evolution by saying that it is incompatible with the Bible when such an incompatibility is unproven. The error of ruling out a scientific theory by saying that it is incompatible with the Bible when such an incompatibility is unproven has been committed by Christians over the centuries, often with disastrous consequences when the theory (e.g. Copernicus' and Galileo's) was subsequently vindicated by further evidences. Often, the errors are due to Christians insisting that certain scriptural passages must be interpreted in a certain way when there is, in fact, no adequate justification for thinking that that is the case for those particular passages. As McGrath (2010) observes, all texts need to be interpreted; the Bible is no exception, and throughout history Christians have recognized different kinds of interpretation, such as literal, metaphorical, symbolic and, accommodation to common, ways of expressions (see next chapter). I shall discuss the interpretation of the relevant biblical texts with regard to these various options in the following chapters.

1.4 Conclusion

In this chapter, I have argued that one can address perceived conflicts between science and religion using a transdisciplinary approach which involves philosophy of religion, natural sciences, social sciences, historical-critical biblical studies and theology. This should be done in a manner which respects each discipline as having its own integrity as a method of enquiry to construct its own model of reality without interference from other disciplines, before attempting to integrate the models constructed by different disciplines together. Concordism Type A (which seeks to extract modern scientific information from ancient scriptural texts) and Type B (which seeks to interpret scriptural texts in the light of modern science) should be avoided, because they arguably involve such a mutual interference by imposing modern scientific meanings onto scriptural texts, rather than interpreting these texts using proper hermeneutical principles such as considering the literary genre, context and so on.

With regard to the so-called Concordism Type C which Alexander advocates, the name 'Concordism' probably should be dropped because, as Alexander (2017b) himself notes, 'as a category it's so broad that one wonders whether the use of the term "Concordism" in this context does any useful work', and that it is open to the possibility of discord. Moreover, as noted earlier, what Alexander advocates is not what most scholars understand by the term 'Concordism'; thus to use the term is to invite misunderstanding. Nevertheless, the project itself is a worthy one, and as Alexander notes is widely practised in academic discussions on science and religion. One should perhaps call it Conversation rather than Concordism, since the project is open to the possibility of discord.

On my Conversation model, compatibility between Science and Christianity is not simply assumed, it has also to be argued for. The project does not submit the Bible to the authority of science nor science to the authority of the Bible; it does not read modern science into or out of the text, nor 'manipulate' the interpretation of the Bible so as to say 'God is right again'. My approach avoids the charge of ad hoc eisegesis of the Bible by affirming that the Bible should be interpreted according to proper hermeneutical principles such as considering the literary genre, literary context, meaning of words, grammatical relationship and the background and concerns of the ancient authors (historical, cultural and theological), rather than 'it depends on what the science says'. Having accomplished the tasks of interpreting the Bible according to proper hermeneutical principles and assessing the scientific data according to proper mainstream scientific methodology, one then proceeds to examine whether the results are in conflict or not, and whether they might complement each other.

To argue that the results are not in conflict in this manner is distinct from Concordism Types A and B. It is one thing to argue that the Bible is conveying modern science (e.g. Big Bang Theory), it is another thing to argue that it could be the case that the Bible is not inconsistent with modern science. The former arguably brings modern scientific ideas into Scripture, the latter argues that Scripture is not inconsistent with modern scientific ideas. To show that the scientific and the biblical models of reality are not contradictory, one does not need to provide an actual model of the past ('it was like this . . .'). Rather, all that is required is to provide a possible and plausible model of the past ('it could have been like this . . .') to show how the scientific and biblical models could coexist.

Moreover, one should note the distinction between Task (A) 'interpreting the Bible', (B) 'showing that the Biblical account is true', and Task (C) 'showing that there is no incompatibility between evolution and Bible'. For Task (A), it is illegitimate to bring in scientific details for which we have no adequate evidence to think that the ancient biblical authors would have thought of. However, as explained earlier, for Task (C) it is perfectly legitimate to suggest a possible and plausible scenario which includes scientific details that the biblical authors may not have thought of, as long as the possibility is not contradictory to what the biblical authors expressed. Just as modern historians studying ancient warfare can draw from modern-day knowledge (e.g. of infectious disease, a knowledge that was unavailable to the ancients) to explain historical events (e.g. why soldiers die from contaminated wounds), it can be argued that later knowledge can be employed in the study of earlier history to fulfil an explanatory function (Kitcher 1998, p. 43). Here, the explanatory function is to show whether the scientific and biblical account of human origins are compatible. Those who think that they are not compatible would then need to bear the burden of proof to exclude the possible scenario proposed in this book. In the following chapters, I shall discuss both Task (A) and Task (C), keeping them distinct and mentioning modern scientific knowledge for the purpose of Task (C) when appropriate. For Task (A), I shall apply the earlier mentioned hermeneutical principles rigorously and provide justifications for my applications to key scriptural passages in the rest of this book.

Finally, as will be argued in subsequent chapters, with regard to Task (A) there are biblical passages which are vague and open to a number of different interpretations, and even after proper hermeneutical principles are applied, the precise meaning and implication of the passages remain indeterminate. In such cases, where Task (C) is concerned, it is legitimate to select a *possible* and defensible interpretation for the purpose of constructing a *possible* scenario. Those who think that a biblical passage is not compatible with modern science would then need to bear the burden of proof to exclude the possible interpretation.

I shall now provide an overview of the rest of this book.

In Chapter 2, I discuss the important theological concept of Divine Accommodation, which has implications for how we should read the biblical texts concerning human origins. I explain that it is based on reasonable inference concerning what it would take for a Divine omniscient being to communicate to cognitively limited human beings. Whether Divine Accommodation results in the affirmation of what we now know are scientific errors is debatable. I shall explain that one can hold an alternative view of Divine Accommodation, according to which the biblical texts use ancient common ways of expressions without affirming scientific errors.

In Chapter 3, I discuss how the biblical genealogies of human ancestry and the Seven Days of Genesis 1–2 are to be understood. I focus on the important recent contributions by John Walton (2009) and John Collins (2018). Walton has argued on the basis of ANE evidences that the Seven Days of Genesis 1–2 can be understood as seven solar days in which the cosmos and living things were organized by God for the setting up of a Cosmic Temple. Where Task (C) is concerned, the implication of Walton's view is that Genesis does not say when the universe (with the sun, the moon, the stars and the living things) began to exist. Thus, Genesis does not exclude the possibility that it could have been millions or billions of years during which God worked out His purposes for other creatures, followed by a seven-day organization process which included the creation of the first humans. I reply to various objections against Walton's Functional Creation interpretation, and develop it further in this and the following chapters. I also discuss Collins's proposal, which offers important modifications of other proposals and opens up a range of possibilities.

In Chapter 4, I discuss whether the process of evolution which postulates that humans and other creatures came from a common biological ancestor is compatible with the biblical doctrine of creation. I discuss a number of biblical passages, reply to various objections (including the problem of evil associated with the evolutionary process) and demonstrate it is possible that God could have chosen to use the process of evolution to bring about various organisms, including human beings.

In Chapter 5, I summarize the scientific evidences for human evolution, and assess whether human evolution is compatible with the biblical account of human origins. This involves an examination of the meaning of the Imago Dei in the Bible, and a discussion of a range of views among Christians concerning the existence of Adam. I shall show that there are good exegetical and theological reasons for thinking that the biblical authors affirm Adam as a historical person, and that contrary to many scholars this conclusion is compatible with population genetics. I demonstrate the latter by developing a new model (in accordance with Task C) which shows that all humans today could have a common ancestor even though they descended from a large population of anatomical *Homo* as indicated by population genetics. This model postulates a distinction between those anatomical *Homo* with the Imago Dei (God's-Image-Bearers) and those without and proposes that God created the first God's-Image-Bearer (=Adam) out of a member of the latter group.

In Chapter 6, I discuss the time frame concerning the common ancestor (Adam) and whether evolutionary population genetics contradict the biblical account that all human beings today are descendants of one family (Noah's) after the Flood. I shall argue that the Flood can be interpreted quite literally as a localized phenomenon which is nevertheless sufficient for wiping out the God's-Image-Bearers group as well as their possessions (including animals within their areas of dominion), leaving only Noah and his family. This leaves open the possibility that many other animals around the globe, including many of those anatomical *Homo* without the image of God, would have survived. Utilizing the theological model developed in

Chapter 5, I argue that it is possible that a number of Noah's descendants (God's-Image-Bearers) mated with non-God's-Image-Bearing anatomical *Homo* after the Flood, thus accounting for the genetic diversity we observe today.

In the concluding Chapter 7, I shall summarize the conclusions of previous chapters and discuss their implications for understanding the relationship between science and religion and for the future of humanity.

Chapter 2

DIVINE ACCOMMODATION AND ITS IMPLICATIONS FOR BIBLICAL ANTHROPOLOGY

2.1 Introduction

In this chapter I discuss the important concept of Divine Accommodation. Many religious scholars understand this to be the claim that God – the Divine author of Scripture – communicated to humans through the Scripture using expressions that were specifically adapted to the original audience. Thus Scripture speaks to humans according to the human mode of understanding, and according to appearances in the common manner, taking into account the human point of view (McGrath 2010, pp. 20–3). How Divine Accommodation is to be understood has significant implications for how the biblical texts concerning human origins are to be understood.

It should be noted at the onset that the concept of Divine Accommodation did not originate as a response to modern science. The concept is based on reasonable inference concerning what it would take for a Divine omniscient being (if He exists) to communicate to cognitively limited human beings, and Jewish and Christian scholars recognized this inference long before the rise of modern science. For example, when considering how to interpret the Mosaic passages that speak of God having hands, arm, face and feet, the mid-second-century BC Jewish philosopher Aristobulus proposed that Moses adopted phrases applicable to things according to their appearance (Frag. 2, §3). Likewise, from early days Christian theologians have argued that biblical descriptions of God having hands, wings, etc. should not be taken literally. Rather, God, who is a Spirit according to Scripture (John 4.24), took into consideration the limitation of human understanding and ways of communication, and accommodated Himself by using lively and metaphorical way of expressions which can be easily understood, much as adults would sometimes try to use 'baby language' to communicate with infants (McGrath 2010, chapter 3). In the third century, Origen (*Frag. On Deut. 1:21*) wrote that God 'condescends and lowers himself, accommodating himself to our weakness, like a schoolmaster talking a "little language" to his children, like a father caring for his own children and adopting their ways'.

2.2 Two different views concerning Divine Accommodation

Whether Divine Accommodation results in the affirmation of what we now know are scientific errors in the Scripture has been debated by scholars. This issue is relevant to the topic of this book, for it might be argued by way of inductive reasoning that, if (1) the scriptural texts affirm erroneous scientific notions with regard to many other issues concerning the physical world (including living things), then it is likely that (2) they affirm erroneous scientific notions with regard to human origins.[1] Indeed, those scholars who hold to (1) usually hold to (2) as well (e.g. Enns 2005; Sparks 2008; Miller and Soden 2012; Parry 2014; Greenwood 2015). The sort of arguments they use and the relevant biblical texts they usually cite have been well summarized in the numerous writings of Denis Lamoureux (2008, 2010, 2016) who has argued that numerous biblical texts affirm what we now know are erroneous scientific notions such as the movement of the sun across the sky, a three-tiered universe and flat earth. A number of these scholars (e.g. Enns and Sparks) have appealed to theologian John Calvin for their view of Divine Accommodation, and they have claimed that the biblical account of Adam is factually erroneous on scientific grounds. However, other scholars have argued it is unlikely that Calvin himself would have thought that Divine Accommodation involves the affirmation of factual errors (Balserak 2006, pp. 163–8; Scott 2009).

On the other hand, many Christians have used the concept of Divine Accommodation to defend the Scripture against the charge of error. They hold to an alternative understanding of Divine Accommodation, according to which the biblical texts use ancient common ways of expressions without affirming errors. For example, consider Ps. 19.5-6 which says that the sun 'rises at one end of the heavens and makes its circuit to the other'. These Christians would argue that passages like this can be understood as an accommodative, phenomenological and common way of expression describing how the movement of the sun appears to people on earth. Such arguments were made by astronomer Johannes Kepler, one of the key figures of the seventeenth-century scientific revolution. Kepler writes:

> The psalmist was unaware that the sun does not go forth from the horizon as from a tabernacle (even though it may appear so to the eyes). On the other hand, he considered the sun to move for the precise reason that it appears so to the eyes. . . . He expressed it so because in either case it appeared so to the eyes. He should not be judged to have spoken falsely in either case, for the perception of the eyes also has its truth. (Kepler 1992, p. 60)

Elsewhere, Kepler states:

> For Scripture does not speak falsely, but affirms with perfect truth that the sense of vision says this, or better, that [Scripture] accommodates to its own purpose

---

1. Lamoureux mentions such an argument to me in personal correspondence.

this thing suggested by the sense of vision. The astronomer, on the other hand, or rather, the optician, convicts the sense of vision of error without any affront. (Optics, p. 338)

Kepler also discusses the well-known passage in Josh. 10.12-13:

Then Joshua spoke to the LORD in the day when the LORD delivered up the Amorites before the children of Israel, and he said in the sight of Israel: 'Sun, stand still over Gibeon; and Moon, in the Valley of Aijalon.' So the sun stood still, and the moon stopped, till the people had revenge upon their enemies. . . . So the sun stood still in the midst of heaven, and did not hasten to go down for about a whole day.

Concerning this passage Kepler observes:

That thoughtless persons pay attention only to the verbal contradiction, 'the sun stood still' versus 'the earth stood still', not considering that this contradiction can only arise in an optical and astronomical context, and does not carry over into common usage. Nor are these thoughtless ones willing to see that Joshua was simply praying that the mountains not remove the sunlight from him, which prayer he expressed in words conforming to the sense of sight, as it would be quite inappropriate to think, at that moment, of astronomy and of visual errors. For if someone had admonished him that the sun doesn't really move against the valley of Ajalon, but only appears to do so, wouldn't Joshua have exclaimed that he only asked for the day to be lengthened, however that might be done? (Kepler 1992, pp. 60–1)[2]

Galileo also utilized the concept of Divine Accommodation during the Galileo Controversy (McGrath 2010, chapter 3). Contrary to many who think that Galileo demonstrated a conflict between science and the Bible, Galileo himself thought that 'The holy Bible can never speak untruth – whenever its true meaning is understood' (*Letter to the Grand Duchess Christina of Tuscany*, 1615).

Collins distinguishes between affirming scientific errors with merely using ancient common ways of expressions in his discussion of the *Letter of Aristeas* in contrast with Leviticus:

2. Kepler suggests that 'God . . . responded by stopping the motion of the earth, so that the sun might appear to him to stop' (Kepler 1992, pp. 60–1). Stopping the earth's rotation, however, would have caused other effects such as huge tidal waves around the globe that would have required Divine intervention to prevent. The alternative suggestion of God responding by creating a mirage which makes it possible for one to perceive sunlight around a corner or over the horizon under certain conditions (Butler 1951) seems to be better.

Leviticus is famous for its catalogue of unclean animals; it never really gives a general rationale for why some are clean and others unclean. The 'weasel' (Lev. 11.29 RV; the ESV has 'mole rat'; the Heb. is holed; the Gk. has γαλῆ, 'weasel') was unclean and thus ineligible for sacrifice and eating. Although Leviticus gives no rationale, the *Letter of Aristeas* explains that it 'conceives through the ears and brings forth through the mouth' (*Letter of Aristeas*, 165–6; see also *Barn.* 10.8). That this was taken to be authentic natural history becomes obvious when we find that Aristotle refuted it, saying that 'Anaxagoras and some of the other physiologers' had alleged precisely this; Aristotle dismissed their work as based on 'insufficient evidence and inadequate consideration' (Aristotle, *Gen. an.*, 3.6 [756b]). (Collins 2018, Section 9.E)

For another example of affirming ancient science (rather than merely using ancient common ways of expressions), consider also Aristotle's argument for the fixity of biological kinds:

If the products were dissimilar from their parents, and yet able to copulate, we should then get arising from them yet another different manner of creature, and out of their progeny yet another, and so it would go on ad infinitum. Nature, however, avoids what is infinite. (*Generation of Animals* 1.1 [715-b])

Collins argues that such scientific and philosophical explanations are not found in the Genesis text; thus we should call Aristotle 'ancient science', but we should not regard Genesis as such (Collins 2018, section 10.A.3). It should also be noted that Aristotle's argument is not compelling given Genesis' account of a cosmic beginning which implies that there has been only a finite time since the beginning, and so mutable kinds would not by now have proliferated to infinity.[3]

A number of contemporary scholars have offered additional arguments for such a view of Divine Accommodation based on their understanding of the ancient Jewish background.

For example, consider biblical passages such as those which state that 'The world is firmly established; it cannot be moved' (Ps. 96.10), 'God set the earth on its foundations; it can never be moved' (Ps. 104.5). Such expressions can be understood as accommodative and figurative expressions to convey the stability of natural order as it appears to people on earth, based on the ancient Jewish theological understanding of the heavens and earth as a temple and/or as an imitation of the four-cornered tabernacle (Beale 2008, p. 213). To illustrate, in Ps. 104.9 God is then said to have 'stretched out heaven like a tent *curtain*' (v.2) and laid 'the beams of his upper chambers' (v. 3). This psalm uses words (e.g. curtain) and phrases which are often associated with the temple in the Old Testament, and it also has similarities with other temple scenes such as portrayed in 2 Sam. 22.7-15

---

3. I thank William Lane Craig for highlighting this to me in personal correspondence. For arguments that time has a beginning, see Loke (2017a, Chapters 2 and 3).

(for these and other examples, see Beale 2008, pp. 210-13). This theological understanding also fits well with Lamoureux's (2016, p. 99) own observation that ancient Hebrews used a tent to describe physical reality, such as a domed canopy of heaven and the flat floor of earth (see Ps. 104.2-3; Ps. 19.4-5; Ps. 18.16; 2 Sam. 22.16). Lamoureux (2020, p. 186) objects that Ps. 104.3 says 'lays the beams of his upper chambers on their waters', which he claims is the waters of the heavenly sea. However, it can also be understood as the waters of the clouds. As Kidner (1973, p. 369) comments, 'the dizzy height of "the waters above the firmament", or the clouds, is pictured as but the base of God's abode.' Lamoureux ignores the poetic genre, and his objection does not deny my argument that these phrases are 'figurative expressions to convey the usual stability of natural order, based on the theological understanding of the heavens and earth as a temple and the earth as an imitation of the four cornered tabernacle'. He also objects that the curtain is that of a domed canopy of tent, not a Jewish temple with flat roof (2020, p. 186). However, the Hebrew word *yeriah* does not necessarily mean a tent curtain; Lamoureux fails to note Beale's (2008, pp. 211-12) observation that it can also refer to curtain in a temple and that canopy can be a synonym for temple.

While Lamoureux (2016, p. 90) claims that the Scripture affirms a three-tiered universe, Harris (2013, p. 104) notes that the cosmos is described in the Scripture 'not in terms of tiers so much as realms of habitation', and that 'the world is conceived of as a well-known dwelling of ancient times, with the earth and the sky as its main structures, not tiers so much as boundaries which envelop and secure the dwelling space for creatures and humankind' (p. 43). Harris observes that the writings of the rabbis of the early centuries contained evidence of cosmological speculation which involves not three tiers, nor four, but many tiers – seven heavens and seven earths to begin with, as well as water' (p. 104). This indicates 'the shortcomings of the three-tiered model as a literal description of the ancient Hebrew cosmology' (p. 104). Additionally, 'most of the cosmological statements which are interpreted as evidence in its favour are in fact metaphorical allusions to God's relationship with the world' (p. 104). For example, consider Solomon's prayer of dedication to the Jerusalem Temple (1 Kgs 8). Harris comments:

> Solomon implores Yahweh to hear his prayer 'in heaven your dwelling place' (v. 30), while at the same time expressing the awareness that God will no more dwell in the Temple which Solomon has just built than literally in heaven: 'But will God indeed dwell on the earth? Even heaven and the highest heaven cannot contain you, much less this house that I have built!' (1 Kgs 8.27). This is one of the clearest indications in the Old Testament that a primary function of the references to God being in the heavens is to point metaphorically to God's utter transcendence over the world. (2013, pp. 106-7)

Among the many problems with Lamoureux's arguments is his failure to do proper hermeneutics by an adequate consideration of the genre of the biblical texts in question, the meaning of the original biblical words, etc. For example, referring to biblical passages which speak of stars falling from heaven (Mt. 24.29; Isa. 34.4; Rev. 6.12-14),

Lamoureux (2016, pp. 100–1) claims that the biblical texts imply that stars are tiny specks attached to a solid firmament which is part of a three-tiered universe. However, various commentators (e.g. Beale 1999; France 2007) note that these passages belong to Jewish apocalyptic in which stars often symbolize evil human or angelic powers, and thus these passages are likely figurative in which language of cosmic collapse symbolizes God's judgement resulting in political reversal. Citing Mt. 4.8, 'The devil took Jesus to a very high mountain and showed him all the kingdoms of the world,' Lamoureux (2016, p. 96) argues that this verse makes sense only if it assumes that the world is flat. However, other commentators (e.g. Manson 1979, p. 44 cf. *1 En.* 24-25; *2 Bar.* 76.3) have noted that this passage can be understood as a visionary experience; thus it is not intended to convey information about physical geography. In support of his view that the Bible affirms a flat earth, Lamoureux (2016, p. 94) notes that numerous passages in the Bible state that the earth has 'ends' (e.g. Isa. 41.8-9; Gen. 11.31). However, he fails to observe that the Hebrew word most often translated 'earth' in the Old Testament is *'erets*, which is often used to refer to some specific nation or territory, like the 'land of Havilah' (Gen. 2.11), or to a defined plot of land, like the one purchased by Abraham (Gen. 23.15) (Holding 2013). (For other problems with Lamoureux's arguments regarding the movement of the sun, a solid firmament, flat earth, his reading of three tier universe in Phil. 2.10, the end at the horizon, the ends of the earth, the earth set on water, circular trench, the 'underworld', etc., see Loke [2018a; 2020c]. Compare with Lamoureux [2019; 2020]. Lamoureux's latest reply [Lamoureux 2020] misrepresents my arguments on various points; for a detailed response, see Loke (2021b). Parts of the response can be found elsewhere in this chapter and in Chapters 3 and 5).

The problems with Lamoureux's arguments undermine his claim to have succeeded in showing that the Scriptural texts affirm erroneous scientific notions with regard to many other issues concerning the physical world. This undermines the premise of his inductive reasoning (noted at the beginning of this chapter), namely, establishing the claim that the Scriptural texts affirm erroneous scientific notions with regard to many other issues concerning the physical world would increase the likelihood that they affirm erroneous scientific notions with regard to human origins. Alternatively, one might reply that, even if the Bible affirms scientific errors concerning a number of other issues, this does not entail that the Bible affirms scientific errors on all issues such as those concerning human origins. After all, the ancients did not get everything wrong. They understood, for example, that evaporation of water from earth forms clouds from which rains upon the earth come (Job 36.27-29; see earlier). Likewise, they could have correctly passed down the knowledge that humanity originated from Adam from their ancestors (this depends on how they understood humanity to be; see discussion in Chapters 5 and 6). Other Christians who do not hold to Biblical Inerrancy (see later) might also object to the inductive argument by arguing that, while God allowed the biblical authors to commit a number of errors concerning other issues in the process of accommodation, He preserved them from errors with regard to more important issues such as the origins of humanity.

Contemporary Biblical Inerrantist Woodbridge (1982, p. 34) argues that 'The principle of accommodation carries with it no logical concomitant to an errant Biblical text. . . . A father, particularly an omnipotent and omniscient One, can speak true thoughts simply.' He and other Biblical Inerrantists believe that the omniscient and omnipotent God who inspired the Scripture would be able to guarantee the truthfulness of Scriptural statements, and they believe that He had, indeed, done so when He inspired the biblical texts thousands of years ago. They would often attempt to show that their belief in biblical inerrancy is warranted as a deduction from other premises such as concerning the deity of Christ which they argue for on other grounds (see, for example, the discussion in Craig 2007, who nevertheless goes on to explain that Biblical Inerrancy is not a central doctrine of Christianity; thus even if a person should discover an error in the Bible one day, this does not imply that he/she has to give up his/her Christian faith. Craig argues that the central doctrines of Christianity such as the existence of God, the resurrection and the deity of Jesus, etc. can still be affirmed, and that the evidences for those doctrines are not dependent on complete Biblical Inerrancy).

Other Christians might object that the biblical texts themselves (such as John 20.30-31[4] and 2 Tim. 3.15-17[5]) affirm that the declared purpose of the Bible is to instruct for salvation through faith in Christ Jesus, and that this purpose requires the Bible to be inerrant only with regard to theological statements concerning salvation, but not with regard to statements concerning the physical world. However, Biblical Inerrantists might reply that, while the declared purpose of the Scripture is to instruct for salvation through faith in Christ Jesus, there is no verse in the Scripture which says that the truthfulness of Scripture is restricted only to matters concerning salvation. They would argue that, on the contrary, the truthfulness of the Scripture with regard to other issues is related to salvation because the Biblical message is a holistic one in which the spiritual and physical are not compartmentalized (Montgomery 2010).

Biblical Inerrantists have also argued against the theological adequacy of a restricted inerrancy view by referring to passages such as Mt. 5.18,[6] 24.35[7] and John 10.34-36,[8] which they interpret as assuming the claim that what Scriptural

---

4. 'Now Jesus did many other signs in the presence of his disciples, which are not written in this book. But these are written so that you may come to believe that Jesus is the Messiah, the Son of God, and that through believing you may have life in his name.'

5. 'And how from childhood you have known the sacred writings that are able to instruct you for salvation through faith in Christ Jesus. All scripture is inspired by God and is useful for teaching, for reproof, for correction, and for training in righteousness, so that everyone who belongs to God may be proficient, equipped for every good work.'

6. 'For truly I tell you, until heaven and earth pass away, not one letter, not one stroke of a letter, will pass from the law until all is accomplished.'

7. 'Heaven and earth will pass away, but my words will not pass away.'

8. Jesus answered, 'Is it not written in your law, "I said, you are gods"? If those to whom the word of God came were called "gods" – and the scripture cannot be annulled – can you

texts affirm are factually true.[9] One might object that Mt. 5.18 refers to ethics, John 10.34-35 is about a theological issue while Mt. 24.35 is about historical events; none of these verses supports the claim that what the Bible says about scientific matters is to be taken as inerrant. However, a Biblical Inerrantist might reply that Mt. 24.35 is not just referring to theological statements but to events that happened or will happen in the world, and issues such as the creation of the world, living things and human beings belong to this category. The context of John 10.34-35 concerns human nature: Jesus was arguing that humans can in some sense be called gods (Köstenberger 2007, p. 466). While the context of Mt. 5.18 concerns ethics, a Biblical Inerrantist might argue that the underlying assumption is that the Scripture is telling the truth in whatever matters it touches on, such as events (Mt. 24.35), human nature (John 10.34-35) and ethics (Mt. 5.18). The question is not whether the Bible teaches science, but whether the Bible is truthful in all that it affirms (Grudem 2017, p. 825).[10]

Against the view that Biblical Inerrancy began as a reaction among American Fundamentalists in response to the challenge of modernists' arguments, Woodbridge (1982) observes that many theologians throughout church history – including early church theologians such as Justin Martyr, Irenaeus, Theophilus of Antioch and Augustine of Hippo – were concerned to defend the factual accuracy of the Scripture. For example, he notes Augustine's statement that 'whatever they (the men of physical science) can really demonstrate to be true of physical nature, we must show to be capable of reconciliation with our Scriptures' (*Gen.ad.litt.*2.18.38). Anglican scholars Anthony Hanson and Richard Hanson, who are not Biblical Inerrantists, nevertheless acknowledge that the belief in the inerrancy of Scripture has deep historical roots and that the rejection of inerrancy among Christians is a recent phenomenon. They write:

> Again, as we have seen, the writers of the New Testament certainly believed in the inerrancy of the Old Testament, which constituted for them the scriptures. The Christian Fathers and the medieval tradition continued this belief, and the Reformation did nothing to weaken it. On the contrary, since for many reformed theologians the authority of the Bible took the place which the Pope had held in the medieval scheme of things, the inerrancy of the Bible came to be more firmly maintained and explicitly defined among some reformed theologians that it had ever been before. Only since the very end of the seventeenth century, with the rise of biblical criticism, has this belief in the inerrancy of Scripture been widely challenged among Christians. (Hanson and Hanson 1989, pp. 51–2)

say that the one whom the Father has sanctified and sent into the world is blaspheming because I said, "I am God's Son"?'

9. http://defendinginerrancy.com/historical-evidence-for-inerrancy/.

10. Non-Inerrantists sometimes point to grammatical errors in the Greek of the NT, but these are irrelevant because such errors do not imply an affirmation of factual errors.

One must be careful to note, however, that the kind of inerrancy the early church theologians affirmed is not necessarily the same as what many Christians today affirm. For example, Franke (2013, pp. 77–8) observes that Origen often used non-literal interpretation and defended only the inerrancy of deeper spiritual meaning. In fact, Origen claimed that the biblical texts are often incoherent so as to compel us to find the deeper spiritual meaning. Likewise, Augustine prior to his conversion rejected the Bible until he encountered the spiritual allegorical interpretations of Ambrose (2013, pp. 77–8). While Augustine did eventually believe that truths concerning the natural world should be reconcilable with Scripture, he was willing to do this by Reading Genesis 1 in a figurative way as something other than a straight chronological account. Augustine also said that questions about 'the motion of the heavens . . . how the stars are fixed in it', etc. are not matters relevant to salvation, and so he did not discuss them (*DGaL* 2.10).

Nevertheless, many contemporary scholarly defenders of Biblical Inerrancy are aware of the need to consider non-literal interpretations, though they would argue that there are cases where a literal interpretation should be preferred (e.g. concerning the bodily resurrection of Jesus; see Merrick and Garrett ed. 2013). A contemporary Biblical Inerrantist may or may not agree to Augustine's figurative reading of Genesis 1, but he/she would argue that his/her motivation is nevertheless the same as Augustine's, namely, to refrain from attributing error to the Scriptures. Augustine's refusal to discuss some matters that are not directly relevant to salvation is not contrary to this motivation, which Lamoureux et al. do not share. Contemporary defenders of an unrestricted inerrancy view who do share this motivation include not only Protestant Evangelicals but also many (though not all) Roman Catholics[11] and Eastern Orthodox[12] Christians (with reasonable qualifications about the need to consider various interpretations [literal and non-literal] and the distinction between the errancy of our understanding and the inerrancy of Scripture).

It is beyond the scope of this chapter to settle the complicated debate concerning the motivations for Biblical Inerrancy. Suffice to note that it is of importance for many Christians today and that their motivations for holding it cannot be so easily dismissed on theological grounds. Against the assumption that biblical texts should be treated like any other ANE texts, Wenham (1987, p. xlvii) observes that Genesis 1–11 (for example) is often highly critical of ideas current in the ancient world about the natural and supernatural world (concerning whether the biblical authors borrowed ideas from ANE mythology, see Chapter 3). Those who object to Biblical Inerrancy must be careful not to beg the question against the Inerrantist's view of Divine Inspiration by assuming that the Bible would contain erroneous science simply because it is an ancient text. Rather the objectors would have to cite evidences to prove that the Bible contains erroneous science, and, indeed, many have attempted to do so while others have responded as noted earlier.

11. https://www.catholic.com/magazine/print-edition/is-scripture-inerrant.
12. http://www.orthodoxcanada.org/qa_archives/question7.html.

Concerning my citation of Wenham, Lamoureux objects by claiming that it ignored Wenham's assertion that Genesis 1-11 is 'a polemic against many of the commonly received notions about the gods and man' (ibid). Lamoureux (2020, p. 184) adds: 'In other words, these biblical chapters are criticising ANE theology and anthropology, not cosmology.' He then cites Wenham (1987, p. xlvii), 'at certain points biblical and extra biblical thought are in clear agreement. . . . Genesis 1-9 records a bare outline of world history from its creation to the flood that finds a parallel in the Atrahasis epic and Sumerian flood story.' Lamoureux adds: 'These prominent similarities include the cosmology' (2020, pp. 184–5).

Both of Lamoureux's additional comments are misleading. Lamoureux ignores Wenham's (1987, p. xlviii) subsequent qualification that 'these similarities between biblical and non-biblical thinking, however, are overshadowed by the differences'. Commenting on Gen. 1.14, Wenham notes that cosmological entities such as the sun, moon and stars which were regarded powerful deities according to pagan mythology are not regarded as such in Genesis (1987, p. xlix). This shows that Genesis' criticism of ANE theology does involve cosmology. Lamoureux also ignores Wenham's observation that the nature of *rāqîaʻ* is disputed (1987, pp.19–20). Contrary to Lamoureux's unwarrantedly confident assertion that it is a solid dome, Wenham writes, 'quite how the OT conceives the nature of the firmament is less clear . . . since the most vivid descriptions occur in poetic texts, the language may be figurative. Certainly Gen 1 is not concerned with defining the nature of the firmament, but with asserting God's power over the waters' (ibid). Lamoureux also did not reply to my argument that in Gen. 1.8 the *rāqîaʻ* was named *shamayim* 'heaven(s)' in which the birds fly (Deut. 4.17); this seems to indicate that it is not solid.

Concerning *rāqîaʻ*, I had previously pointed out that Lamoureux's citation of *rāqaʻ* and *riqqûaʻ* ignores Walton's warning that nouns and verbs of the same root do not necessarily contain the same semantic range or character. Lamoureux acknowledges this but says there are other cases (e.g. *zeraʻ* and *zaraʻ* in Hebrew) where they do (2020, p. 185). Which I do not deny. The question is why think that this point applies to *rāqîaʻ*, *rāqaʻ* and *riqqûaʻ*? In reply to my previous objection that 'Lamoureux citation of Job 37:18 ignores Walton's point that the word translated "skies" is not *rāqîaʻ* – it is *šeḥaqim*' (Loke 2018, p. 129; see the Excursus on Job 37 in Walton 2012), Lamoureux (2020, p. 185) acknowledges this but complains by stating that Walton says that the ancient Israelites believed in a solid sky. However, Lamoureux fails to note the point I explained in Loke (2018a; 2020c) that we need to draw a distinction between what the text affirms and what the ancient author believed. Thus Lamoureux's complaint is irrelevant and fails to substantiate his claim that the text affirms a solid sky. (For other responses to Lamoureux's other arguments, see Loke [2018a; 2020c; Loke 2021b].)

The question concerning the reliability of the Bible continues to be debated to this day, with a number of scholars (e.g. Haught 2008, pp. 31–3) dismissing those who hold it as naïve, while others have continued to defend it vigorously (e.g. Arnold and Hess 2014; Cowan and Wilder 2013). A comprehensive assessment of the debate is beyond the scope of this book, which focuses on addressing the arguments of atheists/agnostics, Judaists, Roman Catholics, Mainline Protestants, Eastern Orthodox Christians and Evangelicals regarding the compatibility between science and the traditional understanding of the biblical account of human origins in its canonical form. Regardless of the possible historical sources of the biblical text, it is the canonical form which is regarded by the majority of Christians throughout history as divinely inspired (Longman III and Dillard 2006, p. 51; Brevard Childs's influential work [1979] has shown that a canonical approach can yield interpretative insights for historical-critical studies as well).

Additionally, regardless of their views on Biblical Inerrancy, many Christians would still be concerned to uphold the biblical account of human origins on the basis of its integral relationship with the exposition of the Gospel in theological tradition. For example, the Roman Catholic Church does not have an official position on whether God used the process of evolution to create various life forms. However, Pope Pius XII insists that, while God could have created the human body using an evolutionary process, the human souls are immediately created by God (Pius XII, *Humani Generis* 36). The pope also states – with a footnote referring not only to Scripture (Rom. 5.12-19) but also the Council of Trent, Session V, Canons 1–4 – that Adam was a real historical individual from whom all human beings descended. He writes:

> the faithful cannot embrace that opinion which maintains either that after Adam there existed on this earth true men who did not take their origin through natural generation from him as from the first parents of all, or that Adam represents a certain number of first parents. Now, it is in no way apparent how such an opinion can be reconciled that which the sources of revealed truth and the documents of the teaching authority of the Church proposed with regard to original sin which proceeds from a sin actually committed by an individual Adam in which through generation is passed onto all and is in everyone as his own. (*Humani Generis* 37)

While some Roman Catholic theologians have rejected Adam as a real historical individual (e.g. Haught 2008; O'Collins 2016, p. 41) and argued that the doctrine of Original Sin can be understood in other ways (O'Sullivan 2016, citing Pierre Teilhard de Chardin, Karl Rahner and John Haught, among others), others have continued to affirm that Adam is a real historical individual and the ancestor of all human beings on the basis of various theological arguments (e.g. Riches 2017).[13]

---

13. See also, for example, the Roman Catholic International Theological Commission's statement on *Communion and Stewardship: Human Persons Created in the Image of God* (2004), https://web.archive.org/web/20140621050711/http:/www.vatican.va/roman_curia/congregations/cfaith/cti_documents/rc_con_cfaith_doc_20040723_communion-stewardship_en.html. Accessed 13 February 2018. See also https://www.catholic.com/tract/adam-eve-and-evolution.

The Eastern Orthodox Church does not have any official prohibition against the theory of evolution, and different Orthodox theologians have different views regarding the compatibility between evolution and Christian faith. Nevertheless, many of those who are open to the theory of evolution would still affirm the existence of Adam in view of theological tradition.[14]

The importance of a historical Adam who is the ancestor of all human beings is also affirmed in the Judaist tradition. For example, the rabbis argue that it is important for the peace of humanity:

> But a single man was created [first] ... for the sake of peace among mankind, that none should say to his fellow, 'My father was greater than your father'. Again, [a single man was created] to proclaim the greatness of the Holy One, blessed is he; for man stamps many coins with the one seal and they are all like one another; but the King of kings, the Holy One, blessed is he, has stamped every man with the seal of the first man, yet not one of them is like his fellow. (*Sanhedrin* 4.5)

The Islamic tradition likewise revered Adam's role as the father of the human race; his creation from dust is specifically mentioned in the Quran (3.59).

Lamoureux et al. would regard the arguments against the historicity of Adam to be a clear and theologically important case for their view, and many articles and books (e.g. Lamoureux 2008b; Enns 2012; Venema and McKnight 2016; Cole-Turner 2016, 2020) have been written calling for a re-evaluation of the biblical message concerning Adam in the light of our present scientific knowledge. On the other hand, many Christians have resisted their arguments and conclusion on theological and exegetical grounds (see, for example, the editorial in *Christianity Today*,[15] and the debate between James Hoffmeier, Gordon Wenham and Kenton Sparks in Halton ed. 2015), but offer no good response to the scientific objections. This debate has upset many Christian communities, leading to the dismissal of professors from seminaries, for example. In the following chapters, I shall show that all such calls for re-evaluation are unnecessary, for they are based on problematic inference of scientific data and unwarranted interpretation of Scripture.

2.3 Conclusion

Divine Accommodation is based on reasonable inference concerning what it would take for a Divine omniscient being (if He exists) to communicate to cognitively limited human beings. While some have argued that Divine Accommodation resulted in the affirmation of what we now know are scientific errors (including

---

14. See, for example, this article by Fr. George Nicozisin published by the Orthodox Research Institute http://www.orthodoxresearchinstitute.org/articles/dogmatics/nicozisin_creationism.html. Accessed 24 February 2018.

15. http://www.christianitytoday.com/ct/2011/june/noadamevenogospel.html.

errors concerning human origins) in the biblical texts, others have argued for an alternative view of Divine Accommodation, according to which the biblical texts use ancient common ways of expressions without affirming scientific errors. In any case, regardless of their views of Divine Accommodation and Biblical Inerrancy, many Christians (including not only Evangelicals but also a large number of Roman Catholic and Eastern Orthodox Christians) would still be concerned to uphold the Scriptural account of human origins on the basis of its integral relationship with the exposition of the Gospel in classical theological tradition. In the rest of this book I shall assess whether this account is compatible with modern science, beginning with the issue concerning the time span of creation.

Chapter 3

THE TIME SPAN OF CREATION

3.1 Introduction

When did our biological species begin to exist on earth? From a scientific point of view, this question is not easy to answer. According to the Smithsonian, 'the species that you and all other living human beings on this planet belong to is *Homo sapiens*.'[1] However, the term 'human' is ambiguous with reference to the distant past when other members of the *Homo* genus existed, and some have argued that the whole *Homo* genus is really one species[2] (see further, Chapter 5). Regardless of these disputes, most scientists agree that humans and other creatures evolved from a common biological ancestor over a long period of time. Different Christians have different views concerning this time span and the process of evolution. I shall address the issue of time span in this chapter and the process of evolution in the next. The conversation between science and Scripture concerning the issue of time span involves a consideration of the scientific evidences concerning the dating of the cosmos and living things, as well as how the biblical accounts of the genealogies of human ancestry and the creation of the cosmos during the Seven Days of Genesis 1–2 are to be understood.

3.2 Scientific evidences

On the basis of various methods of calculation which provide multiple independent confirmations, scientists have concluded that the universe is approximately 13.8 billion years old, the earth 4.5 billion years, and *Homo sapiens* around 300,000 years old.[3] Very briefly, these methods include the following:

---

1. http://humanorigins.si.edu/evidence/human-fossils/species/homo-sapiens.
2. I thank Joshua Swamidass for highlighting this point.
3. This is based on recent fossil discoveries in Jebel Irhoud, Morocco (Hublin et al. 2017). See further, Chapter 5.

1. Starlight from faraway galaxies: This method uses distances of galaxies and the speed of light to calculate that the light has travelled from distant galaxies for billions of years before reaching the earth. YEC have replied by utilizing the concept of time dilation (e.g. Humphreys 1994). However, Gordon (2014) points out that there have been no expected leftover effects from gravitational time dilation of such a huge scale observed on other stars; moreover, the heavy elements in our sun indicate that it is at least a second-generation star, which indicates that the universe would have existed for billions of years before our solar system came to be.[4]
2. Dating stars: This method calculates the ages of stars based on scientific understanding of how stars are born, evolve and die. After a star exhausts the nuclear fuel in its core, it loses its gaseous outer layers into space leaving behind a small core known as white dwarf, which cools over billions of years. By measuring the temperature of white dwarfs, astronomers can determine how long they have been cooling down. The results indicate that the oldest have been cooling for 12 to 13 billion years.[5]
3. Radiometric dating[6] of rocks from both the earth and outer space (e.g. from the moon and of meteorites recently fallen to the earth) yields consistent results in pointing to about 4.5 to 4.7 billion years for the age of the earth (Young 1982; Young notes that the dating of materials from outer space could not have been affected by Noah's flood as many YECs used to believe). Meteorites are particularly helpful for finding out when the earth and the solar system were formed, for they were formed early in the history of our solar system and they have changed little since their creation (Christian 2011, p. 67). Gordon (2014) notes that 'There are more than forty different radiometric dating methods in common use as well as a number of non-radiometric methods, all of which allow for independent cross-checks of the date yielded by any given method'.
4. Other methods such as the study of sedimentary rocks, coral reefs, fossil patterns, seafloor spreading and magnetic reversals, volcano layers and annual

---

4. Ham (2017, p. 42) acknowledges that YEC scientists do not yet have a solution to the distant starlight problem, but he claims that opponents of YEC face the 'horizon problem', namely, 'even given 13.8 billion years for the age of the universe there has not been enough time for the light to get equally distributed to produce the uniform background radiation temperature (2.7 degrees Kelvin) that is observed everywhere astronomers look'. Ross (2017, p. 53) replies that this problem is solved by cosmic inflation.

5. https://stardate.org/astro-guide/age-universe-0.

6. A number of different isotopes are used in the calculation, such as the decay of uranium 235 to lead 207 and uranium 238 to lead 206. To determine the amount of lead 207 and lead 206 present in the 'original', it is observed that common lead contains proportions of four isotopes which are nearly constant, and that the isotope lead 204, which is not produced by radioactive decay, can thus provide a measure of the 'original' lead (http://hyperphysics.phy-astr.gsu.edu/hbase/Nuclear/clkroc.html).

ice layers, genetic molecular clocks, the migrations of life forms (including humans) and the dating of Palaeolithic and Mesolithic fossils and tools.

In response to the evidences for Old Earth, YECs, such as Ham (2017, p. 67), claim that historical science is fundamentally different and less reliable than experimental science, and that 'all old-earth origin scientists ignore (or worse, twist) God's eyewitness testimony in Genesis in their efforts to interpret the physical evidence from events of the past' (p. 212).

Old Earth Creationists would object that Ham's statement concerning 'God's eyewitness testimony in Genesis' assumes that the Bible teaches YEC, but this is not proven (see later). On the other hand, sceptics would ask what reasons there are for thinking that Genesis is a reliable record of God's eyewitness testimony of creation. They would argue that, if the YECs are right in their interpretation of Genesis, then there is reason to doubt that this is, indeed, a reliable record of God's eyewitness testimony of creation, given the contradictions between YEC's interpretation and scientific evidences for the age of the universe. Ham's dismissal of the evidences of 'historical science' is unjustified, for as Haarsma (2017, p. 56) explains:

> historical and experimental sciences are closely tied together. For example, astronomical observations of gasses in galaxies, the light of which originated millions of years ago, are regularly compared to lab experiments on similar gasses today. Genetic methods that have proven reliable in studying today's cancer are the same methods used to measure genetic changes in evolution.

Ham's point concerning 'eyewitness testimony' seems to assume that, unless we were there to see it (as he claims God did), we cannot be justified in coming to a conclusion; indeed, Ham makes this assumption explicit in his debate with Bill Nye.[7] However, as a commentator of the debate points out, such an assumption would undermine Ham's own belief system, for Ham himself wasn't there to see God create the universe, and neither was he there to witness God inspiring the writing of His eyewitness testimony. In any case, the assumption is unwarranted, for as Haarsma (2017, p. 134) explains:

> If no people were there to see it, how can we even study the universe scientifically? The short answer is, using the evidence left behind. A scientist is like a detective who gathers evidence to determine how a crime was committed. Even without an eyewitness, a detective uses evidence such as footprints, DNA, and phone records to build a strong case. Similarly, scientists can piece together what happened from the evidence we measure today. While such historical science has differences from experimental science (one can't bring a galaxy into the lab for an experiment!), it is similar in the most important respects. Just like an experimental scientist, the historical scientist builds a hypothesis, tests it against

---

7. https://www.youtube.com/watch?v=l71_zflVA4U&t=27s.

observations, then modifies the hypothesis as needed. And like the detective, when multiple lines of evidence all confirm the same hypothesis, scientists become confident that we know what happened. Historical science is reliable.

Some YECs have claimed that the universe is young even though it appears to be old, because it was created in a mature state. Others object that it is implausible that a God of truth would create a universe with a multitude of evidences which provide multiple independent confirmations of old age when it is, in fact, young (Rusbult 2006). One might agree with YECs that in some cases a mature state would have been functionally necessary given their scenario. For example, if God wanted Adam to be able to have dominion immediately as indicated by Gen. 1.26-28, God would have to create Adam as a mature adult rather than as an infant. However, evidences such as starlight coming from 170,000 light years away indicating a supernova explosion (Rusbult 2006) are difficult to explain from YECs' perspective. YECs might say that God desired humans to observe supernova explosions which declare His glory (Ps. 19.1). However, Ps. 19.1 does not indicate that declaring God's glory has to involve supernova explosions. On the other hand, given that God foreknew that scientists would discover supernova explosions one day and calculate an old age on this basis, a Young-Earth view would imply that God wanted to mislead us by providing so many independent evidences to the contrary without providing an indication of His intention for doing so.

3.3 Biblical interpretation

3.3.1 The possibility of alternative interpretations

As noted earlier, the underlying motivation for the YECs' view is their interpretation of the Bible. Many non-YECs such as professing Christians Denis Lamoureux, Peter Enns and Paul Seely as well as many non-Christians would also agree with YECs' interpretation of the Bible, but they would disagree with YECs' conclusion that the earth is therefore really young; that is, unlike YECs they think that the biblical account is erroneous.

Many other Christians have argued that, in a manner similar to those who objected to Galileo's interpretation of the Bible, YECs have failed to give adequate consideration to the possibility that the relevant passages in the Bible can be legitimately interpreted in various ways (see the discussion on Divine Accommodation in Chapter 2). Some might wonder whether the suggestion of alternative interpretations is a case of rationalization or theology in retreat as science advances. In reply, rationalization is a loaded word; it implies that excuses are being made to avoid the true interpretation. Saying that this is a case of rationalization assumes that the 'true interpretation' is 'young earth', which begs the question. In fact, as will be argued later, the young-earth view is based on unwarranted assumptions; the progress of science has led to a better understanding of the Bible by forcing a closer examination of the Bible which reveals these unwarranted assumptions.

Contemporary YECs claim tradition in their favour, arguing that most Christians prior to the modern era interpret the Bible as saying that God created the cosmos a few thousand years ago (Mook 2008). However, most Christians prior to the modern era also interpret the Bible as saying that the sun rotates around the earth, but not many YECs today would agree with that. The interpretations of those pre-modern Christians who affirmed geocentricism were influenced by their understanding of the world. In particular, they were informed by Ptolemy's model and were not aware of the scientific evidences (such as those discovered by Galileo later) which contradict the geocentric view, and which might have compelled them to examine the Scripture more carefully (for interpretation of passages related to geocentrism, see Loke 2018a).

In view of this, one might also ask whether the translations and interpretations of Genesis by those pre-modern Christians who affirmed that God created the cosmos a few thousand years ago were likewise influenced by their understanding of the world, rather than based on sound biblical exegesis (Rusbult 2008). As noted in Chapter 1, to interpret any text properly, one should follow hermeneutical principles such as considering the literary genre, literary context, meaning of words, grammatical relationship and the background and concerns of the authors (historical, cultural, theological) (e.g. Klein, Blomberg and Hubbard 2017; Thiselton 2006). However, many of the early church fathers lacked an adequate understanding of the Jewish background of the Old Testament and the Hebrew language; this is a well-established fact acknowledged by YEC.[8] The interpretations of the early church fathers were often influenced by Hellenistic ideas (compare their exegeses of Genesis with, say, for example, the careful analysis of Hebrew terminologies and Jewish background of Genesis by contemporary Old Testament scholars such as John Walton and John Collins; see later). Moreover, YECs themselves admit that a number of those pre-modern Christians were also influenced by the popular Millennial Day Theory which is motivated by the desire to date the time of Christ's return (Mook 2008), and which is based on problematic exegeses of Scriptural texts. In addition, those pre-modern Christians were not aware of the scientific evidences (such as those explained earlier) which contradict the YEC view, and which might have motivated them to examine the Scripture more carefully.

3.3.2 Calculations based on biblical genealogies and biblical phrases concerning creation

There is no passage in the Bible which states that the cosmos began a few thousand years ago. A number of Christians such as the seventeenth-century Archbishop

---

8. See, for example, YEC Robert Bradshaw's chapter https://robibradshaw.com/chapter1.htm accessed 13 April 2018. After summarizing the evidences Bradshaw concludes that 'in its knowledge of Hebrew modern Christian scholarship has the edge over the church of the third and fourth centuries'.

Ussher have argued for this conclusion based on their interpretation and calculation of biblical genealogies. Others have objected that such interpretation and calculation involve a number of problematic assumptions. For example, the Hebrew terms for 'begat', 'father' and 'son' in the genealogies do not necessarily express a relationship separated by a single generation. (To illustrate, Mt. 1.8 said that Joram is the father of Uzziah, but among them there is a gap of three generations in 2 Kings 8–15. Luke 3.35-36 states that Shelah is the son of Cainan who is the son of Arphaxad, but Gen. 10.24 states that Arphaxad [Arpachshad] is the father of Shelah.) While some have argued that 'the seventh from Adam' in Jude 14 requires an absence of gaps between Adam and Enoch, others have replied that in the biblical genealogies 'only prominent names are sometimes recorded. For example, St. Matthew refers to three lots of "fourteen generations" (Mt. 1.17) meaning significant generations; and I see no reason why on this precedent Jude 14 should not likewise mean the seventh significant generation' (Gavin McGrath 1997).

Some YECs have argued that, even if there are missing names in the genealogies, there are no missing years because the age of the ancestor is given when the descendant is born. For example, even though there might be genealogical gaps between Enosh and Kenan, some YECs claim that Gen. 5.9 states that Kenan was born when Enosh was ninety years old (Sexton 2015). Other Old Testament scholars have rejected this claim, arguing that verses such as Gen. 5.9 can be understood as causing the begetting of the descendant by setting off a chain of actions by fathering a son. That is, the Hebrew text of Gen. 5.9 does not necessarily imply the birth of Kenan, for it could mean the begetting of an ancestor of Kenan. The causative verbs which are used allow for a temporal gap between the causation of the situation and the result. 'That is, one can "cause" a situation at a certain time, even if the situation itself does not transpire until much later' (Steinmann 2017, p. 146; see also Collins 2018, who explains other factors which make Sexton's exegesis unconvincing, such as the semantics of 'fathered' and the structure of the two genealogies in Genesis 5 and 11). In support of Sexton, YEC Mortenson (2016) argues it is an error to think that, since there may be gaps, there must be gaps. However, Mortenson fails to note that, since the YECs cite the biblical genealogies to support their case, the burden of proof is on them to rule out the alternative possibilities mentioned earlier. In other words, an opponent of YEC does not have to argue 'since there may be gaps, there must be gaps'. Rather, the burden of proof is on the YEC to show that there are no gaps, and they have failed to do so.

In support of the view that the genealogies of Genesis are not intended to be complete, Green (1890) observes that there are evidences of abridgement in other biblical genealogies; moreover, there is no summing up of the ages of the persons listed nor any deduction of chronological statement concerning the time that elapsed from the creation or from the Flood, such as the case concerning the time between the descent into Egypt and the Exodus (Exod. 12.40). Stott (1984) observes that the genealogies never claim to be complete, and that the purpose of the biblical genealogies was more to establish the line of descent (e.g. Jesus was descended from David) than to provide a comprehensive family tree. Provan (2016, p. 108) notes the use of genealogies as abbreviated stories, encapsulating much history in a few words.[9]

In any case, even if there are no missing years in the genealogies as Sexton argues, that does not prove that YECs are correct in their interpretation of Genesis; it only proves that Genesis affirms a Recent Adam the existence of whom – it may come as a surprise to many – is arguably consistent with Old Earth and Evolutionary Creationism (see the discussion on the Most Recent Common Ancestor in Chapter 6). It depends on how the other passages of Scripture are interpreted.

YECs often cite 'But from the beginning of the creation God made them male and female' (Mark 10.6) and 'so that the blood of all the prophets, shed since the foundation of the world, may be charged against this generation, from the blood of Abel to the blood of Zechariah' (Luke 11.50-51 NASB) to argue that Adam and Eve and Abel existed near the beginning of the cosmos and not billions of years after. For example, Mortenson (2008) argues that biblical phrases similar to 'from the beginning of the creation' are also used elsewhere, and in a number of these cases they refer to the creation of heaven and earth in the 'creation week'. One example Mortenson cites is Mark 13.19: 'For those days will be such a *time of* tribulation as has not occurred since the beginning of the creation which God created until now, and never will *again*' [NASB]).

In reply, it is not clear that Mark 13.19 is referring to the creation of heaven and earth rather than the human race (which suffer tribulation). Mortenson (2008) argues that 'which God created' modifies 'creation' rather than 'beginning', but this does not imply that 'creation' refers to the entire creation week or the creation of heavens and earth. Mortenson (2008) also argues that Jesus was thinking that present human experience and present cosmos will end at the same time (cf. v.31 'heaven and earth will pass away') imply that they also began at the same time in the past. However, this is a non-sequitur.

More importantly, similar phrases can have different meanings in different contexts, as Mortenson (2008) himself realizes when he states that some similar biblical phrases are irrelevant for the consideration for Mark 10.6 because in those cases the context refers to something else such as when the readers first heard the apostles' preaching (e.g. 1 John 2.7). Thus the meaning of 'from the beginning of the creation' in Mark 10 should be determined by its context. Now the context of Mark 10.6 is focusing on humanity rather than on the cosmos or other living things. Thus 'the beginning of the creation' may well be referring to the creation

---

9. With regard to the long ages of the patriarchs in the genealogies, Walton notes that the Sumerian kings in their lists were said to have lived even longer (e.g. eight kings reigned for 241,200 years), and he argues that we do not know enough about the rhetorical function of the numbers in such genealogies to know how to read them.

and beginning of humans with the image of God, rather than the creation and beginning of time or of the cosmos or of the earth or of all other living things. The context of Luke 11.50-51 is referring to humanity's story from Abel onwards (Ross 2017, p. 51).); 'the foundation of the world (Greek *kosmos*)', can refer to the 'human world' (*kosmos* can refer to the worldly system of humankind rather than the entire creation).

Finally, even if Mark 10.6 refers to the creation of heaven and earth in the 'creation week', this does not imply that Adam and Eve existed near the beginning of existence of the cosmos. For given the viability of the Functional Creation interpretation (see Section 3.3.3.2), the (functional) creation of heaven and earth in the 'creation week' does not imply the ontological beginning of existence of the cosmos. A similar problem beset YEC Minton's (2008) argument based on Rom. 1.20: 'For since the creation of the world His invisible *attributes*, that is, His eternal power and divine nature, have been clearly perceived, being understood by what has been made, so that they are without excuse' (NASB). Minton thinks that this passage implies that humans have perceived the evidence for God from the very beginning of the creation of the world, which implies that humankind is (nearly) as old as the earth and the cosmos itself. In reply, the conclusion does not follow. For if 'creation of the world' refers to the six days of creation which includes the creation of humankind on Day Six (as YEC argues), then 'since the creation of the world' would imply from the time after the cosmos and humankind were created onwards. However, this does not imply that humankind is (nearly) as old as the earth and the cosmos itself. Rather, it depends on how long each of the 'Six Days' are (is it a solar day, or could it be analogous for a longer period of time as Collins 2018 argues?), and whether the cosmos could have pre-existed before the six days of (functional) creation as Collins (2018) and Walton (2009; 2015) argue (see the discussion on Walton's and Collins' views in Section 3.3.3.2). It should also be noted that since the YECs cite the above-mentioned biblical passages to support their case, the burden of proof is on them to rule out the above-mentioned alternative interpretations.

3.3.3 Interpretation of the opening chapters of Genesis

3.3.3.1 Overview of issues YECs argue that the universe was created within six solar days (Mortenson and Thane eds. 2008; Mortenson eds. 2016). They think that each of the enumerated 'day' in Genesis 1 refers to a solar day, and that this interpretation is confirmed by the repeated refrains 'And there was evening and there was morning'. While YECs often claimed that their interpretation is the traditional one, Moberly (2009, p. 6) points out that a study of the history of interpretation of the first chapters of Genesis indicates that there was no clear consensus among early Christians about how certain details within this material is to be understood. An extensive survey by Andrew Brown demonstrates that various possible interpretations of the creation narrative have a long pedigree.

3. The Time Span of Creation 41

For example, a vague form of an earlier phase of earth's history postulated by the so-called Gap theory – together with a vague form of Functional Creation view – has roots all the way prior to the Renaissance. In the Medieval theologian Peter Lombard's *Sentences* 2.12.1, he wrote:

> In the beginning God created heaven, that is, angels, and earth, namely the material of the four elements as yet mingled and unformed, which is called *Chaos* by the Greeks, *and this was before any day*. Next God *distinguished* the elements, and gave to individual things their proper and distinct types according to their kinds; which he *formed* not at once, as seemed best to certain of the holy Fathers, but through intervals of time and the measures of six days, as it seemed to others. (italics mine)

The non-literal interpretation by Philo of Alexandria in the first century subsequently influenced a number of early Christian theologians such as Irenaeus (who suggests that each day of Genesis 1 represented one thousand years) and Origen, long before the rise of modern science (Brown 2014). Origen wrote:

> For who that has understanding will suppose that the first, and second, and third day, and the evening and the morning, existed without a sun, and moon, and stars? And that the first day was, as it were, also without a sky? . . . And if God is said to walk in the paradise in the evening, and Adam to hide himself under a tree, I do not suppose that any one doubts that these things figuratively indicate certain mysteries, the history having taken place in appearance, and not 'literally'. (*De Principiis IV*, 16)

A number of modern scholars have offered further arguments in support of non-literal interpretation of certain details. For example, Wilkinson (2009, p. 138) argues that Genesis 1 has a liturgical form with repeated refrains, and that it is a complex interweaving of literary genres, poetry, hymn and doctrine in narrative mode; this implies that it is wrong to think that science can be simply lifted from the text. Concerning the Days of Genesis, Augustine writes, 'What kind of days these are is difficult or even impossible for us to imagine, to say nothing of describing them' (*City of God* 11.6.48). He warns:

> In matters that are so obscure and far beyond our vision, we find in Holy Scripture passages which can be interpreted in very different ways without prejudice to the faith we have received. In such cases, we should not rush in headlong and so firmly take our stand on one side that, if further progress in the search for truth justly undermines this position, we too fall with it. (*De Genesi ad Litteram*)

The conclusion that there are plausible alternative interpretations of the text concerning the peripheral details does not imply that the text is totally ambiguous. As noted in Chapter 1, to properly interpret any text (scientific, historical, religious, etc.), one needs to consider the literary genre, context, word meaning, grammatical relationship and background and concerns (historical, cultural, theological). Applying these principles to the opening chapter of Genesis, commentators realize that the main message is clear (even though some of the finer details are vague): God is the Creator of the cosmos, and He has a special plan for humankind. Former archbishop of Canterbury Rowan Williams (2006) observes that '[For] most of the history of Christianity there's been an awareness that a belief that everything depends on the creative act of God, is quite compatible with a degree of uncertainty or latitude about how precisely that unfolds in creative time'.

Some might raise the objection that, if the Bible was divinely inspired, why didn't God tell us clearly that the universe was billions of years old, etc.? Moreover, why would God leave a number of details in the Genesis text ambiguous such that they are subjected to different interpretations – including apparently waffling interpretations – which have been debated by scholars for centuries? The second question expresses the concern of many YECs who regard their interpretation as the 'plain sense' of the Genesis text and who are sceptical of alternative interpretations.

A Christian who believes in the Divine Inspiration of the Bible may reply that the objector neglects the fact that the Bible was first written for people thousands of years ago with very different sets of concerns compared to a twenty-first-century individual. Moreover, people were not aware of the evidences back then, and such statements would have made the Bible seem implausible to them. In addition, as explained in Chapter 1, scientific details were not the main concern of the biblical authors. Their primary intention was to record what they regard as the revelatory and salvific acts of God in human history, and passages in the Bible encourage people to study the physical world and find out the details themselves. By focusing on our twenty-first-century understanding of science, the objector also neglects the fact that science is constantly progressive. The quote from Lennox (2011, p. 30) already cited in Chapter 1 is worth repeating here:

> Suppose, for instance, that God had intended to explain the origin of the universe and life to us in detailed scientific language. Science is constantly changing, developing. . . . If the biblical explanation were at the level, say, of twenty-second-century science, it would likely be unintelligible to everyone, including scientists today. . . . Rather than scientific language, the Bible often uses what is called phenomenological language – the language of appearance. It describes what anyone can see.

Robinson (1988, p. 39) observes that 'If ancient people had consciously set out to articulate a worldview congenial to science, it is hard to imagine how, in terms available to them, they could have done better'.

With regard to why God would leave a number of details in the Genesis text ambiguous, one might reply that – given the progressive nature of science – a text that would appear sensible to people for thousands of years (including people living 3000 years ago, during the medieval period, and in the twenty-first century – think about the vastly different scientific views they had about the cosmos) would have to be open to different interpretations. Unlike other ANE texts (e.g. *Enuma Elish*) which no one today takes seriously because of their clearly fanciful mythological details, the marvel about the Genesis text is that it is still being taken seriously by many people today and the details can (arguably) still be interpreted in a way that is in accordance with proper hermeneutical principles and yet compatible with modern science (as, for example, this book and many others have attempted to show). Thus, instead of understanding the existence of various interpretations (including apparently waffling interpretations) as evidence against the Divine Inspiration of the text, one might even argue that these can be regarded as evidence for the Divine Inspiration of the text. That is, one might argue that they can be understood as evidence of the act of God who in His wisdom had left a number of details in the text vague and open to different interpretations such that they can (arguably) be interpreted in a way that is compatible with what people from different eras understand to be factually correct about the cosmos, yet kept a number of details clear such that people can clearly perceive its central message (e.g. that 'everything depends on the creative act of God' [Rowan Williams]). In answer to the question why God would make it so difficult for people to understand His word, Walton (2009, p. 171) writes:

> Given God's decision to communicate, he had to choose one language and culture to communicate to, which means that every other language and culture has their work cut out for them. As readers from a different language and culture, we have to try to penetrate the original language and culture if we are to receive the maximum benefits of God's revelation. . . . God is not superficial, and we should expect that knowledge of him and his Word would be mined rather than simply absorbed. This means that all of us will be dependent on others with particular skills to help us succeed in the enterprise of interpretation. This is not elitism; it is the interdependence of the people of God as they work together in community to serve one another with the gifts they have.

Collins (2013a, p. 234) explains the moral and spiritual values of such a process of learning to serve one another, and he argues that, instead of making the teachings of scripture clearer,

> God has left it up to the persistent, ongoing efforts of humans to understand and apply the revelation in scripture, something that allows for connections of appreciation between those who through persistent effort have gained spiritual understanding, developed better translations of scripture, and so on, and those who are the beneficiaries of these efforts.

A number of scholars have objected that the opening chapters of Genesis should not be regarded as conveying factual information in view of their parallels with the ANE literature. For example, Harlow (2010) claims that the author(s) of Genesis found it desirable to 'borrow and transform sequences, themes, and motifs from pagan myths' (p.182), citing examples of parallels with ANE texts such as *Gilgamesh Epic, Atrahasis Epic, Enki and Ninhursag*, and *Adapa*. He argues that the parallels he cites establish that 'virtually all of the narrative details in Genesis 2–8 are borrowed from Mesopotamian mythology but transformed to craft new stories with a decidedly different theology' (p.184), and notes that no one today takes *Gilgamesh* and others as historical writings. He concludes that since the early chapters of Genesis borrowed details from them, those chapters should not be taken as historical either.[10]

There are a number of problems with his argument.

First, there are important differences between Genesis and other ANE texts. For example, Harlow (2010, p. 182) claims that the Garden of Eden in Genesis parallels the Sumerian myth of *Enki and Ninhursag* (third millennium BC), which features a pure, clean and bright land called Dilmun where predation and death were unknown. However, unlike Genesis, the concept of a garden of God for human and Divine interaction is absent from the Sumerian myth (Walton 2015, p. 119). On the other hand, certain fanciful mythic details in the Sumerian account such as Ninḫursag giving birth to a deity for each of Enki's hurting parts (head, hair, nose, mouth, throat, arm, ribs and sides) are absent from the Genesis account (Walton 2015, p. 119). While Harlow (2010, p. 182) claims that the giving birth of Ninti for Enki's hurting ribs parallels the creation of Eve from Adam, Walton points out that the alleged parallel is unconvincing: 'All the characters are gods, not humans. Ninti is only one in a series of deities associated with various parts of the body, and the goddesses are given birth, not formed. Ninti has no continuing association with Enki. . . . The inclusion of "rib" is incidental' (Walton 2015, p. 119; Walton discusses a number of other examples in his book). By ignoring important differences one might be able to draw various kinds of parallels with a large number of unrelated literature.

Second, parallels do not prove that Genesis borrowed from Mesopotamian mythology (Arnold 2009, pp. 31–2, 41). Lambert (1965, p. 289) observes that parallels to Genesis 'can also be sought and found among the Canaanites, the ancient Egyptians, the Hurrians, the Hittites and the early Greeks. When the parallels have been found, the question of dependence, if any, has to be approached with an open mind.' It could be the case that both descended from a common tradition, the Mesopotamian version got corrupted by myths to conform to the polytheistic religions of its people (Longman III and Dillard 2006, p. 52), and the

---

10. Harlow (2010) also offers another argument by claiming that the first creation account in Gen. 1.1–2.3 contradicts the second one in Gen. 2.4b–2.25. For discussion, see what follows.

Genesis version aims to counter these myths and reaffirm the original version. On the one hand, there is a paucity of evidence dating from earlier eras to rule out this possibility. On the other hand, Kitchen (1966, p. 89) argues that, in fact, the contrast between the simple creation account in Genesis and the more elaborate ANE creation epics indicates that the Genesis account had earlier roots, for it is generally the case that simple accounts or traditions give rise (by accretion or embellishment) to elaborate legends.

It should be noted that the doctrine of Divine Inspiration of the Bible does not exclude the possibility that the inspired biblical authors made use of earlier sources. Many Evangelical scholars recognize this point as well. For example, Longman III and Dillard (2006, p. 51) note that 'Evangelical scholars recognize that the Pentateuch contains pre-Mosaic sources as well as post-Mosaic glosses . . . it is possible to affirm the substantial Mosaic authorship of the Pentateuch in line with the occasional internal evidence and the strong external testimony, while allowing for earlier sources as well as later glosses and elaboration.'[11] The doctrine of Divine Inspiration also does not deny the value of studying the biblical account in the context of ANE texts. The avoidance of unjustifiably imposing ANE structures onto the biblical texts is compatible with citing parallels that may help us understand the text better (Averbeck 2013).

For example, comparing Genesis 1 with the Ugaritic cosmogony reveals something very different: In Genesis 1 'the lack of any conflict, even any personification of the cosmic oceans or waters, heightens the picture a powerful God who but speaks and the divine will is accomplished . . . even the old role of cosmic forces as domesticated has been downplayed, even depersonalized. These cosmic monsters are no longer primordial forces opposed to the Israelite God at the beginning of creation. Instead, they are creatures like other creatures rendered in this story. The narrative encloses the order of the divine creation around these monstrous enemies and, by omission, transforms them into another part of creation' (Smith 2001, p. 38).

The Babylonian creation text *Enuma Elish* has also often been compared with the Genesis account. The *Enuma Elish* begins this way:

---

11. One example of post-Mosaic gloss is the ending of Deuteronomy, which comments on what happened after Moses' death. While many have argued that the (final) author of Genesis 1 was a member of Israel's priestly caste who lived during the post-exilic period, others have argued that he lived during the pre-exilic period (see Weinfeld 2004, pp. 95–109). Theories concerning the sources of the book of Genesis have a complicated history since the Enlightenment period. For an overview, see Longman III and Dillard (2006, pp. 42–51); Arnold (2009, pp. 12–18), and Westermann (1984). The traditional Graf–Wellhausen hypothesis, which postulated four sources J, E, D and P for the Pentateuch, has been widely criticized by scholars in recent decades, but this criticism should be understood as a refinement rather than a rejection of the research concerning the issue of sources altogether.

> When skies above were not yet named
> Nor earth below pronounced by name,
> Apsu, the first one, their begetter
> And maker Tiamat, who bore them all,
> Had mixed their waters together,
> But had not formed pastures, nor discovered reed-beds;
> When yet no gods were manifest,
> Nor names pronounced, nor destinies decreed,
> Then gods were born within them.
> Lahmu (and) Lahamu emerged, their names pronounced.
> As soon as they matured, were fully formed,
> Anshar (and) Kishar were born, surpassing them.
> They passed the days at length, they added to the years.
> Anu their first-born son rivalled his forefathers:
> Anshar made his son Anu like himself,
> And Anu begot Nudimmud in his likeness.
> He, Nudimmud, was superior to his forefathers:
> Profound of understanding, he was wise, was very strong at arms.
> Mightier by far than Anshar his father's begetter,
> He had no rival among the gods his peers.
> The gods of that generation would meet together
> And disturb Tiamat, and their clamour reverberated.
> They stirred up Tiamat's belly,
> They were annoying her by playing inside Anduruna. (Dalley 2000, p. 233)

The text goes on to describe the god Marduk's victory over the sea monster Tiamat and forming the heavens and the earth from her dead body, and killing her consort Kingu and forming humans from his blood and the clay of the earth. Understanding this context may help us perceive the implicit polemic in Genesis 1–2 against these myths (Longman III and Dillard 2006, p. 52). The absence of certain fanciful mythic details (e.g. the sea monster as the source of heaven and earth in the Babylonian account) in the Genesis account is significant here as well. On the other hand, the presence of features such as saying that there are 'lights' (or lamps) in the sky in Gen. 1.14 as opposed to naming them sun and moon indicates 'a rejection of any trace of divinity in the sun . . . to describe the sun and the moon constantly as lights or lamps is to put the heavenly bodies as a whole in the context of creation' (Westermann 1984, p. 129).

Brown (2010, p. 49) observes:

> Compared to the rough-and-tumble, divinely micromanaged, theogonic world of Mesopotamian creation, Genesis 1 is an exercise in mythological reduction, on the one hand, and an acknowledgement of creation's freedom and integrity, on the other. Creation in Genesis is replete with dynamic order and structure, cosmic qualities readily discerned by science.

When considering the genre of Genesis one should be careful to distinguish between the intention of the ancient author(s) and the perception of modern scholars, many of whom may have been influenced by a naturalistic world view very different from that of the ancient author(s), and which would exclude any miraculous event whatsoever. Many modern scholars have labelled the genre of all or parts of Genesis as novella, legend, fable, myth or saga (Van Seters 1992, pp. 10–23;[12] Coats 1983, pp. 5–10; for saga, see the influential writings of Gunkel 1901; 1902; 1910). Other scholars have objected that, on the one hand, the intention of ancient author(s) to convey events which he/they thought took place can be seen from the chronological structure of the text, the use of the so-called *waw* consecutive verbal form which is the basic characteristic of narrative in the Hebrew Bible, and the use of the *tôledôt* formulae (Gen. 2.4; 5.1; 6.9; 10.1; 11.10, 27; 25.12, 19; 36.1, 9; 37.2), a structural device which has been translated as 'these are the generations', 'this is the family history', and 'this is the account' (see Longman III and Dillard 2006, pp. 54–5 and the sources cited; see also the debate between various positions in Halton ed. 2015). Whether the author(s) accomplished his/their intention (e.g. concerning human origins) is a separate issue (see further, Chapter 5). On the other hand, a number of scholars have noted that the naturalistic world view has been sharply criticized in recent years and that there has been 'an increasingly rigorous philosophical and theological defence of the possibility of miracles' (Twelftree 2011, pp. 2518–19),[13] as well as the 'recognition that the miracle traditions have not arisen in an entirely credulous world' (Twelftree 2011, n.10).

Concerning the genre of Genesis 1–11, Wenham observes:

> The backbone of Gen 1 – 11 is an expanded linear genealogy: ten generations from Adam to Noah and ten generations from Noah to Abram. Most figures in these genealogies are simply known by their names and their age when they fathered their first-born and their age at death. But a few of them have extra details attached to them such as Lamech's prayer for his son Noah or the observation that Enoch walked with God. At other times the additional comments balloon into long accounts about the garden of Eden or the flood, but this does not obscure the point that these stories are add-ons to the chronological backbone of the genealogy. This

---

12. Van Seters himself affirms the historical intentionality of the author(s) through comparing the text with Greek historiography, though he does not believe that the author(s) was/were correct in many instances.

13. For example, philosophers Moreland and Craig have argued that, instead of understanding a miracle as 'a violation of the laws of nature', a miracle should be understood as 'an event which would not have been produced by the natural causes operative at a certain time and place' (Moreland and Craig 2003, pp. 566–8). Therefore, unless we assume that causes other than natural causes do not exist – which would be begging the question against the existence of God – miracles are possible. For a critique of arguments against the plausibility of miracles by David Hume and others, see further, McGrew (2009, 2013), Loke (2020a, Chapter 8).

> interest in chronology and the causal explanation of the sequence of events in the dim and distant past makes protohistory a better description of Gen 1 – 11 than myth on the one hand and history on the other. (Wenham 2015, pp. 95–7)

Saying that the ancient author(s) intention to convey events which he/they thought took place does not deny that they could have used a variety of forms such as poetry, hymn and narrative. In addition, one needs to note the distinction between 'historical' and 'literal'; a text may be essentially metaphorical or symbolic and still retain historical features or elements that reflect real events in time and space (Arnold 2014, pp. 34–5). While many scholars have argued that the garden, the trees and the serpent are symbols, by itself this does not prove that they are not real. For example, a country's flag is a symbol, but it is also something real (Walton 2015, pp. 116, 226).

Many have regarded the talking snake in Genesis 3 as a feature of fairy tales in which animals talk. However, Collins (2011b, p. 12) observes that the only other example of a talking animal in a biblical narrative (Balaam's donkey in Numbers 22) attributes that speech to some kind of interference with the animal's proper nature. Unlike fairy tales, the biblical author(s) did not portray a world in which donkeys naturally speak, but says/say that the Lord 'opened the mouth of the donkey', which is what enabled it to speak (Num. 22.28). Given this observation and the portrayal of the serpent's knowledge and motivation in Genesis 2 (e.g. urging disobedience to God's solemn command, implying that God is a liar and insinuating that God's motives cannot be trusted), it is reasonable to conclude that the biblical author(s) intended to convey that the snake talked as a result of some kind of interference by an evil personal agent which the Jewish and New Testament tradition (e.g. Wis. 1.13, 2.24; John 8.44; Rev. 12.9, 202) identifies as 'Satan' or 'the devil'. Collins notes:

> to deny this by insisting that Genesis never mentions the Evil One is actually a poor reading, because it fails to appreciate that biblical narrators generally prefer the laconic 'showing' to the more explicit 'telling', leaving the readers to draw the right inferences from the words and actions recorded. If we read the story poorly like this, we will miss a crucial part of the story. (2011b, p. 12)

Some scholars interpret the serpent in Genesis 3 as symbolic rather than literal, noting that it is a well-known symbol of evil in the ancient Near East (Longman 2017). However, it should be noted that the fact that the serpent is a well-known symbol of evil in the ancient Near East does not exclude the possibility that the author of Genesis intended to write about a literal serpent which was also symbolic of evil. On the other hand, one should not assume that all the details in the early chapters of Genesis are literal. For example, Collins (2018, section 7.A.2) comments that 'eat dust' (3:14) when used of the snake

> would probably not have evoked the snake's diet; we have to suppose that at least some Israelites had seen them eating rodents, lizards, or other snakes. The

expression conveys, then, not a diet, but humiliation and defeat (Mic. 7:17; Isa. 49:23; Ps. 72:9). Likewise, to 'go on the belly' (also in 3:14) may refer to travel in some contexts (Lev 11:42), but in this heightened speech is better suited to describe the cringing of a beaten foe.

Craig (2021) has argued, based on his analysis of the genre of Gen. 1–11, that while the existence of Adam is intended to be taken literally in view of the genealogies, details such as the talking snake and the trees should not be taken literally. The model for the origin of humanity defended in this book is not committed to denying or affirming the view of Craig. (I will be engaging with the work of Craig in Loke forthcoming. See also Section 5.8.5.)

Against the conclusion that the ancient biblical author(s) intention was to convey events which he/they thought took place, some might claim that the first creation account in Gen. 1.1–2.3 contradicts the second one in Gen. 2.4b-2.25. For example, the first account says that plants were created on the third day (Gen. 1.11-13) and birds and animals on the fifth day (Gen. 1.20-23) before humans on the sixth day (Gen. 1.26-27), while the second account says that God created man first (Gen. 2.7) followed by the plants and trees (Gen. 2.5-6, 9), birds and animals (Gen. 2.19), and then woman (Gen. 2.21-22).

The problem of apparent contradictions in these passages is not new; Harlow (2010, p. 185) observes that the recognition of two distinct accounts goes back to the first-century Jewish exegete Philo of Alexandria (citing Philo, *De Opificio Mundi*, 134–5). From very early times, scholars have discussed various ways of reconciling the apparent contradictions, and such attempts continue to this day. For example, Collins argues that, on the one hand, while it has been claimed that the two creation accounts come from separate sources, it has been objected that none of these putative sources is actually known to exist; the only text we have is the one that places these two accounts together. In any case, the final author/editor of the text who did not smooth out the apparent contradictions would have invited ancient readers to seek ways to 'recognize the truthfulness of *both* narratives' (Collins 2011b, p. 8; citing James Barr 1999, p. 6). On the other hand, a version of the traditional Rabbinic interpretation regards Gen. 1.1–2.3 as the overall account of God creating and preparing the earth as a suitable place for humans to live, and Gen. 2.4-25 as elaborating the events of the sixth day of Gen. 1.25 (James Barr 1999, pp. 108–12, Collins 2006, pp. 121–2; Collins provides a grammatical justification [e.g. the chiastic structure of Gen. 2.4] which shows how Gen. 2.4-7 links the two stories.). For example, while the first account does not specify the number of human beings created on Day Six, the second account elaborates that God created one man followed by one woman. Given that the differences can be understood as complementary rather than contradictory (see later), there is inadequate justification for regarding them as discrepancies.

Hamilton (1990) notes that the plants in Genesis 1 are those that are able to grow wild, whereas those in Genesis 2 refer to those that require human cultivation through planting and artificial irrigation. Concerning Gen. 2.19, Kitchen (1966, p. 119) argues that the first verb concerning the formation of animals can be rendered as the pluperfect 'had formed'. This implies that the animals had already been formed prior to humans. (Thus ESV: 'Now out of the ground the LORD God had formed every beast of the field and every bird of the heavens and brought them to the man to see what he would call them.') There is nothing strained about such an attempt to reconcile the two accounts; the attempt follows quite naturally from consideration of context, word meaning and grammar.[14] Even if there is no reason to prefer this reading over the alternative, there is no good reason to exclude it either.

While many biblical scholars today disparaged such attempts at reconciling accounts, such attempts are, in fact, widely utilized in historical studies. For example, historian Gilbert Garraghan (1973, p. 314) notes that 'almost any critical history that discusses the evidence for important statements will furnish examples of discrepant or contradictory accounts and the attempts which are made to reconcile them'. Thus, unless one assumes that the author of Genesis does not intend to convey historical information (which begs the question), one should not dismiss the attempts which have been made. Wenham (1992, p. 128) observes that, while strained harmonization is worthless, many biblical scholars 'give up too easily' instead of doing the necessary spadework, noting that the harmonistic approach 'enables one to ponder long and conscientiously over every detail of the narrative and to see how one account illuminates and modifies another. Gradually (without fudging) people and events take shape and grow in solidity and the scenes come to life in one's mind.'

The process of harmonization does not silence the diversity of voices present within the biblical canon; rather, it reveals the unity within the diversity of voices within the biblical canon.

Other differences between Gen. 1.1–2.3 and Gen. 2.4-25 can be easily accounted by the view that the latter retells part of the story of the former from a different angle, elaborating on some details without repeating all the details. For example, concerning the creation of humankind, Gen. 1.1–2.3 does not mention the sequence that Eve was created after Adam, but it does not exclude that sequence either. Gen. 2.4-25 elaborates Gen. 1.26-27 by detailing the sequence. N. T. Wright

---

14. Kitchen explains further: 'As pluperfect meaning is included in the perfective, we cannot a priori deny it to contextual equivalents of the Perfective. Hebraists and others should also remember that no special pluperfect tenses exist in the Ancient Semitic Languages (or in Egyptian), this nuance being covered by perfective forms and equivalents interpreted on context as here in Hebrew' (1966, p. 119).

He further adds examples from Scripture to support this argument:

The meaning of any Waw-Consecutive-Imperfective must be settled on context, not by appeal to abstract principles.... For Hebrew Waw-Consecutive-Imperfectives that require a pluperfect standpoint in English, cf: Exod. 4.19 (picking up 4.12, not 18); Exod. 19.2 ('having departed... and come... they pitched...' picks up 17.1, not 19.1; these examples, courtesy Dr W. J. Martin). Perhaps more striking, Josh. 2.22 ('now the pursuers had sought them...') does not continue immediately preceding verbs' (1966, p. 119).

notes that ancient writers who intended to tell others what actually happened took for granted that they were not obliged to mention every event, nor every detail of an event. Wright observes, for example, that 'When Josephus tells the story of his own participation in the various actions that started the Jewish-Roman war in AD 66, the story he tells in his Jewish War and the parallel story he tells in the Life do not always correspond in detail' (Wright 2003, pp. 648–9).

3.3.3.2 Various interpretations of Genesis 1–3 and two important recent contributions by Walton and Collins Other than YEC, various interpretations of the opening chapters of Genesis have been offered in the literature over the centuries, such as

- Day-Age creation (e.g. Ross 2017; this regards each of the seven days of Genesis 1 as a duration of time which can be much longer than a solar day);
- Gap theory/gap of unknown duration of time between each 'day' of Genesis 1 (e.g. Lennox 2011);
- Literary framework view (e.g. Waltke 2001; see in what follows);
- Functional Creation (e.g. Walton 2009; see in what follows) and
- Various forms of non-literal interpretations (e.g. Philo of Alexandria, Origen and Augustine as noted previously).

The amount of literature on these interpretations is huge, and it is beyond the scope of this book to provide a detailed assessment of them all (for surveys, see Westermann 1984; Wenham 1987; Barton and Wilkinson eds. 2009; Charles ed. 2013; Halton ed. 2015; Stump ed. 2017). In what follows I shall focus on two important recent contributions by Old Testament scholars John Walton (2006; 2009; 2015) and C. John Collins (2018). (Another important recent contribution based on the analysis of the genre of biblical texts has been made by Craig (2021). See my engagement with Craig in Loke (forthcoming).)

Walton's (2006; 2009; 2015) 'Functional Creation' interpretation has been widely discussed in recent literature, and while many are appreciative of his insights, others remain critical.[15] I think that many of the criticisms are based on misunderstandings, while others can be adequately responded to with some clarifications and perhaps slight modification of his views. The result is that a plausible interpretation of Genesis 1 which is exegetically defensible, which avoids the problems associated with Concordism (see Chapter 1) and which is also relevant to the creation–evolution controversy can be offered. I would like to emphasize that the model concerning the origins of humanity which I am defending in this book is not dependent on Walton's interpretation. Even if one disagrees with Walton's interpretation, one can consider C. John Collins's interpretation (see later) which is also compatible with my view.

---

15. Walton has replied to a number of objections in subsequent publications, for example, in Walton (2015).

According to Walton, the Seven Days of Genesis 1–2 can be understood as seven solar days (Walton 2009, p. 108) during which the pre-existing cosmos, the earth and living things were ordered by God to function in a way that provided a suitable home (a 'cosmic temple') for the first humans (Walton 2015, p. 104). Functional Creation is understood as making a pre-existing thing function or appear functional (i.e. in a phenomenological sense) in a certain way. This often involves an ordering process, for example, the separation or shaping of pre-existing thing(s). This is in contrast to creating something out of nothing (ex nihilo), and in many cases it is also in contrast to the beginning of existence of something, although in other cases it may involve the beginning of existence of a new thing as well. To elaborate, on the Functional Creation view, commanding things 'to be' – for example, 'Let there be light' (v.3) on Day One – does not necessarily mean that light begins to exist only on Day One. Rather, with respect to Gen. 1.5, the light is called 'Day' rather than 'light'. Calling it 'Day' emphasizes the functional and phenomenological aspect: the light can now be seen on the earth's surface to mark daytime. On Day Two (Gen. 1.6-8), 'Let there be an expanse . . . and God made the expanse (ESV)', this involves the creation of a space by the separation of pre-existing waters (see my discussion on *rāqîa'* in Loke 2018a).

Some scholars have accused Walton of interpreting creation as functional apart from material. For example, Collins (2013, p. 180) writes, 'I do not understand why Walton thinks that material and function provide a meaningful antithesis . . . after all it is things with material existence that perform the functions.' Likewise, Averbeck (2013, p. 171) remarks that when a person makes a functional clay pot he is making something material. I think this accusation is due to the fact that Walton uses the word 'material' in a confusing way. If, instead of contrasting functional with material creation, we contrast Functional Creation (making a pre-existing thing function in a certain way) with creating something out of nothing (ex nihilo), the problem disappears (e.g. a clay pot is of course material, but it is not created out of nothing). This is consistent with Walton's intent. For example, Walton (2015, p. 37) notes that, even though the creative activities involve components of the material world (waters, dry land, plants), the verbs do not describe God making any of those objects (i.e. not making them ex nihilo). 'The seas are gathered, the dry land appears and the plants sprout. This is the work of organization and ordering' (2015, p. 37). By Functional Creation Walton intends to convey, not merely specifying functions, but also the idea of organizing pre-existing things as well.[16] Walton is not saying that the already existing physical entities do not have any function at all prior to the Creation Week – surely the animals had been feeding! – rather, Walton is saying that, prior to the Creation Week, they have no function *with respect to the Cosmic Temple*. Unlike YEC, Walton's view does not exclude the possibility that there were already physical entities prior to the Seven Days which were organized – not with respect to *the Cosmic Temple*, but

---

16. Thus Walton's idea of Functional Creation involves both Aristotle's idea of efficient cause (bringing about an effect; that is, things get organized) and final cause (teleology).

for other purposes (which, for example, allowed for the existence of dinosaurs for millions of years) – and which were subsequently organized into things to which functions were assigned *with respect to the Cosmic Temple* in six literal days. While creation involves the origination of certain physical properties, this does not necessarily mean 'the beginning of existence of something', because it can also mean 'a preexisting thing taking on certain new physical properties' as it is being made functional.

Walton (2009, p. 169) thinks that his interpretation is a literal reading of the text: the days are taken literally as solar days, while 'create' is taken literally as Functional Creation, in accordance with an understanding of the Hebrew language and ancient Israelite culture. Moreover, the Garden of Eden is regarded as an archetypal sanctuary, with features that are found in later sanctuaries such as the Jerusalem Temple (Walton 2009, pp. 81–2).

Walton does not deny that the material universe had a beginning and that God is the First Cause who brought the universe into existence. On the contrary, he argues that there are other passages in the Bible (e.g. Col. 1.16-17)[17] which affirm God's creation of the material cosmos ex nihilo (Walton 2009, p. 97; As Copan and Craig observe, the implication of saying that Christ is before all things in Colossians 1.16-17 is that 'there was a state of being in which Christ existed and the universe did not' [Copan and Craig 2004, p. 85]. Paul affirms that all things come from 'God' (1 Cor. 8.6; Rom. 11.36), and not from 'God and another pre-existent entity'; see the discussion in Loke (2021c)).[18] However, Walton thinks that creation ex nihilo is not necessarily the message of the opening chapters of Genesis, the focus of which is on the setting up of the Cosmic Temple. According to Walton's theological view, the creation ex nihilo event happened first (as portrayed by Col. 1.16) and provided the pre-existing material for the Functional Creation as portrayed by Genesis 1–2. However, the creation ex nihilo event is indicated by other Bible passages and not by Genesis 1–2 which nevertheless does not rule an earlier creation ex nihilo event either. Contrary to Hamilton (1990 p. 105) who claims that the standard alternatives are either monotheism (only God is eternal) or eternal dualism (God and matter are eternal), saying that Genesis does not convey creatio ex nihilo is compatible with saying that, unlike other ANE

---

17. 'For in him all things in heaven and on earth were created, things visible and invisible, whether thrones or dominions or rulers or powers – all things have been created through him and for him. He himself is before all things, and in him all things hold together.'

18. In an influential study, Gerhard May (2004) claims that the doctrine of creatio ex nihilo was not found in Scripture at all, but arose in the second century CE as a response to the Greek and Gnostic idea that the world was formed out of eternal matter. However, his argument suffers from a failure to distinguish between words and concepts (Osborn 2001, p. 66; Osborn observes that the concept of creation from nothing can be present without the formula, and vice versa). 'The meaning and substance of the doctrine, though not the terminology, is firmly rooted in scripture and pre-Christian Jewish literature' (Bockmuehl 2012).

cosmologies, Genesis does not affirm the *eternity* of pre-existing matter either. (Concerning the relationship between Gen. 1.1 and New Testament creation texts such as John 1.1-3, see later.)

Walton (2009, pp. 110–11) compares his view with the literary framework hypothesis, which recognizes that literary parallels exist between days one and four, days two and five, and days three and six of Genesis 1, with the first three days defining realms of habitation and the second set of three filling these realms with inhabitants, and concluding that the six days are a literary device.[19] Walton thinks it is implausible that the ancient Israelites thought of this text in only literary/theological terms. However, he observes that his Functional Creation view does not require an abandonment of a literary framework, but adding to it the understanding of Functional Creation.

I shall now discuss the evidences Walton offers for his interpretation, address a number of objections others have raised against his interpretation and discuss the implications of Walton's interpretation. It should be noted that citing Walton's views concerning Functional Creation – which I find insightful – does not imply that I agree with him on every detail concerning the interpretation of Genesis. Where appropriate, I shall insert the interpretation of the details by other scholars in what follows.[20]

Walton argues that ancient Hebrews focused more on function and phenomenology, noting, for example, that Gen. 1.5 calls the light 'Day'.

Walton also notes that, while the Hebrew word *bārā'* which is translated as 'create' in Genesis 1 (Gen. 1.1, 21; 2.3) can mean creating something out of nothing, it can also mean Functional Creation, that is, to make a pre-existing thing function in a certain way. This is not a new observation; for example, back in the medieval period the Jewish commentator Ibn Ezra (1089–c.1167) already noted that *bārā'* does not of itself denote the creation of something out of nothing (Sarna 1989, p. 5). Other scholars have observed that *bārā'* is frequently used together with other verbs (e.g. *asah*; Gen. 1.26-27) which often do mention the material out of which something is made; and that its meaning is not unlike the use of yatsar in Gen. 2.7 (Arnold 2009, p. 37; it should be noted that Gen. 2.7 states that human was formed of dust, which was a pre-existing material). The main distinction between *bārā'* and other verbs is that *bārā'* highlights the initiation of something new (Averbeck

---

19. Cf. Westermann (1984, p. 88)'s comments on the eight works of creation over six days: 'The universe with all its not suddenly established by one sweeping act; it is set into the categories of time and space. A distinction is made between the world as such (the first three works) and what is in the world and upon the earth (works three to eight), and again between animate and inanimate life.'

20. While Walton's claim that ANE creation stories (e.g. Egyptian and Mesopotamian) are more concerned about assigning functions than material origins have been challenged (Currid 2017), many of the evidences that Walton cites are based on Hebrew Scriptures rather than Egyptian and Mesopotamian myths, as noted later.

2013, p. 11); this point remains regardless of whether pre-existing material is involved.

Citing detailed studies of *bārā'* which is used about fifty times in the Hebrew text of Scripture (Walton 2009, pp. 36–43; 2011, pp. 127–39), Walton (2015, pp. 29–30) concludes that 'Although a number of occurrences could refer to material creation, many of them cannot'.[21] He argues that those that do not refer to material creation fit into the category that describes activity bringing order, organization, roles or functions to pre-existing entities, such as the creation of the blacksmith and ravager in Isa. 54.16[22] (2015, pp. 29–30; other examples include the creation of a clean heart in Ps. 51.20 and the creation of Israel in Isa. 43.1).

Walton notes that in Hebrew usage the adverb 'beginning' typically introduces a period of time rather than a point in time (e.g. in Job 8.7 which speaks of the early part of Job's life, and Jer. 28.1 which refers to the beginning period of Zedekiah's reign) (Walton 2009, p. 43). 'The heavens and the earth' is a Semitic *merism*[23] for the entirety of physical reality, for which there is no separate word in Hebrew (Sarna 1989, p. 5); in a merism, words coupled together means something different than the words taken individually). Hence, Gen. 1.1 does not imply that the earth existed 'in the beginning'. In the subsequent verses 'heaven(s)' refers to 'sky' (Gen. 1.8, 9, 14, 15, 17, etc.) while 'earth' refers to 'land' (Gen 1.11, 12, 22, 24, 25, etc.).

The syntactical features of Gen. 1.1-3 present many difficulties (Bauks 1997) and the relationships between these verses have been heavily debated in the literature (Westermann 1984, pp. 93–8). The result is a number of possible interpretations which are helpfully classified by Copan and Craig (2004, p. 38) as follows:

1. Reading v.1 as a clause subordinate to v.2: 'In the beginning when God created the heavens and the earth, the earth was a formless void and darkness covered the face of the deep, while a wind from God (or while the spirit of God) swept over the face of the waters. Then God said, "Let there be light"; and there was light.' (NRSV)
2. Reading v.1 as a clause subordinate to v.3, with v.2 as a parenthetical comment: 'In the beginning when God created the heavens and the earth (now the earth was a formless void and darkness covered the face of the deep, while a wind from God (or while the spirit of God) swept over the face of the waters'), God said "Let there be light"; and there was light.'
3. Reading v.1 as an independent clause and not as a subordinate clause and regarding v.1 as an introductory formula summarizing all the events

---

21. Walton also notes that 'deity' is always either the subject or the implied subject (in passive constructions) of *bārā'* in the Old Testament.

22. 'See it is I who have created (*bārāṭî*) the smith who blows the fire of coals, and produces a weapon fit for its purpose; I have also created (*bārāṭî*) the ravager to destroy.'

23. In a merism, words coupled together means something different than the words taken individually.

described in vv.2–31: that is, 'In the beginning, God created the heavens and the earth, and this is how it happened.'
4. Reading v.1 as an independent clause describing the first act of creation.

It is beyond the scope of this book to provide a detailed assessment of the huge amount of literature arguing for or against each of these possible interpretations. Suffice to note that they are all compatible with the model I am defending in this book.

Walton's interpretation fits the description of Type (3) in the classification by Copan and Craig mentioned earlier. Walton (2011, pp. 123-4) explains that the arguments against taking v.1 as an independent clause are not compelling. Observing the fact that throughout Genesis sections begin with a literary introduction (Gen. 2.4; 5.1; 6.9; etc.), Walton (2015, p. 27) interprets Gen. 1.1 as a literary introduction: 'In the inaugural period [this is the nature of the Hebrew word "beginning"], God created the heavens and earth, and this is how he did it.'[24] The actual account begins in Gen. 1.2, where we find the description of the pre-creation situation with material (earth, seas) already present, which was then organized to function in the way God intended. The mentioning of the heavens and the earth in Gen. 2.1-3 comes back to the introduction in Gen. 1.1 in its summary as it indicates the completion of the creation activities over the seven-day period (Walton 2009, p. 45).

Collins, however, interprets v.1 as an independent clause describing the first act of creation (Type 4 in the classification by Copan and Craig). He argues that in v.1 *bārā'* is in the perfect tense and establishes the background, while the first verse in the storyline tense (*wayyiqtol*) appears in v.3: 'And God said . . .' (see Collins 2013, p. 89 and the sources cited). Collins explains that his view that whole narrative sections can begin with a *wayyiqtol* is supported by the recognition that the *wayyiqtol* can be understood as an actual past tense (connected to the *preterite* form attested in other Semitic languages) rather than as an imperfect tense, and by discourse grammar. Collins elaborates,

> this is the normal usage of the syntax we find here. That is, our pericope is a narrative that uses the *wayyiqtol* tense for its storyline; the *wayyiqtol* sequence begins in 1:3. In 1:1 we have an adverbial ('in the beginning') that opens the verse, and the clause's verb is in the perfect tense form (ארב, *bārā'*, 'created'). In such cases the clause designates a background action that took place before the main storyline got under way. (Collins 2018, section 7A1)

Collins (2013, p. 181) himself thinks that his view can incorporate Functional Creation. On his view, Gen. 1.1 describes, 'the initial bringing into existence of all things, v.2 gives the condition under which the first day began, the Seven Days are God's activity of shaping physical reality to provide a suitable place for mankind to

---

24. Cf. the translation of Gen. 1.1 in the NRSV: 'In the beginning *when* God created the heavens and the earth' (italics mine).

live, to love and to serve.' He concludes that 'The main event of "material origin" is in 1.1; the rest is mostly shaping the material that is already there'.

On the other hand, reading v.1 as a subordinate clause ('When God began to create...') is compatible with a Functional Creation view as well. Sarna (1989, p. 5) observes that the Mesopotamian Creation epic *Enuma Elish* also commences the same way – in fact, *Enuma* means 'when'. It is true that the differences in theology between the *Enuma Elish* and the Genesis account are quite marked; nevertheless, the opening style of the *Enuma Elish* can be understood as a conventional opening style for cosmological narratives (1989, p. 5). On this Reading Genesis 1 does not convey creatio ex nihilo and thus the creation would be functional. (However, it should be noted that neither does this reading preclude the possibility of an earlier creatio ex nihilo event; it is just that creatio ex nihilo is not conveyed by the text according to this reading; see Arnold 2009, p. 36.)

As noted earlier, according to Walton, during the Seven Days of Genesis 1 God ordered the pre-existing cosmos to form a cosmic temple, which Genesis 2 clarifies as having its centre in the Garden of Eden (Walton 2015, p. 104). Given this and the functional and phenomenological emphasis of the text, the details of Genesis 1 should therefore be viewed from the perspective of the place which was later to become the habitat for the first humans. Thus, for example, the initial darkness (v.2), the mixing of waters prior to separation (Gen. 1. 6-8) and waters covering the land (Gen. 1.9-13) do not have to be interpreted as (what we understand today to be) a 'worldwide phenomenon'. Rather, the perspective is phenomenological and viewed from a particular place on earth which was to become the centre of the Cosmic Temple.

The initial state of the earth was *tōhû wābōhû* (Gen. 1.2). This is often translated as 'formless and void', but Walton argues that it should be understood as 'lacking order and purpose' (Walton 2015, p. 28). The place which was later to become the habitat for the first humans was covered by darkness.

On Day One (Gen. 1.3-5), God created a period of light that interrupted the darkness and which was to alternate with periods of darkness, and He named these periods Day and Night (Walton 2011, p. 153). With respect to Task (C), it should be noted that Walton's interpretation does not exclude the possibility that there were already days and nights in an earlier period prior to the time the place was covered by darkness; it only implies that God intervened to set up a time cycle in that place.

On Day Two (Gen. 1.6-8), God created a space[25] between the heaven and the earth which separated the waters below and the waters above (Walton 2011, p. 159; for the meaning of *rāqîa'*, see the discussion in Loke (2018a; 2020c; 2021b)). One might assume that prior to the separation these waters were mixed together at the place which was later to become the habitat for the first humans, perhaps in the form of a thick cloud portrayed in Job 38.9 ('made the clouds its garment and wrapped it in thick darkness' (Ross 2017, p. 49). Following Beale, I had previously

---

25. For the meaning of the word *rāqîa'*, see the discussion in Loke 2018a.

argued in Loke (2018a) that the writer of Genesis 1 is focusing on the setting up of water cycle, thus he uses the word for water (which ancients knew composed the *clouds*) consistently. Lamoureux objects that the Old Testament has well-known words for rain and clouds but none of these words appear (2020, p. 186). But my argument applies here too: the writer of Genesis 1 is focusing on the setting up of water cycle, thus he uses the word for water (which ancients knew composed the *rain and clouds*) consistently. Lamoureux then objects that *rāqîa'* is found twelve times in the OT outside Day Two, but it is never associated with rain or clouds (ibid). But that is because (as he noted) the context of those other passages do not concern the hydraulic cycle (ibid). They are just referring to the expanse, whereas the context of Day Two does have something to do with water. Concerning Lamoureux's question why Day Two is not called good, one plausible answer is that the Second Day not only concerns the setting up of water cycle but also the separation of waters which (as Wenham 1987, p. 19 notes) is only completed on Day Three (v.10).

On Day Three (Gen. 1.9-13), God made dry land appear in that place which was previously covered by water, and He called the dry land Earth (v.10), while the waters surrounding it are called seas. Against Walton's interpretation, John Day (2013, p. 4) objects that we cannot envisage the description of the vegetation on the third day as merely functional since Gen. 1.11 declares 'let the earth bring forth vegetation', which can only refer to its creation, and it is only on the parallel sixth day in Gen. 1.29-30 that its function as food for humanity and animals is declared. However, Functional Creation does not have to be tied to the declaration of function; the initiation of an ordering process with respect to the place where the first humans would dwell would suffice. The land concerned was previously 'lacking order and purpose' (Gen. 1.2; Walton 2015, p. 28) and covered by water, but is now commanded in v.11 to bring forth vegetation (cf. Walton 2015, p. 37: 'The function of plant growth is initiated. This ordering provides the basis for food production'). There is therefore the beginning of existence of vegetation in that place which was later to become the habitat for the first humans, but with regard to Task C, this does not exclude the possibility that the vegetation in that place could have come from the seeds, spores, etc. of the vegetation which may have had already existed outside of that place.

On Day Four (Gen. 1.14-19), God created the sun, moon and stars for the purpose of separating the day from the night, serving as 'signs and for seasons and for days and years . . . for lights in the expanse of the heavens to give light on the earth' (vv.14–18). Again the emphasis is on the functions.

With respect to Task (C), many have wondered why Gen. 1.1-2 states that the earth was already present on the First Day, while Gen. 1.14-19 seems to imply that the sun, moon and stars appear only on the Fourth Day. In reply, 'made' (*'āśâ*, v.16) can be understood in accordance with the Functional Creation view, according to which the text is not trying to say that the sun, moon and stars only begin to exist on Day Four. Rather, it is only from Day Four onwards that the sun, moon and stars began to function as luminaries that 'separate the day from the night', serving as 'signs and for seasons and for days and years . . . for lights in the expanse of the heavens to give light on the earth' (vv.14–18). These verses indicate that the focus is on the functions. Moreover, from the context of the passage, the frame of reference is from the earth's surface – Gen. 1.2, 'The Spirit of God was hovering over the waters [of Earth]' (Ross 2011, p. 81). Using the idea of Functional Creation, 'Let there be light' (v.3) on Day One does not mean that light begins to exist only on Day One. Rather, as noted earlier with respect to Gen. 1.5, the light is called 'Day', emphasizing the functional aspect: the light can now be seen on the earth's surface to mark daytime. This is consistent with the light appearing after a period of darkness. In addition, Job 38.9 portrays that God 'made the clouds its [the sea's or the waters'] garment and wrapped it in thick darkness'. This can be understood as affirming an opaque primordial atmosphere, not the sun's non-existence, as the cause of darkness 'over the surface of the deep' (Ross 2017, p. 49).

In view of these hermeneutical insights, one may suggest, in accordance with Task (C) (see Chapter 1), that perhaps whatever had caused darkness to be over the surface of the earth (v.2) had been sufficiently dispersed by Day Four, such that from the frame of reference of the earth's surface, the pre-existent sun, moon and stars would have become visible enough to serve as functionaries for time measurement in preparation for the first humans who would be created later. The fact that light already appears on Day One before the sun was clearly seen explains why plants could have already existed on the third day before Day Four; the light would have been sufficient for the growth of the plants.

Regarding the creation of sea creatures on Day Five (Gen. 1.20-21), Walton (2013, p. 150) argues that 'let the waters teem with swarms' (NASB) is functional placement; in v.22 God's blessing gives them a functional role of filling the sea ('God blessed them, saying, "Be fruitful and multiply and fill the waters in the seas, and let birds multiply on the earth."') Interpreters have pondered on the significance of the use of the verb *bārā'* in Gen. 1.21 ('God created [*bārā'*] the great creatures of the sea'), which is only used elsewhere in Genesis 1 in v.1 (referring to the creation of the cosmos) and v.27 (the creation of humankind). Walton (2015, pp. 39–40) argues that this should be understood in light of the ANE view of the sea as the very embodiment of non-order. He notes that 'the *tannîn* referred to here (NIV: 'great creatures of the sea') are counted among the chaos creatures in the Old Testament (see Job 7.12; Ps. 74.13; Isa. 27.1; 51.9; Ezek. 32.2; cf. the Ugaritic chaos creature *tunnanu*)' (2015, pp. 39–40). Thus the use of the word *bārā'* indicates (as in Gen. 1.1) that the instillation of order that also brings about the fruitfulness of filling the seas (i.e. Functional Creation) is in view here, rather than the beginning of existence of these creatures. (For the phrase 'Let the waters bring forth' (v.2), see what follows.)

With regard to the creation of animals on Day Six, God made (*'āśâ*, Gen. 1.25) them by commanding the earth to 'bring forth living creatures of every kind: cattle and creeping things and wild animals of the earth of every kind' (Gen. 1.24). Walton argues that the text concerns the functional role of filling the land (Walton 2013, p. 150). Walton (2009, p. 66) cites the ANE text *The Exploits of Ninurta* 1.6.2:

> Let its meadows produce herbs for you. Let its slopes produce honey and wine for you. Let its hillsides grow cedars, cypress, juniper and box for you. Let it

make abundant for you ripe fruits, as a garden. Let the mountain supply you richly with divine perfumes. . . . Let the mountains make wild animals teem for you. Let the mountain increase the fecundity of quadrupeds for you.

The passage portrays the earth as a sustaining source of life (the ancient people evidently knew that animals depend on plants for food, and the plants depend on the land), and indicates a continuing process of fruitful generation of living things, not the initial creation or beginning of existence of all living things. Likewise, Gen. 1.24-25 does not have to be interpreted as the initial creation and beginning of existence of all living creatures on planet earth. Rather, it can be understood as Functional Creation with respect to the place where the first humans would dwell. (Note that 'earth' in Gen. 1.24 refers to the dry land which was called Earth earlier in v.10.) The place concerned was previously 'lacking order and purpose' (Walton 2015, p. 28). In Gen. 1.24-25 God causes its land to be fruitful for the continuing generation of animals that would fulfil their functional role of filling the land, just as He causes the sea to be fruitful for the continuing generation of sea creatures that would fulfil their functional role of filling the sea around the land (this is how the phrase 'Let the waters bring forth' (v.20) can be understood).

With respect to Task (C), it should be noted that Gen. 1.20-25 does not have to be interpreted as the initial creation and beginning of existence of all living creatures on planet earth. Thus, the text is compatible with the possibility that there may already be pre-existing animals and sea creatures prior to the Seven Days of Functional Creation, some of which subsequently moved into the place where the first humans would dwell as well as the sea surrounding this place, as these areas were made habitable from Day One to Day Six. This is compatible with Walton's idea of 'moving into the home'[26] and 'installing functionaries in the way that furniture fills a room and beautifies it but also carries out the functions of the room. Here, the birds beautify the space established on day two, and the sea creatures beautify the waters below' (Walton 2015, p. 39).

With respect to Task (C), it has been objected that the order of appearance of living things in Genesis does not fit with the fossil record (Day 2013, p. 3). For example, Genesis 1 says that birds were created on Day Five and land animals on Day Six, but fossil evidence indicates that terrestrial life appeared before birds. However, advocates of Functional Creation can reply that the order of appearance of living things in Genesis is not ontological but functional. Thus the text does not exclude the possibility that terrestrial life existed before birds, but the functional

---

26. https://biologos.org/blogs/archive/reflections-on-reading-genesis-1-3-john-waltons-world-tour-part-1. Walton is referring to humans moving in, but the idea is also compatible with creatures moving in. With regard to humans, as explained in Chapters 5 and 6, Walton thinks that there could already be human beings made in the image of God before Adam, with which I disagree; I think there could be anatomical *Homo sapiens* who moved into the Garden of Eden, and God made one of them to become a human being in His image.

organization of pre-existing birds happened before the functional organization of pre-existing terrestrial life. Alternatively, one might also argue that 'land animals' might not be referring to all terrestrial life but perhaps only to certain kinds of animals that the ANE people are familiar with, for example, domesticated animals, rodents and others (Ross 2017). As noted earlier, Genesis 1 is not intended to provide a complete record; thus, one should not expect Genesis 1 to detail the creation of all terrestrial life.

One of the Scriptural passages most often cited by YECs is Exod. 20.8-11:

> Remember the Sabbath day, and keep it holy. Six days you shall labor and do all your work. But the seventh day is a Sabbath to the LORD your God; you shall not do any work – you, your son or your daughter, your male or female slave, your livestock, or the alien resident in your towns. For in six days the LORD made heaven and earth, the sea, and all that is in them, but rested the seventh day; therefore the LORD blessed the Sabbath day and consecrated it.

YEC Ham (2017, pp. 21-2) argues that God's commandment of six days of working and the seventh day of resting in Exod. 20.8-11 indicates that each of the enumerated days in v.11 is a solar day. He claims that the commandment makes no sense if the days are not literal in v.11 as they are in vv.8-10, that v.11 implies that the first day begins in Gen. 1.1 (when God created the earth), that there was no time before v.1, and that millions of years cannot be inserted into each of the days or between the days or before the days.

In reply, the Hebrew verb translated as 'made' is 'āśâ, which can be understood as 'formed', that is, Functional Creation. The emphasis on function in the Functional Creation view is compatible with the emphasis on the Sabbath in this passage. With respect to Task (C), this does not exclude the possibility of a pre-existing cosmos and time prior to the six solar days, and that during these six days the pre-existing cosmos was organized by God to function in a way that was ideal for the appearance of the first humans. Such a possibility would be compatible with Exod. 20.11 – 'For six days the LORD made ('āśâ) the heavens and the earth, the sea, and all that is in them.' (Alternatively, Collins [2018] might argue that God functionally created (āśâ) physical reality ('the heavens and the earth') in six *analogical* days (Collins 2018, section 7.A.1), and that the first day begins in Gen. 1.3 which is distinct from (and could have happened sometime after) the initial creation (bārā') of 'the heavens and the earth' in Gen. 1.1. See the explanation on Collins' view).

Day (2013, p. 4) objects that Walton is certainly wrong to understand the narrative wholly in functional terms, arguing that it is quite unnatural to deny that Gen. 1.1 gives us an account of the creation of the material universe which is the way all other interpreters have understood it over the past 2000 years. Walton (2017) replies that the earliest commentaries of Genesis are found in other biblical texts such as Psalms 8 and 104, and he interprets these as affirming ordered functions. By the time of the intertestamental period, the commentaries were already occupied with the concern to respond to Hellenistic ontological views by interpreting Genesis as affirming creatio ex nihilo, and that became the way Genesis has been translated and understood by many scholars since then (see also Westermann 1984, pp. 109–10). Walton (2009, p. 170) writes:

> The worldview of antiquity was lost to us as thinking changed over thousands of years, and the language and literature of the ancient world was buried in the sands of the Middle East. It was only with the decipherment of the ancient languages and the recovery of their texts that windows were again opened to an understanding of an ancient worldview that was the backdrop of the biblical world. This literature and the resulting knowledge has made it possible to recover the ways of thinking that were prominent in the ancient world and has given us new insight into some difficult biblical texts.

Even then, other possibilities regarding the details were occasionally noted, for example, by the medieval commentator Ibn Ezra concerning *bārā'* (see earlier). Harris (2013, pp. 90–1) observes that 'Genesis 1:1 has not always been read as describing the absolute beginning of all things including time' noting that

> the Jewish rabbis whose thoughts are recorded in the *Genesis Rabbah* (a midrashic document from the third to the sixth centuries CE) maintained that many things existed before the 'In the beginning' statement of Genesis 1:1, and time itself had existed long before the evening and morning of the first day in Genesis 1:5 (*Genesis Rabbah* III. 7). The rabbis contended that God had experimented with making many worlds before ours. . . . Or a related rabbinic interpretation: God created Wisdom and Torah two thousand years before the creation of the heavens and earth, together with other features important to Judaism such as Paradise, Hell, the Messiah's Name, and Repentance (*Genesis Rabbah* I. 4). (2013, pp. 90–1)

YEC Steve Ham (2015) asks why New Testament texts that are clearly alluding to Gen. 1.1 also depict it in terms of material origins (John 1.1–3; Heb. 11.1–3). To this question it can be replied that New Testament writers alluding to Old Testament texts do not always intend to comment on and explain what those texts mean; they sometimes convey additional meanings as well in light of additional 'revelatory insights' and in engagement with contemporaneous views (e.g. Hellenism, the apocalyptic views of Second Temple Judaism) (Beale 2012, pp. 14–18). For example, Hurtado observes that the author of John's Gospel could have modified terms and categories they inherit from their 'parent' traditions. In modifying the term 'Logos', the author of John's Gospel intends to convey beyond what was previously affirmed in the Word, Wisdom or Divine name traditions. This can be seen, for example, by his claim that 'the Word was God' and that 'the Word became flesh' (Hurtado 2003, pp. 366–7). One might therefore suggest the possibility that, while Genesis 1 is speaking of functional origins in its original context, the authors of John 1.1–3 and Heb. 11.1–3 alluding to Genesis 1 intend to make the additional point (in light of additional 'revelatory insights' and in engagement with Hellenistic views) that the Logos was also responsible for the material origins of the cosmos. Making this point does not require the material and functional origin of the cosmos to have occurred at the same time.

Even if one disagrees with Walton's interpretation of Gen. 1.1 and affirms that *bārā'* in Gen. 1.1 implies the creation of the cosmos out of nothing, the interpretation can still be compatible with my model, by considering (for example) Collins's (2013) interpretation mentioned earlier, which I shall now elaborate.

As noted earlier, according to Collins (2013, p. 181), Gen. 1.1 describes 'the initial bringing into existence of all things, verse 2 gives the condition under which the first day began, the Seven Days are God's activity of shaping physical reality to provide a suitable place for mankind to live, to love and to serve'. 'The main event of "material origin" is in 1:1; the rest is mostly shaping the material that is already there' (2013, p. 181). His view can be understood as:

- Allowing for a time gap between Gen. 1.1 and 1.2 and between 1.1-2 and 1.3 without the problems of the traditional Gap theory (problems such as interpreting 1.2 as 'became' formless and void). On Collins's view, Gen. 1.1-2 describes the background conditions to the narrative; the narrative of the Seven Days begins in 1.3, and there is no implication that v.3 happens quickly after v.1 or v.2. 'The text-grammatical features are entirely non-committal as to how long before the work week the whole universe is supposed to have come into being' (56Collins 2018, section 7.A.1).

  Against the view that the narrative begins in v.1 and not v.3, Collins makes his case that the narrative begins in v.3 on the basis of the recognition that the *wayyiqtol* in v.3 is the simple past tense (rather than the imperfect tense) and the rise of discourse grammar, and his observation that whole narrative sections can begin with a *wayyiqtol* (ibid).

  Collins clarifies that the grammar of Genesis 1 does not entail that the event described by Gen. 1.1 is simultaneous with or immediately followed by the condition described in Gen. 1.2. He interprets the *waw* disjunctive at the beginning of 1.2 as an explanatory clause for 1.3 rather than for 1.1.[27] Where Task C is concerned, this means that the grammar of Genesis 1 does not exclude the possibility of a 'gap' of undefined length between Genesis 1.1 and 1.2. The difference between Collins' view and that of the traditional 'Gap Theory' is that the latter involves seeing the formless and empty condition of the earth as the result of a primeval rebellion, interpreting 1.2 as 'And the earth *became* formlessness and emptiness'. Collins agrees that the Hebrew grammar does not support that reading and that *tohu wabohu* need not have resulted from judgment, but that does not mean that there is no gap between Gen. 1.1 and 1.2.

---

27. Personal correspondence.

- Allowing for each of the seven days of creation to be analogous to a twenty-four-hour day but not necessarily to be of the same length, and without the problems of the traditional Day-Age theory (problems such as assuming the Hebrew word *yom* to mean something more than a twenty-four-hour day in Genesis 1). Collins notes that the Sabbath (Gen. 2.1–3) of the Divine work-week has no ending (as indicated by the lack of a concluding formula for Day Seven in Genesis 2)[28] and that God does not get tired, thus

> the presentation here and elsewhere (such as Exod 31:17) is analogical: God's work and rest are like human rest and work in some ways and unlike it in other ways (for the audience to ascertain). That is, these creation days are God's workdays, and, since the divine Sabbath does not correspond in length and character to a human Sabbath, we need not concern ourselves with the exact relationship of this work week to a human work week. (Collins 2018, section 7.A.1)

Thus the Seven Days of Genesis 1 are understood as real historical periods; each period was like a twenty-four-hour day (*yom*) but not necessarily equivalent to a twenty-four-hour day. The six periods of work followed by one period of rest is analogous to a human work-week. The Seven Days of Genesis 1 are mentioned to set a pattern of six periods of work followed by one period of rest, which according to Exodus should be observed by the Israelites in the form of six twenty-four-hour periods followed by one twenty-four-hour period.

- Allowing for the description of creation to be functionally oriented (as Walton affirms) but which (unlike Walton) does not deny creation ex nihilo in 1.1, and
- Synthesizing all of the above insights without the error of Concordism.

In summary, Walton's and Collins's interpretations provide a number of plausible and illuminating perspectives on the biblical texts. These perspectives are not guilty of Concordism (see Chapter 1) because they can be argued for on the basis of hermeneutical principles noted in Chapter 1. The implication of these perspectives is that Genesis does not say when the universe (with the sun, the moon, the stars and the living things) began to exist ontologically. Thus the Genesis text is compatible with the view (proposed in accordance with Task (C), see Chapter 1) that the universe could have existed for billions of years (during which God worked out His purposes for other creatures [e.g. angelic beings] while causing life to evolve) before the creation of the first humans (concerning evolution, see further, Chapter 4). With regard to early creatures such as dinosaurs, in accordance with Task (C) one may say, as Walton (2009, p. 168) does, that these

---

28. It is also arguably implied by Heb. 4.4-9: For in one place it speaks about the seventh day as follows, 'And God rested on the seventh day from all his works.' And again in this place it says, 'They shall not enter my rest. . . . So then, a sabbath rest still remains for the people of God.'

creatures could be part of the pre-functional cosmos which preceded the Seven days of Genesis 1–2.

Embracing the Functional Creation perspective does not imply that one has to accept other aspects of Walton's exegesis. For example, Walton (2015, pp. 63–7) notes that some scholars have claimed that the first creation account in Gen. 1.1–2.3 contradicts the second one in Gen. 2.4b–2.25. Walton argues that one possible solution is to locate Genesis 2 chronologically after the Seven days rather than as an elaboration of the creation of humans on Day Six. Walton's solution would imply that Adam was not the first to be created in the image of God but was created in Gen. 2.7 after (or alongside) other God-image-bearers who were created in Genesis 1. Some have argued that this interpretation is inconsistent with other passages which imply that Adam was the first human being, while others have defended this interpretation (see section 6.3.1). In any case, as explained earlier (see Section 3.3.3.1, 'Overview of Issues'), other viable solutions are available for the apparent contradictions between the two creation accounts.

3.4 Why take billions of years?

It might be asked, 'Couldn't God have accomplished His creation of the earth, animals, humans, etc. quickly? Why take billions of years?'

There are a number of possible answers to this question (these answers are not mutually exclusive).

(1) Of course, an omnipotent God could have accomplished His creation immediately if he wanted – He did not even need six solar days, but could have done it in a shorter period of time. However, according to the Scriptures God often chooses to use a process to accomplish his purpose, for example, in forming humans in their mother's womb over a few months (Ps. 139.13), or inspiring the Scriptures over the centuries. God's perspective of time is different from ours; to God a thousand years is as one day (2 Pet. 3.8) and 13.8 billion years is but a hair's breadth for Him. Some might complain, 'But it seems so inefficient!' In reply, philosopher Thomas Morris (1986, p. 78) points out:

> What reason do we have to hold that efficiency is a great-making property at all? ... What is the property of being efficient, anyway? An efficient person is a person who husbands his energy and time, achieving his goals with as little energy and time as possible. Efficiency is a good property to have if one has limited power or limited time, or both. But apart from such limitations, it is not clear at all that efficiency is the sort of property it is better to have than to lack. On the Anselmian conception of God, he is both omnipotent and eternal, suffering limitations with respect to neither power nor time. So it looks as if there is no good reason to think that efficiency is the sort of property an Anselmian being would have to exemplify.

(2) Other Christians may reply by suggesting the possibility that God used a long period of time to work out His purposes involving other creatures, such as angels. Dan. 10.12-14 offers an interesting theological perspective that sometimes 'delays' can be related to events in the angelic realm:

> He said to me, 'Do not fear, Daniel, for from the first day that you set your mind to gain understanding and to humble yourself before your God, your words have been heard, and I have come because of your words. But the prince of the kingdom of Persia opposed me twenty-one days. So Michael, one of the chief princes, came to help me, and I left him there with the prince of the kingdom of Persia, and have come to help you understand what is to happen to your people at the end of days. For there is a further vision for those days.'

The Scriptures indicate that the human realm is not all that God is concerned with; the angelic realm is an object of God's concern too.

(3) Peels suggests that God might have reasons not to let his existence be too obvious to everyone,[29] and that God's existence would be too obvious 'if we had strong evidence to think that biodiversity and humanity came into existence out of nothing, say, a few thousand years ago' (Peels 2018 – for the arguments of divine hiddenness, see further, Loke 2022b, chapter 7).

(4) God might have chosen to create such a long period of time – just as He has chosen to create such a vast universe – in order to let humans discover their finitude even as their knowledge of astronomy progresses. (Indeed, the average human life span of seventy to eighty years is like nothing within 13.8 billion years.) Therefore, instead of becoming proud as the result of increasing scientific knowledge, one should become humble and realize the insignificance of one's life apart from a relationship with the eternal and infinite God (cf. Pss 8.3-5).[30] Thus, in this sense the billions of years and the billions of galaxies are not wasted; on the contrary, they have the potential to teach us humility.

---

29. Philosopher J. P. Moreland suggests one reason as follows: 'God maintains a delicate balance between keeping his existence sufficiently evident so people will know he's there and yet hiding his presence enough so that people who want to choose to ignore him can do it. This way, their choice of destiny is really free' (Moreland 1998, p. 263).

30. 'When I look at your heavens, the work of your fingers, the moon and the stars, which you have set in place, what is man that you are mindful of him, and the son of man that you care for him? Yet you have made him a little lower than the heavenly beings and crowned him with glory and honor.'

Chapter 4

THE PROCESS OF EVOLUTIONARY CREATIONISM

4.1 Introduction

Many people – Christians and non-Christians – think that evolution is incompatible with the biblical doctrine of creation.[1] The situation among Evangelical Christians, however, is not as simple as what Dawkins seems to think. Christians from a wide variety of denominational perspectives have been divided over evolution since 1859, and it may come as a surprise for many that a number of leaders of the 'Fundamentalist' movement actually subscribed to a form of theistic evolution (Donald 2009, pp. 15–19). Quite a number of leading Christian theologians, biblical scholars, apologists, philosophers, scientists and church leaders past and present who have been identified as Evangelicals, such as J. I. Packer, John Stott, Alister McGrath, John Walton, Bruce Walke, Alvin Plantinga, William Lane Craig, Owen Gingerich, Francis Collins and Dennis Alexander have answered in the affirmative. Among non-Evangelicals, leaders of the Roman Catholic Church[2] and a number of mainline Protestant denominations such as the Lutheran World Federation and the United Presbyterian Church have argued that evolution merely describes a process which God could have chosen to use over a long time (see previous section) to create various biological life forms.

Nevertheless, there are other Christians who remain unconvinced. Debate concerning creation and evolution has existed among Evangelicals for some time (see, for example, Moreland and Reynolds eds. 1999) and has flared up in recent years (e.g. Barrett and Caneday 2013; Stump ed. 2017). The objectors point out that the issue cannot be settled simply by saying that 'God could have created through evolution', and many of them claim that there is insufficient evidence (for example, the lack of transitional fossils) to show that all modern creatures came

---

1. While a Gallup poll in 2017 indicates that there is an increase in the number of people who think that belief in God and evolution are compatible, this remains in the minority at 38 per cent: http://www.gallup.com/poll/210956/belief-creationist-view-humans-new-low.aspx.

2. See http://www.vatican.va/holy_father/pius_xii/encyclicals/documents/hf_p-xii_enc_12081950_humani-generis_en.html (accessed 21 January 2013).

from a common ancestor (macroevolution). They also argue that one needs to look at the details of the case and assess whether those are compatible with biblical Christianity.

In order to assess the debate we need to clarify the notion of evolution. Yale biologist Keith Thomson has noted that in contemporary biology the term 'evolution' can refer to (1) change over time, (2) universal common ancestry and (3) the natural mechanisms that produce change in organisms (Thomson 1982). Now hardly anyone would object to the occurrence of genetic variation and natural selection resulting in certain minor changes to living organisms over generations. This can be understood as biological adaptation (also sometimes called 'microevolution') and is very much inconsistent with the notion that God created creatures with the ability to adapt. Nevertheless, the word 'evolution' is usually used to refer to something more (as in this book), namely, the process, involving[3] the variation of offspring and natural selection, by which the present diversity[4] of living organisms came from a common ancestor (this process is sometimes labelled as 'macroevolution').

The above-mentioned notion of evolution should be distinguished from other notions of evolution, such as

- Weak Naturalistic Evolution, which affirms macroevolution and claims that a natural process is sufficient to explain how the present diversity of living organisms came from a common ancestor (without denying that the common ancestor or the universe may be created by God).

---

3. The degree of involvement of the mechanism of variation of offspring and naturalistic selection can vary, and other mechanisms such as endosymbiosis (an organism living within another organism) can be involved as well. Celia Deane Drummond (2017, p. 212) notes that in recent years 'evolutionary biology is, to a large extent, undergoing something of a paradigm shift such that narrow proscriptions of behavior according to a genetic deterministic model of evolutionary theory are being replaced by a four-dimensional model that includes not just genetics, but also epigenetics, behavior, and symbol-making'. See Jablonka and Lamb (2005), Pigliucci (2010), and http://www.nature.com/news/does-evolutionary-theory-need-a-rethink-1.16080?WT.ec_id=NATURE-20141009.

4. In biology, 'similar species are grouped together in *genera*, related genera are grouped into families and superfamilies, and these, in turn, are classified within orders, classes, phyla, and, finally, kingdoms and even superkingdoms' (Christian 2011, p. 120). Christian also states that 'A single species consists of individual organisms that are so similar biologically that they can, in principle, interbreed with each other, but not with members of other species' (Christian 2011, p. 120). However, there are difficulties with this definition: for example, it is difficult to apply to many bacteria which reproduce mainly asexually by binary fission; additionally, many plants and some animals form hybrids – it's not so surprising that these blurry places exist – after all, the idea of a species is something that we humans invented for our own convenience! (http://evolution.berkeley.edu/evolibrary/article/evo_41).

- Strong Naturalistic Evolution = Atheistic Evolution, which affirms macroevolution and denies that there is a God who is involved at any stage in cosmic history.
- Deistic evolution, which affirms macroevolution and also affirms that there is a God who created the universe and perhaps fine-tuned the initial conditions of the universe to such an extent that a common ancestor would form and evolve into other organisms, but who does not intervene after the universe is created. This view is inconsistent with Scripture which affirms that God acts in creation after the beginning of the universe (Grudem 2017 argues that the affirmation that God 'rested' in Gen. 2.1-2 implies that there was some special activity of God in the creation of different kinds of fish, birds and land animals portrayed in Genesis 1 from which He rested).
- Theistic Evolution or Evolutionary Creationism, which affirms macroevolution and affirms that there is a God who created the universe and also intervened in the history of the universe. Different interventions have been affirmed by different proponents, for example:

1. God intervenes in the creation of the first common ancestor (the first living thing).
2. God intervenes in the process of macroevolution.
3. God intervenes in the creation of the first human.
4. God intervenes in the acts of Special Revelation (e.g. resurrecting Jesus).

Thus, for example, Francis Collins (2006, p. 200) acknowledges that there are variants of theistic evolution, but defends a version that affirms 3 and 4 and is open to 1. In particular, he states that 'humans are also unique in ways that defy evolutionary explanation and point to our spiritual nature. This includes the existence of the Moral Law (the knowledge of right and wrong) and the search for God that characterizes all human cultures throughout history' (2006, p. 200), and calls the view of Pope Pius XII who affirms that 'the spiritual soul is created directly by God' an 'enlightened' one (p. 202). He also writes that 'the precise mechanism of the origin of life on earth remains unknown' but rejects 2 by stating that 'once evolution got under way, no special supernatural intervention was required' (p. 202). On the other hand, 2 is affirmed by the American botanist Asa Gray who used the term 'theistic evolution' in his *Essays and Reviews Pertaining to Darwinism* (1876) and argued that a number of beneficial variations were caused by God. The contemporary Harvard astronomer Owen Gingerich has likewise affirmed 2 by arguing that

> Most mutations are disasters, but perhaps some inspired few are not. Can mutations be inspired? Here is the ideological watershed, the division between atheistic evolution and theistic evolution, and frankly it lies beyond science to prove the matter one way or the other. Science will not collapse if some practitioners are convinced that occasionally there has been creative input in the long chain of being. (Gingerich 2006, p. 69)

- Methodological Naturalistic Evolution, which affirms macroevolution and denies the scientific detectability of divine intervention in the history of macroevolution. Theistic Evolutionists may or may not subscribe to this. Those who subscribe to this would claim that God intervened in scientifically undetectable ways, as Gingerich does when he says in the above-mentioned quote that 'it lies beyond science to prove the matter one way or the other'. Those who do not subscribe to this would embrace evolution and argue for (say) evidence of intelligent design in biology (e.g. Ratzsch 2001).

From the above clarifications, it is evident that, while Atheistic Evolution involves evolution, it is not equivalent to it. Darwin himself was never an atheist (McGrath 2011, pp. 157–60; in various editions of *The Origin of Species* he stated that the first life was created by a Creator), and scientists who accept evolution might not accept Atheistic Evolution.

4.2 Is evolution undirected?

On the one hand, David Christian (2011, p. 125) claims that evolution has no pre-planned direction – this might seem to be inconsistent with the notion of Divine Creation. On the other hand, Christian notes that evolution is not a purely chancy process,[5] noting the analogy that the odds of a monkey typing the entire Bible by tapping away randomly for millions of years are almost infinitely low. 'But if a rule is added saying that each time a correct letter is typed it is locked into position, then the odds change radically, and we can expect a Bible to be produced within a decade' (2011, p. 100). With regard to evolution, one may ask where the rule comes from. The theist might argue that intelligence is involved in setting the rule and the initial conditions of the evolutionary process, and that 'evolution' (see the discussion of definition in the previous section) is compatible with divine intervention at various points of the universe's history. For example, it is compatible with the view that God created the universe, created and fine-tuned its laws, created the first life, causing certain beneficial mutations which appear random (perhaps by acting at a quantum level), directed the natural forces[6] such that certain biological traits are selected, and (as will be explained in the next chapter) specially created the first human in His image. Thus understood, evolution is compatible with the Cosmological Argument (e.g. Loke 2017a)

---

5. Eminent Cambridge Palaeobiologist Simon Conway Morris (2008, 2015) has likewise argued against evolution being a purely chancy process, citing evidences of convergent evolution in which two or more lineages have independently evolved similar structures and functions (e.g. the aerodynamics of hovering moths and hummingbirds and the use of silk by spiders and some insects to capture prey). See also Sweetman (2015).

6. Cf. the Biblical portrayal of God using the strong east wind to drive the sea back, turning it into dry land and dividing the waters in Exod. 14.21.

and the Teleological Argument (e.g. Swinburne 2004; Gingerich 2006, 2014; Polkinghorne 2006, 2011; Lewis and Barnes 2016), as well as a number of other arguments for theism (Craig and Moreland 2009). It is even compatible with certain projects undertaken by members of the Intelligent Design movement (see the discussions in Nelson 2002; Behe 2008; Kojonen 2013, 2021), such as arguing that it is improbable that life originated without the supervisory control of a Designer (e.g. Dembski and Ruse ed. 2007; Meyer 2010, 2013, 2017a; see also the essays on Intelligent Design in Moreland et al. eds. 2017). A number of theists (see Plantinga 2011) have also argued that there is no real conflict between creation and evolution; rather, the real conflict lies between evolution and naturalism, for if both are true we cannot rationally believe either of them.

Therefore, it is not necessarily the case that believing in evolution allows people to explain life without reference to God or that God makes no difference at all, as Grudem (2009, pp. 9–10) alleges. Charles Kingsley (1874, xxvii), Darwin's contemporary, already argued more than a century ago that the understanding of divine activity had been enhanced by Darwin's theory; it indicates a God so wise that He could make all things make themselves (for his correspondence with Darwin, see Burkhardt 1991, pp. 380, 407, 409; for a contemporary defence of Kingsley position, see Kojonen 2021). This implies the possibility of discovering evidence for *both* design *and* common descent. Within Roman Catholic circles, noted scholar John Henry Newman wrote in 1868 that

> As to the Divine Design, is it not an instance of incomprehensibly and infinitely marvelous Wisdom and Design to have given certain laws to matter millions of ages ago, which have surely and precisely worked out, in the long course of those ages, those effects which He from the first proposed. Mr. Darwin's theory need not then to be atheistical, be it true or not; it may simply be suggesting a larger idea of Divine Prescience and Skill. (Newman 1973)

But why should God need to use an evolutionary process to create? Of course, God does not need to, and the Scripture does not say that He did, but (as I shall argue later) neither can we exclude the possibility that He did choose to use this process.

4.3 Evidences for evolution

Multiple independent lines of evidence have been cited for the common ancestry of all species including humans, in addition to the explanatory and unificatory power of evolution to provide new predictions and its applicability in many fields (Mayr 2002; Finlay 2013; Haarsma 2017). For example, it has been argued that evidence from genetic scars[7] indicate common descent (Finlay 2013, Section 3.2).

---

7. http://biologos.org/blogs/guest/genetic-scars-compelling-evidence-for-human-evolution.

Haarsma (2017, p. 111) argues that 'while common design would explain why similar species share many functional genes, it does not explain why species have the same errors in non-functioning genes or why the insertion points of DNA invasions match precisely when such exact positioning is functionally unimportant' (for details, see Finlay 2013, chapter 4). Genetics show that chimpanzees have twenty-four pairs of chromosomes, while humans have twenty-three pairs, with two chromosomes fused in humans but not in chimpanzees, in line with the prediction that humans and chimps share a common ancestor with chimpanzees (Haarsma 2017, p. 145). Evolution also explains why in the fossil record are so many early forms seemingly a cross between different later forms. While anti-evolutionists emphasize the missing links in the fossil record (e.g. Simmons 2007; Meyer 2013), evolutionists emphasize the links which have been found. For example, they argue that a number of fossils predicted by evolutionary theory, as well as fossil intermediates such as *Archaeopteryx* (dinosaurs to birds; recent evidences indicate that dinosaurs had feathers)[8] and *Tiktaalik* (between fish and amphibians (e.g. frog)) have been found. There are organisms with half-developed yet useful organs, such as rudimentary 'eyes'.[9] Many fossils have been found for several species between land mammals and whales, showing a group of creatures that led to the whales we know today (Haarsma 2017, pp. 175–6); the evolution of whales is further supported by independent embryological evidence which shows limb buds for all four limbs just like land mammals (Haarsma 2017, p. 141, noting that 'as the embryo grows, the hind limbs do not fully develop. In some species, only a pelvic bone remains in the mature whale.')[10] The geographical distribution of species also fits the prediction of evolution (e.g. no kangaroos in England, and no pandas in Australia (Christian 2011, p. 86). On the other hand, Dawkins (2010) claims that what would be evidence against evolution would be the discovery of even a single fossil in the wrong geological stratum, for example, fossil rabbits in the Precambrian, and this has not been found. The pattern of chronology of fossils fits the common descent model better than the separate origination model. While mutations are often harmful, some are not.[11] Additionally, it is not always true that evolution occurs slowly; if environments change more rapidly, species can evolve and diversify very quickly when environments change rapidly; an example would be the evolution of bacteria in response to the challenge of antibiotics (Christian 2011, p. 93).

---

8. http://news.nationalgeographic.com/news/2014/07/140724-feathered-siberia-dinosaur-scales-science/; http://news.nationalgeographic.com/news/2014/07/140715-four-winged-raptor-dinosaur-science/.

9. http://evolution.berkeley.edu/evolibrary/article/evo_53.

10. Ham (2017, p. 159) objects that one palaeontologist has changed his conclusion about transitional whale fossils but Haarsma 2017, p. 175) replies that this example merely shows 'the proper workings of science, as researchers modify and develop their understanding in response to new data'.

11. http://www.talkorigins.org/indexcc/CB/CB101.html.

4.4 Interpretation of some relevant Bible passages

Many atheists think that the evolutionary story is inconsistent with the Bible which 'seemed to say that species were created by God, about 6,000 years ago, and that they remained essentially as God had created them' (Christian 2011, p. 84). However, it has been explained in the previous chapter that the Bible does not claim that the creation of species happened 6,000 years ago. As for species remaining essentially as God had created them, one might cite the biblical expression that God created creatures 'after their kind' (Gen. 1.24-25 'Then God said, "Let the earth bring forth living creatures after their kind: cattle and creeping things and beasts of the earth after their kind"; and it was so. God made the beasts of the earth after their kind, and the cattle after their kind, and everything that creeps on the ground after its kind; and God saw that it was good'; see also Gen. 1.11-12, 20-22). However, in the original Hebrew (a single letter lamed ('to'), followed by *mîn* ('kind')) this expression can be understood as simply saying that God created various kinds of cattle, creeping things and beasts, etc., without asserting or implying that each plant and animal reproduced exactly as what preceded it (Hess 2012). Hess notes that

> The traditional interpretation in Genesis 1 is to relate the phrase to the verb of creation. Thus God created 'according to their kinds,' and they are to reproduce 'according to their kinds'.... However, this approach does not enable a meaningful understanding of the phrase in the flood story. In Genesis 6:20 Noah is to bring into the ark every kind of bird and every kind of animal. Here the phrase modifies the noun, to describe what kind of bird or what kind of animal.... The same is true in Leviticus 11 and Deuteronomy 14. So Leviticus 11:14 does not discuss 'the black kite according to its kind,' but 'every kind of black kite.' The emphasis is on the various sorts of black kites, ravens, hawks, etc. None of these classes or kinds of animals can be eaten. They are all unclean.... Thus the phrase in which *mîn* appears in Genesis 1 emphasizes the great variety of kinds of plants and animals. It does not assert that each plant and animal reproduced exactly as what preceded it. It says nothing about that point. Instead, the biblical text emphasizes the diversity of life – plants and animals – with which God filled the sky, the sea, and the dry land he had created.

Thus the expression 'after their kind' does not specify the process of creation, nor does it exclude the possibility that God could allow certain creatures of particular kinds to evolve into other kinds in various places so as to bring about various kinds of creatures.

McGrath (2009) points out that early Christian writers noted how Genesis (e.g. 1.24) speaks of the earth 'bringing forth' living creatures and concluded that this pointed to God's endowing the natural order with a capacity to generate living things. Where some might think of creation as God's insertion of new kinds of plants and animals ready-made into an already existing world, Augustine rejects this as inconsistent with the overall witness of Scripture. Rather, God must be thought of as creating in that very first moment the potencies for all the kinds of living things to come later, including humanity. In Augustine's *The Literal Meaning of Genesis*, he argues that God endowed the created order with the capacity to develop using the image of a dormant seed: God creates seeds, which will grow and develop at the right time. One can think of the created order as containing divinely embedded causalities that emerge or evolve at a later stage.

Old Testament scholar Bruce Waltke (2001, p. 75) observes,

> Genesis is concerned with ultimate cause, not proximation. . . . When the psalmist says 'You knit me together in my mother's womb' Ps 139:13, he is not intending to comment on genetics or immediate cause. In Genesis . . . the narrator only tells us that God commands the earth to bring forth life. He does not explain how that bringing forth occurs.

The process of bringing forth can be left for science to discover, and the discovery of the evidences for the theory of evolution can be understood as a discovery of the evidences of the process. One might object to why many strange creatures in the fossil records are not mentioned in the Bible (Christian 2011, p. 85), but this objection is based on the assumption that the biblical authors intend to write a complete record of the creation of biological life, which as explained in previous chapters is a fallacious assumption, for the Bible is accommodated to the ANE Hebrews 3,000 years ago, and mentions creatures with which those people would have been familiar.

Others may ask 'Doesn't Genesis 1:30 imply that all creatures were vegetarians at the beginning, which is contradicted by the fossil record which indicated carnivorous and omnivorous animals existing before the time of Adam and Eve?'

In reply, Gavin McGrath (1997) argues that Gen. 2.10-14 supports the view that the Garden of Eden was a segregated geographical area rather than a planet-wide phenomenon, and that Gen. 1.30 may be referring only to creatures in the Garden of Eden rather than creatures on the entire earth.

> Because the reference to vegetarian animals is placed after the focus on the creation of humans (Gen. 1:26-30), rather than after the focus on the animals (Gen. 1:20-25), I think this lends itself to the interpretation that these vegetarian animals are those of the humans' world, i.e., Eden and its environs, rather than the larger planetary world. But since Gen. 1 generally refers to the planetary world, and in this immediate passage reference is made to humankind's dominion 'over all the earth', Gen. 1:30 also indicates God's future plan to expand Eden and its environs to cover the planet. (Gavin McGrath 1997)

The view that the Garden of Eden occupies a limited space on earth is not new; it has been suggested previously by Calvin, who writes of the Garden as 'a particular region, not extended over all the earth . . . a specific place in which the things narrated in Genesis 2 and 3 took place'(Calvin 1981, p. 114). Provan (2017, pp. 222–3) objects by claiming that Eden is meant to stand for the whole earth, arguing that otherwise the command in Gen. 1.28 comes to depend on human sin for its fulfilment by way of the expulsion from the Garden. In reply, the fulfilment of Gen. 1.28 could also have been fulfilled by obedient humans expanding Eden to cover the planet; in any case the notion of expulsion already implies that it is a limited area.

McGrath (1997) goes on to suggest that, likewise, the absence of rain (Gen. 2.5-6) has a regional focus on the human-inhabited 'earth' of Eden's world. 'Thus while God had not caused it to rain upon that world's "earth" after he cleared it in preparation to make it the Garden of Eden (Gen. 2:8, 9, 19), Gen. 2:5, 6 does not refer to either this land before he so designated and cleared it, or to other parts of the planet earth' (McGrath 1997).

In summary, after his creation Adam was placed in a divinely protected environment (Eden) which occupied a limited geographical area on the earth, and outside the divinely protected environment carnivores, etc. already existed. Humans were supposed to multiply and extend the boundaries of Eden and subdue the earth. Sadly, after Adam sinned, the ground on which he lived was cursed in the sense that it no longer had that divine protection. According to the scenario I am proposing, death (though not to human beings=God's-Image-Bearers; see next chapter) had, indeed, occurred before Adam. Scriptural passages such as Rom. 5.12-21, 'Therefore, just as sin came into the world (*kosmos*) through one man', pose no insurmountable problem to my view, for the Greek word translated as 'world' (*kosmos*) can refer to the human race (i.e. descendants of Adam, see Chapter 5), thus the passages can be understood as affirming that *death to human beings* (rather than death in general) began as a consequence of Adam.[12] The eating of green plants in Gen. 1.30 indicates that there was already biological death (i.e. death of the eaten plants) prior to the sin of Adam. As explained in Chapter 3, given the understanding of the Seven Days of Genesis 1 as God ordering the pre-existing cosmos to form a cosmic temple which Genesis 2 clarifies as having its centre in the Garden of Eden (Walton 2015, p. 104), the details of Genesis 1 should be viewed from the perspective of the place which was later to become the habitat of the first human beings. Thus, the vegetarianism portrayed in Gen. 1.30 does not have to be interpreted as (what we understand today to be) a 'worldwide phenomenon'. The view that Gen. 1.30 is not intended to convey a 'worldwide phenomenon' also fits better with other Scriptural texts which indicate that carnivores such as 'the young lions roar after their prey and seek their food from God' were made 'in wisdom' by God (Ps. 104. 21, 24; see also Job 38–42), rather than as a result of the curse of Genesis 3 as YECs think.[13] It is noteworthy that both Augustine (*The Literal Meaning of Genesis*, 1.3.16) and Aquinas (*Summa Theologica* 1.96.1 'For the nature of animals was not changed by man's sin') did not think that carnivores resulted from human sin.

---

12. Adam's sin resulted in physical and spiritual death, the latter referring to alienation from God.

13. https://answersingenesis.org/death-before-sin/death-not-good/.

One might suggest the possibility that there was no lion in the Garden of Eden. Alternatively, Gavin McGrath (1997) proposes that in the Garden of Eden the lions were of a different nature compared to those outside of the Garden, which existed earlier. Just as God can miraculously cause the lions in the future messianic kingdom not to eat meat (Isa. 11.7), God can also miraculously cause the lions in the original Garden of Eden to be vegetarians. McGrath explains,

> In the first Eden and its environs, death was unknown (Gen. 2:17), humans were vegetarians (Gen. 1:29), and so were the animals (Gen. 1:30). Likewise in the second Eden, 'they shall not hurt nor destroy in all my holy mountain' (Isa. 11:9). Therefore, in both the first and second Edens, the lamb and lion lay down together, for God also gave the animals in the first Eden and its environs the same nature they will have after the Second Coming (Isa. 11:6,7). But on my model, this was not so outside Eden and its environs.

YECs object that the existence of animal predation, suffering and death before human sin contradict the Bible which declares that the initial creation was very good (Ham 2017).

In reply, 'very good' may just be referring to the localized state in the Garden of Eden. On the other hand, 'very good' does not mean 'perfect' (Provan 2014, p. 283); the same description *ṭôb mĕ'ōd* ('very good') is used of the Promised Land in Num. 14.7, though the land is filled with enemies and wicked inhabitants (Walton 2015, p. 57), and death of animals, plants, human beings, etc. was present in that land too. Alexander (2014, p. 341) warns that

> we should be careful not to imagine the pre-fallen world as if it were already the new earth that God has planned for the redeemed, where there will be no more death or suffering – this would be a kind of reverse eschatology. Instead the present world was created as a good world, fit for God's plan and purposes, looking forward to another good world to come, which will be good in a different and more complete sense.

Ham (2007, p. 25) claims that the only thing declared 'not good' before the fall was Adam being alone before God created Eve (Gen. 2.18), but he neglects God's command to humans to subdue the earth in Gen. 1.27. As Stump (2016, p. 150) observes, if everything is already perfect why does it need subduing? Stump (2016, p. 150) further points out that, by charging humans to multiply and to subdue the earth before the account of the Fall,

> God seems to have delighted in creating the natural world in a state where there was still work to be done. We might say there was 'non-order' or incompleteness that humans were to work on bringing into alignment with God's will. God must have reasons for wanting to partner with humanity in this work.

Ham (2017, p. 43) objects that the animal death described in Genesis 3 could not have been a covering for the sin of Adam and Eve if deaths of animals already occurred before Adam's fall, but his conclusion does not follow. The postulation that death as a sacrifice is required for sin does not imply that all deaths are the result of sin.

Mortenson (2012) objects that 'nothing in the context warrants reading into "subdue it [the earth]" the idea that the creation had been filled with natural evil (death, disease, extinction, asteroid impacts, tsunamis, etc.) for millions of years prior to man'. However, it should be noted that I am not claiming that the text warrants this interpretation (see the distinction between Tasks A and C in Chapter 1). Rather, what I am claiming is that 'very good' does not mean 'perfect' and that 'subduing the earth' indicates that there was a certain 'non-order', which does not exclude the possibility of the presence of prior animal deaths.

YECs argue that Rom. 8.19-23 implies that death and decay started only after Adam sinned. The text states:

> For the creation waits with eager longing for the revealing of the children of God; for the creation was subjected to futility, not of its own will but by the will of the one who subjected it, in hope that the creation itself will be set free from its bondage to decay and will obtain the freedom of the glory of the children of God. We know that the whole creation has been groaning in labor pains until now; and not only the creation, but we ourselves, who have the first fruits of the Spirit, groan inwardly while we wait for adoption, the redemption of our bodies. (NRSV)

YECs interpret this text as saying that God was the one who subjected creation to futility and bondage to decay, and that this happened when God cursed the ground after Adam and Even sinned (Gen. 3.17) (Smith 2007; Mortenson 2012; Ham 2017, p. 102). However, Ross (2017, p. 75) points out that Genesis 1 and 2 indicate that metabolism (e.g. the digestion of food) and human work predated human sin, and that these processes as well as the deaths of plants indicate that decay (a phenomenon of which the ancient people were well aware, and which we now know is due to the Second Law of Thermodynamics) is already present prior to Gen. 3.17.

Moreover, the portrayal of creation groaning in labour pains in Rom. 8.22 may well be connected with Jer. 4.23-31, which portrays the plight of the earth which resulted from the moral and spiritual failure of God's people in the Old Testament (the Israelites) (Morledge 2015):

> I looked on the earth, and behold, it was without form and void; and to the heavens, and they had no light. . . . For I heard a cry as of a woman in labor, anguish as of one giving birth to her first child, the cry of the daughter of Zion gasping for breath, stretching out her hands, 'Woe is me! I am fainting before murderers.' (Jer. 4.23-31 ESV)

The Hebrew words translated as 'without form and void' (i.e. *tōhû wābōhû*) in Jer. 4.23 are the same words used in Gen. 1.2, which describes the state *before* the cursing of the ground in Gen. 3.17 (Morledge 2015).

Thus what the biblical writers are trying to convey may well be this: God subjected creation to futility and bondage to decay, to be subdued by God's people (this does not exclude a purpose for angels too, see O'Halloran 2015) who sadly failed to accomplish their mission due to their moral and spiritual failures. This brought death to the human race (Rom. 5.12) and resulted in creation being left in a state of groaning, which will finally be liberated at the final redemption of God's people.

YECs might object that the foregoing arguments have not proven that their interpretation of the Bible is wrong, and thus they have not been persuaded to give up their interpretation.[14] In reply, the foregoing arguments are not intended to prove that the YEC interpretation of the Bible is wrong; rather, they are intended to show that YECs have not proven that their interpretation of the Bible is correct. Thus, it is not necessary for a 'Bible-believing Christian' to hold on to YEC.

Many people have been troubled by the problem of evil associated with the evolutionary process (Southgate 2008; Astley 2009). Indeed, this was Darwin's own objection (Draper 2011). As he wrote to Hooker: 'what a book a devil's chaplain might write on the clumsy, wasteful, blundering, low and horribly cruel work of nature!' (Darwin 1990, p. 178). In another letter to Asa Gray he wrote: 'I cannot persuade myself that a beneficent and omnipotent God would have designedly created the contrivances of parasitoids for consuming their hosts alive' (Darwin 1993, p. 224).

Darwin's objection concerns the problem of suffering which is a philosophical and theological issue rather than a scientific one, and thus it has to be addressed using philosophical and theological arguments.

In his response to the problem of evil, Alvin Plantinga (1974) distinguishes between a 'defence' and a 'theodicy'. He regards a theodicy as an attempt to provide an account of why God actually permits the evils in the world, while a defence merely seeks to show that atheists have failed to prove their case that evil is incompatible with God's existence. Since this issue is raised as an argument against the existence of a perfect God, the objector bears the burden of proof. The theist only has to suggest possible and plausible solutions (without having to prove that any of these solutions are actual) in order to show that the objector has failed to prove his case.

Much work has been done in recent philosophy of religion and philosophical theology concerning both theodicy and defence, and it is practically impossible to discuss all the relevant arguments in this chapter. A detailed assessment would require a book of its own, (see Loke 2022b). What follows is a brief summary; readers are encouraged to check out the sources cited for details.

Some philosophers have argued that those creatures which do not have a nervous system do not suffer pain, while those which do may not truly suffer phenomenological pain (similar to cases of blindsight) (Murray 2008, citing

---

14. Influential Christian leader Albert Mohler made this remark in his debate with John Collins. https://www.youtube.com/watch?v=kGETfOQgNI4.

Rilling 2014; Murray notes that the objector bears the burden of proof to rule out these possibilities). Even if animals do truly suffer phenomenological pain, it could be that this suffering would ultimately work for the good of these creatures. For all we know, these creatures might enter into an afterlife, in which they might experience a state of eternal glory that would outweigh all the transient suffering they experience in this life (see Sollereder's photo mosaic analogy discussed later and Sollereder 2018, chapter 6 for responses to objections).[15] As explained in Chapter 1 concerning Task C, there is no need to justify such possibilities by citing passages in the scriptures; rather one only needs to say that this possibility has not been ruled out. Given that the issue of suffering is raised as an argument against the existence of a perfect God, it is the objector who bears burden of proof to rule out this possibility; the theist does not need to bear the burden of proof to prove that such an afterlife for animals exists.

The postulation of an afterlife for animals has deep roots in the Christian theological tradition. John Wesley puts it this way:

> May it not answer another end; namely, furnish us with a full answer to a plausible objection against the justice of God, in suffering numberless creatures that never had sinned to be so severely punished? They could not sin, for they were not moral agents. Yet how severely do they suffer! – yea, many of them beasts of burden in particular, almost the whole time of their abode on earth; so that they can have no retribution here below. But the objection vanishes away if we consider that something better remains after death for these creatures also; that these likewise shall one day be delivered from this bondage of corruption, and shall then receive an ample amends for all their present sufferings. (Wesley 1998, p. 251)

It is important to note that according to the Scriptures, Christ's death has the potential to reconcile *all things* to the Father (Col. 1. 20). Based on passages such as Isa. 11.6-7 ('the lion will eat straw like the ox'),[16] 65.25 and Rom. 8.19-22, a number of theologians such as Wesley, John Calvin and Martin Luther have held that other animals would be redeemed in the future (Murray 2008, pp. 122–9). These animals may well include those hominids which did not have the image of God (see next chapter).

---

15. As explained in Chapter 1 concerning Task C, there is no need to justify such possibilities by citing passages in the scriptures; rather, one only needs to say that this possibility has not been ruled out.

16. Alexander (2014) argues that this passage should be understood symbolically, citing another passage in Isaiah (35.9) which states that 'no lion shall be there'. However, the context indicates that the passage is saying that no lions shall be at 'a roadway ... the Highway of Holiness' (v.8); it does not say that no lions will be found anywhere in the eternal state.

Others (e.g. Collins 2013a) argue that God created conscious agents (e.g. angels, humans) which can affect the welfare of other creatures so as to allow for the possibility of eternal bonds of appreciation, contribution and intimacy. Certain evolutionary evils could have resulted from free decisions by angels (O'Halloran 2015; Lloyd 2018; Betty 2005) or non-human animals (Moritz 2014; Sollereder 2018, chapter 4; cf. Lloyd 1998) which set the conditions for these evolutionary evils. Rom. 5.12 'Therefore, just as sin came into the world (*kosmos*) through one man' does not contradict this view, for the Greek word translated as 'world' (*kosmos*) can refer to the human race (i.e. descendants of Adam, see Chapter 5) and therefore does not exclude the possibility of other creatures sinning before Adam.

The parable of the wheat and the tares (Mt. 13.24-30),[17] which indicates the perils of rooting out evil immediately because evil props up so much of the good during this present dispensation, might serve as a useful hermeneutical lens for understanding the tragedy and beauty of evolutionary history, and the mixture of good and corruption in nature (Creegan 2013). Schloss (2006, p. 202) points out that 'every work of art is every engineer's waste', and that there is still 'grandeur in this view of life' as Darwin (1963, p. 445) himself observed. Compared to the view of life portrayed by YEC, this view of life is far more adventurous and exciting.

As noted at the end of Chapter 3, Peels suggests that God might have reasons[18] not to let his existence be too obvious to everyone; thus He used an evolutionary process to create. For God's existence would be too obvious 'if we had strong evidence to think that biodiversity and humanity came into existence out of nothing, say, a few thousand years ago' (Peels 2018). Peels also suggests that choosing to care for the weak, lonely and vulnerable is a harder thing for humans to do in a Darwinian world, and this makes moral behaviour such as freely choosing to care for those in need to be of great value, and hence God chose

---

17. 'He put before them another parable: "The kingdom of heaven may be compared to someone who sowed good seed in his field; but while everybody was asleep, an enemy came and sowed weeds among the wheat, and then went away. So when the plants came up and bore grain, then the weeds appeared as well. And the slaves of the householder came and said to him, 'Master, did you not sow good seed in your field? Where, then, did these weeds come from?' He answered, 'An enemy has done this.' The slaves said to him, 'Then do you want us to go and gather them?' But he replied, 'No; for in gathering the weeds you would uproot the wheat along with them. Let both of them grow together until the harvest; and at harvest time I will tell the reapers, "Collect the weeds first and bind them in bundles to be burned, but gather the wheat into my barn."'

18. Philosopher J. P. Moreland suggests one reason as follows: 'God maintains a delicate balance between keeping his existence sufficiently evident so people will know he's there and yet hiding his presence enough so that people who want to choose to ignore him can do it' (Moreland 1998, p. 263). Partial hiddenness may be good for fostering certain virtues for humans (e.g. truth-seeking) and for connection building (see Collins 2013).

to create a Darwinian world in which moral behaviour that is of such great value can exist (Peels 2018; see also Swinburne 2018; Loke 2022b, chapter 7).

While an omnipotent God could have created a universe with different laws and constants, He chose to create one in which suffering and death are present. One of the purposes may be to indicate the futility of biological life if there is no God and eternal life. A reflection of life's cycles and the inevitability of suffering and death led the author of Ecclesiastes to comment that 'all is vanity and a chasing after wind' (Eccl. 1.14). Harris (2013, p. 67) notes that

> Despite the fact that these sentiments were first recorded well over two thousand years ago, there is much that resonates here . . . with Darwin's idea of natural selection through survival of the fittest. Nature develops through cycles of endless struggle and competition, oblivious to the fate of the individual or even of whole species. If the seeming futility of this view of life inspires the New Atheists to argue in our day against religion, then it is worth noting that the author of Ecclesiastes acknowledged the same sense of futility thousands of years before, but concluded that it made religion and the confession of God, who is above everything, all the more important. (Eccl. 12.13)

Another purpose may be to provide an object lesson that God can work things out for good. That is, despite the suffering (which may be apparent rather than real, as explained earlier), creation as a whole evolved into all kinds of beautiful and amazing creatures including human beings. Sollereder explains that

> the death of a creature is never wasted. Most of the lives cut short are brought to an end because they are eaten by something else – the lives lost are directly involved in the flourishing of another. Even when they are not directly eaten, the energy and materials stored in their bodies are eventually recycled and reused by other organisms . . . 'the evils are redeemed in the ongoing story'. (2016, p. 105, citing Rolston)

Following Irenaeus (*Against Heresies* IV. 38) who argued that humans were not made perfect in the beginning, Harris (2013) proposes that 'the original creation was never "good" in the sense of perfect, but "good" in the sense of "fit for purpose", and ready to grow towards perfection in the eschatological future' (p. 160)

> through Christ who completes ('recapitulates') all things in himself. . . . It suggests that the 'shadow side' of creation is entirely natural and intended by God, but will become unnecessary in the fullness of time because of the miraculous and eschatological process of resurrection . . . we must accept evolutionary suffering but hope for the future. This is entirely consonant with the pervading apocalypticism of the New Testament: creation can only be understood from the perspective of its eschatological fulfilment (Fergusson 1998: 87). . . . Hence, if it is said of Christ's life (which, of course, includes his suffering on the cross) that it is God's answer to suffering creation, then it should be emphasized that this will

only become fully realized from a perspective in the future, which is essentially the perspective provided by Christ's risen life. Resurrection is the key for the whole cosmos, not just for humans. (p. 156)

Another object lesson is explained by Alexander (2014, p. 376) as follows: the animal world with its competition and survival of the fittest is not there to instruct our moral ethical systems concerning how we should treat one another, nor to provide examples for us to follow in our moral decision making, but, rather, to provide a 'back-cloth against which freely made human decision-making should stand out even more sharply as a unique feature of human existence'. This conclusion can be inferred from the Scriptural affirmation that humans are created in the image of God and hence are uniquely different from animals (see next chapter).

One might ask what consolation there is for those weak creatures which suffered and did not have a chance to live fulfilling lives. Sollereder (2016, pp. 104–7) replies that such creatures may be comforted by God's presence in their suffering, and in the afterlife, they would have a chance to flourish, and that the glories of those creatures whom they had contributed to will be reflected back on them who suffered and made these achievements possible. They would acquire new capacities and share in the glory of the whole – including that of redeemed humans – to which they contributed. Sollereder describes it beautifully as follows:

> The image I use for redemption is that of a photo mosaic. Most of us have seen the computer-generated images in which a picture is made up of hundreds or thousands of pixels, each of which is a full picture itself. Our lives, and the lives of all living creatures, are like those pixel-pictures. Each is a whole in itself, unique and necessary. No other picture could bring the exact arrangement of light, shadow, and color that each picture contributes. God arranges the stories one against another in order to bring out larger redemptive patterns: an image of universal harmony. . . . And because each pixel or narrative is a necessary component of the whole, the beauty, harmony, and glory of the whole reflects back onto each individual part. (2016, p. 106; see further Sollereder 2018)

4.5 Conclusion

In this chapter, I have responded to a number of arguments against the compatibility of creation and evolution and argued for the possibility of discovering evidences for both. In particular, I have argued that Darwinian evolution is compatible with the view that God created the universe, created and fine-tuned its laws, created the first life, controlled the natural forces such that certain biological traits are selected, and specially created the soul of the first human in His image. Hence, creation and evolution are not necessarily mutually exclusive; rather, God could have chosen to use the process of macroevolution to bring about various organisms, including human beings.

Many have thought that the evolutionary account is inconsistent with the Scripture which seemed to say that species were created by God about 6,000 years ago. However, it has been explained in the previous chapter that the Scripture does not claim that the creation of species happened 6,000 years ago. One might cite the biblical expression that God created 'according to their kinds' (Gen. 1.11, 20) and claim that this implies that the species remained essentially as God had created them. However, the expression can be understood as simply saying that God created various kinds of cattle, creeping things, beasts, etc., without asserting or implying that each plant and animal reproduced exactly as what preceded it (Hess 2012). While the problem of evolutionary evil is one of the biggest objections to Evolutionary Creationism, much work has been done in recent philosophy of religion and philosophical theology in response to this problem, and I have summarized some of the main responses in this chapter. In the next chapter, I shall discuss whether the evolution of humanity in particular is compatible with the Scriptural passages concerning the origin of humanity.

Chapter 5

HUMAN EVOLUTION AND THE QUESTION OF ADAM

5.1 Summary of scientific data

Having considered the scientific and theological issues concerning the process of evolutionary creationism in the previous chapter, we now turn our attention to the evolution of humans in particular. According to contemporary evolutionary theory, humans belong to a particular family of primates known as the *Hominoidea*. From this group came the *Homininae* between five and six million years ago. Molecular dating indicates that about six million years ago, there existed somewhere in Africa an animal that was the ancestor of both modern chimps and anatomical *Homo sapiens*, from which, as a result of a series of adaptive radiations, perhaps as many as twenty or thirty different species of hominines have appeared (Christian 2011, p. 154). One key feature distinguishing hominines from apes is bipedalism (Christian 2011, p. 154).

As to why bipedalism evolved, various theories have been suggested: bipedalism enabled hominines to see potential predators from a greater distance in open country; it was more energy-efficient and enabled the searching for food over larger areas; it provided some protection from the midday sun by limiting the area of skin exposed to direct sunlight, which may also explain why hominines became less hairy than the other great apes (Christian 2011, p. 155).

An early bipedal species is *Ardipithecus ramidus ramidus*, whose remains were found in Ethiopia in 1994 and dated to *c.* 4.4 million years ago (Christian 2011, p. 155). Then came the *Australopithecines* dated around 4 million years ago. A number of their fossils have been found, including the famous 'Lucy' (*Australopithecus afarensis*). The structure of their pelvis, the relative length of arms and legs, and the entry point of the spine into the skull (from below rather than from behind) indicate that they were bipedal. However, their skulls indicate that they had small brains of 380 to 450 cubic centimetres, only slightly larger than that of chimpanzees (300 to 400 cubic centimetres) and much smaller than anatomical *Homo sapiens* (1,350 cubic centimetres) (Christian 2011, p. 156).

Our ancestors become distinctly 'anatomically human' in important ways around 2.3 million years ago with the emergence of the *Homo* genus, in particular *Homo habilis*. These had larger brains than those of the *Australopithecines*, ranging from 600 to 800 cubic centimetres, and evidence for the systematic manufacture and use of stone tools were found alongside their fossils as well (Christian 2011, p. 159). While some animals also use tools (e.g. some chimps have been observed inserting sticks into termite mounds), *habilis* seems to have used tools in new ways that required more planning and foresight, such as removing chips from large stones by striking with a 'hammer' stone to create one or two cutting edges (Christian 2011, p. 163).

Homo erectus appeared about 1.8 million years ago, with larger forebrains, the ability to manufacture a more complex type of stone tool known as Acheulian hand axes and a limited ability to use fire. They were able to migrate out of Africa and into southern Asia and Europe by about 700,000 years ago (Christian 2011, pp. 163–4).

Homo heidelbergensis lived from about 700,000 years ago to 200,000 years ago and are regarded by many scientists today as the direct ancestors of *Homo sapiens*, though the evidence is still unclear and debated (see later); moreover, scientists are still uncertain about which species were their direct ancestors.[1]

Homo neanderthalensis first appeared about 400,000 years ago and vanished about 25,000 years ago. They had tougher and stockier bodies, and had brains as large as anatomical *Homo sapiens*. They had the ability to hunt, and their stone tools are more complex than those of *erectus*, but show far less variety and precision than those of *Homo sapiens* (Christian 2011, p. 168). Christian notes that 'There are hints of Neanderthal art or burial ritual, both of which might have signaled an increased use of symbolic communication (but the evidence is ambiguous)' (Christian 2011, p. 168). Studies of the base of Neanderthal skulls suggest that they lacked the capacity to manipulate sounds in the complex ways required by modern human languages; additionally, there is absence of unequivocal evidence for extensive symbolic activity among them (p. 175). A number of factors have been suggested for their extinction, such as transfer of pathogens from *Homo sapiens* (Houldcroft and Underdown 2016), violent conflicts with *Homo sapiens*, interbreeding and absorption into *Homo sapiens* populations and/or climate change (Staubwasser et al. 2018).[2]

In recent years, fossils of other early human species have been discovered, for example, *Homo floresiensis* (nicknamed 'Hobbit'), found on the Island of Flores, Indonesia, in 2003. Their fossils dated between about 100,000 and 60,000 years ago, and are characterized by dwarfish bodies (estimated height around 106 cm), small brain size and the use of stone tools (Sutikna et al. 2016). Another example is *Homo naledi*, discovered in 2013 in South Africa; they had relatively modern

---

1. http://humanorigins.si.edu/evidence/human-fossils/species/homo-heidelbergensis ; http://humanorigins.si.edu/evidence/human-fossils/species/homo-sapiens ; accessed 10 March 2018.

2. Staubwasser et al. (2018) propose that, because Neanderthals relied heavily on protein from large animals, they had trouble adapting when climate change impacted populations of those animals, while *Homo sapiens* were more adaptive because they ate a variety of plants, fish and meat.

human bodies but much smaller brains and dated between 340,000 and 230,000 years ago (Dirks 2017). Other examples include the Denisovans (Warren 2019), and *Homo luzonensis* (Détroit et al. 2019), although there is dispute concerning whether these constitute distinct species rather than locally adapted populations of other species.[3]

Many scientists nowadays would define an anatomical human as the whole *Homo* genus which emerged around 2.3 million years ago (see earlier), rather than just the *Homo sapiens* species. For example, when referring to Neanderthals, Denisovans and *Homo floresiensis*, the noted Harvard evolutionary geneticist David Reich called them 'groups of humans' and writes that 'seventy thousand years ago, the world was populated by very diverse human forms, and we have genomes from an increasing number of them, allowing us to peer back to a time when humanity was much more variable than it is today' (Reich 2018, p. 64).

The scientific account of the origins of the *Homo sapiens* species is currently in a state of constant flux, as a result of the discovery of new fossils coupled with improved analytical tools. For example, it used to be widely held that anatomical *Homo sapiens* appeared somewhere in Africa 200,000 years ago. However, based on recent fossil discoveries in Jebel Irhoud, Morocco, scientists have claimed an earlier date – around 300,000 years (Hublin et al. 2017). It used to be thought that anatomical *Homo sapiens* emerged from a single birthplace somewhere in Africa, perhaps as a result of a process known as allopatric speciation: some groups of a pre-existing species may have entered an area (e.g. a valley) or crossed a river that cut them off from other members of their species. Ceasing to interbreed with other populations of their species, they soon began to diverge genetically from the parent population, a process facilitated by the selective pressures exerted by the ecological conditions of their new home (Christian 2011, p. 177). However, recent fossil, genetic and archaeological evidences indicate a far more complicated picture, namely, that anatomical *Homo sapiens* originated and diversified within strongly subdivided populations across Africa that were connected by sporadic gene flow, a hypothesis called African multi-regionalism (Scerri 2018). This picture is further complicated by hybridization between the lineages of modern humans, Neanderthals and Denisovans (Stringer 2016). Debates concerning how different *Homo* species are related have been fuelled by the discovery of fossils of new species (see earlier) and by advancement in ancient DNA studies (Reich 2018). While it used to be widely held that various *Homo* species arose from earlier species like branches of the trunk of a great tree, ancient DNA studies indicate that a better metaphor would be a trellis: various *Homo* species have split, moved on, remixed and interbred and then moved on again far back into the past (Reich 2018). There are also ongoing debates about the cultural sophistication of human ancestors and other *Homo* species, with some arguing that evidences of clustered distributions of stone tools and other artefacts (material culture) in

---

3. https://www.sciencemag.org/news/2019/04/new-species-ancient-human-unearthed-philippines.

space and through time support the African multi-regionalism hypothesis (Scerri 2018).

Scientists estimate that after *c.* 100,000 years ago humans began to migrate out of Africa and that after *c.* 60,000 years ago humans began travelling into regions where no earlier hominines had settled, arriving in Australia by 40,000 years ago and the Americas perhaps as early as 30,000 years ago (Christian 2011, pp. 180, 194, 202). Migrating into harsh new environments require the development of new technologies such as the control of fire. Fire provided warmth and some protection against predators, and it was used for cooking (which softens fibres and destroys toxins, thus allowing the usage of a wider range of foods) (Christian 2011, p. 194). It was also used to set fire to bushland in regular cycles, clearing away underbrush, and encouraged the growth of new plants that also attracted browsers that could be hunted. Such techniques, known as fire-stick farming, may have been used as early as 45,000 years ago (Christian 2011, pp. 194–5). The last Ice Age ended *c.* 11,500 years ago with a spurt of global warming, and the melting of the ice drowned the land bridges such as those between Siberia and Alaska, Japan and China, Britain and Europe; this threatened to divide humans into separate populations with separate histories (Christian 2011, pp. 210–12). The 'Neolithic revolution' began after the last Ice Age ended with the domestication of a small number of seed plants, the earliest evidence for which comes from Southwest Asia (about 9600 BC) which links Africa and Eurasia (Christian 2011, pp. 219–20).

5.2 Introducing a variety of Christian responses to the modern story of human evolution

As noted in previous chapters, many think that the human evolutionary story outlined earlier is incompatible with the Scriptures. Others, however, have argued for compatibility. There is a range of positions among Christians concerning the existence of Adam in particular. (In the first few chapters of Genesis, the same Hebrew word *'adam* is used to refer to 'humankind', 'the man', and also as a personal name, for example, in Gen. 2.20 'the man' is first called 'Adam'. In this chapter, I am using Adam as a personal name.)

(i) Recent Adam: This view is held by YEC who reject evolution, and also by some Evolutionary Creationists such as John Walton and Denis Alexander who regard Adam as a Neolithic farmer with biological parents. Although 'anatomical *Homo sapiens*' (i.e. creatures with physical features that are identical to those of human beings) appeared in Africa about 200,000 years ago, Alexander postulates the time of Adam's creation to be about 10,000 BC during the Neolithic period (for their reasons, see next chapter).

(ii) Ancient Adam: This view regards Adam to have lived prior to the Neolithic era. It is held by anti-evolutionist Old Earth Creationists such as Hugh

Ross and Fazale Rana (Rana and Ross 2005) and also some Evolutionary Creationists such as Henri Blocher (see next chapter).

(iii) Symbolic Adam: This view denies the existence of a single historical individual Adam. Some claim that Adam and Eve are symbolic of an entire population of humans (Longman 2017). Others claim that the story in the first few chapters of Genesis is a myth, which was written to provide a theological account of the role and importance of humankind in God's purpose, or a retelling of an episode or series of episodes of the beginning of humankind's turning to their Creator in their evolutionary history. While many Christians argue that the New Testament affirms or implies the existence of Adam (e.g. Luke 3.38; 1 Cor. 11.9, 15.22, 45; 1 Tim. 2.14; Jude 14) – in particular, the parallel between Adam and Jesus (a real historical figure) in Rom. 5.12-21 implies that Adam existed and that the doctrine of Original Sin requires a real human ancestor – others (e.g. Venema and McKnight 2017; Harris 2013, p. 142) have objected to these reasons.

It has been argued that non-literal readings of Genesis have had a long pedigree. In particular, David Bentley Hart (2013, pp. 25-6, citing Origen and others) claims that many church fathers thought that the creation narratives of Genesis could not be treated literally, but must be read allegorically as stories whose value lies in the spiritual truths to which they can be seen as pointing. Rowan Williams (2012) asserts that the biblical story about Adam and Eve is not meant to tell the readers exactly what happened thousands of years ago, but to teach the effects of making a wrong choice when faced with temptation.

In reply, on the one hand, the fact that many church fathers thought that the creation narratives of Genesis could not be treated literally does not imply that all the details in Genesis ought not to be read literally. As noted in Chapter 1, to interpret any text properly, one should follow hermeneutical principles such as considering the literary genre, literary context, meaning of words, grammatical relationship and the background and concerns of the authors (historical, cultural, theological) (e.g. Klein, Blomberg and Hubbard 2017; Thiselton 2006). However, as noted in Chapter 2, many of the early church fathers lacked an adequate understanding of the Jewish background of the Old Testament and the Hebrew language. In any case, early church fathers such as Origen (cited by Hart) did not write off the entire Genesis narratives as non-literal, but suggested that there are elements of the narratives which should be understood literally. For example, in *De Principiis* IV.III.7, Origen says that Jacob was 'born of Isaac, and Isaac descended from Abraham, while all go back to Adam', and that Christ 'is the father of every soul, as Adam is the father of all men'. Even though the early church fathers often suggested symbolic and spiritual meanings with regard to the biblical texts concerning Adam, these suggestions were based on the affirmation that Adam existed as a real historical individual. Hart (2013, pp. 25-6) assumes that a literal reading of Genesis will result in contradictions of scientific understanding. However, as argued in the rest of this book, there are details in the Genesis narratives – in particular, the affirmation that Adam was the ancestor of all human beings – which can be interpreted literally without contradiction of modern science.

On the other hand, there are good reasons for thinking that the biblical authors intended Adam to be understood as a historical person, and not merely (as Williams says) to teach the reader about the effects of making a wrong choice when faced with temptation (although the latter is true as well). One of the considerations for determining the genre of a pericope and whether statements should be taken literally or metaphorically is by comparison with other ANE texts. In light of this, a weighty exegetical consideration is offered by Walton. Walton (2015, p. 59) notes that in some cases *'ādām* refers to human beings as a species (e.g. in Gen. 1.27), in others it refers to the male individual of the species, and in some it refers to the designation of a particular individual as the equivalent of a personal name.[4] Nevertheless, he observes that the ANE genealogical lists found so far have only included real people, 'consequently there would be no precedent for thinking of the biblical genealogies differently from others in the ancient world. By putting Adam in ancestor lists, the authors of Scripture are treating him as a historical person' (Walton 2015, p. 102). Walton's conclusion is well established based on extensive studies on ancient genealogies done by himself and others (see Walton 2005; Chavalas 1994). He also makes important distinctions between genealogies and other genres such as king lists which are not genealogies. For example, 'there are lists that start with gods (as Genesis 5 also does). Some Egyptologists believe that the Turin Canon starts with gods and moves to demigods before it begins discussing kings. . . . But it should be noted that this is a king list rather than a genealogy' (Walton 2015, p. 224). Walton (2015, p. 102) observes that 'studies in the ancient world have concluded that genealogies typically are more interested in political unity than in lineage ties, but as such their objectives would not be achieved if imaginary or legendary characters were used'.

This conclusion is not negated by the fact that some of the details in the biblical genealogies (e.g. in Gen. 5.1-5; 1 Chr. 1.1 and Luke 3.38), such as the numbers concerning the ages of the patriarchs, might have been intended to convey

---

4. Walton classifies the different uses of the word *'ādām* in the book of Genesis as follows:

- Generic (some with definite article, some not): Gen. 1.26-27; 2.5; 3.22; 5.1, 2
- Archetypal ('all are embodied in the one and counted as having participated in the acts of that one') (definite article): Gen. 2.7, 18, 21, 22, 23
- Representational agent (definite article): Gen. 2.8, 15, 16, 19, 25; 3.8, 9, 12, 20, 24
- Personal name (no definite article): Gen. 5.1, 3-5
- Anomalous: Gen. 4.1, 25
- Preposition attached: Gen. 2.20; 3.17, 21 (2015, p. 61; noting that 'when it has the definite article, it cannot be understood as a personal name. [Hebrew does not use a definite article with personal names]' (2015, p. 61) and 'when there is an attached preposition, the only determination of whether it has a definite article is in the vowel pointing that the Masoretes assigned in reflection of their received tradition' p. 217).

non-literal and stylistic meanings.[5] Nor is the conclusion negated by the varied uses of genealogies in the ANE and the Bible, since these varied uses (including theological) are compatible with the statements being intended to affirm historical individuals (a theological statement can be historical too).

While the New Testament writers sometimes read the Old Testament symbolically or typologically (Hays 2016), they evidently interpreted some details as historical. For example, consider Mt. 1.4-6's portrayal of Jesus saying,

> Have you not read that the one who made them at the beginning 'made them male and female,' and said, 'For this reason a man shall leave his father and mother and be joined to his wife, and the two shall become one flesh'? So they are no longer two, but one flesh. Therefore what God has joined together, let no one separate.

This passage is clearly commenting on Gen. 2.24, and Waters (2017, pp. 894–5) observes that the

> distinction he draws between the grant of the certificate of divorce through Moses and 'the beginning' (Matt. 19:8) is a fundamentally historical one. Jesus therefore understands the institution of marriage (Gen. 2:24) and the subsequent giving of the law through Moses to exist on a single historical continuum. Furthermore, Jesus' statement, 'but from the beginning it was not so,' independently testifies to the fall of humanity in Adam as marking a decisive shift in the human experiences of marriage.

The theological point that Jesus is portrayed to be making clearly requires Adam to be a real historical individual, and it fits with the consideration that the first-century Jewish community accepted Adam as a historical individual (Collins 2011a, pp. 72–6). This conclusion does not entail affirming that every detail in the Genesis account should be read literally; other details would need to be evaluated

---

5. Harris (2013, p. 100) writes, 'It is now clear that we no longer share much of the Bible's conception and meaning of numbers; sometimes it sees codes and symbols for deeper realities where we might see simply neutral quantities. Many of the dates given in the Bible have clearly been systematized at some stage in the formation of the text. For instance, there is the general trend that most of the generations before the flood are said to have lived between 900 and 1,000 years, while after the flood, the ages given slowly diminish until after Moses, when they reach present-day levels. . . . Apart from the general unlikelihood that such extreme ages should be taken literally, given what we know of human biology, these ages are clearly designed to make the theological point that, since creation, humankind has steadily lost its vitality, withdrawing further and further from divine favour. Looking more closely, there are good indications that the ages of the patriarchs before the flood (Genesis 5) have some kind of symbolic significance, using multiples of 5 and 60, for instance, which also feature in Babylonian numerology.'

case by case using the principles of interpretation noted in Chapter 1 (genre of the passage in question, context, etc.).

5.3 The challenge of population genetics

Figuring out the view of the original biblical authors is one issue, the question of whether it is still the best view to hold for today is another issue (Harris 2018, p. 49). Many scholars would agree with Walton that the authors of Scripture treat Adam as a historical person, but they do not regard these authors to be correct because they assume that it conflicts with the modern scientific understanding of human origins (an assumption which is challenged in the rest of this book). For example, with regard to Paul's reference to Adam in Romans and 1 Corinthians, Enns writes:

> Paul, as a first-century Jew, bore witness to God's act in Christ in the only way that he could have been expected to do so, through ancient idioms and categories known to him and his religious tradition for century upon century. One can believe that Paul is correct theologically and historically about the problem of sin and death and the solution that God provides in Christ without also needing to believe that his assumptions about human origins are accurate. The need for a savior does not require a historical Adam. (Enns 2012, p. 143)

The challenge from science to the idea of monogenism (human species originated from one original human couple) was acknowledged by Roman Catholic theologian Pierre Teilhard de Chardin in the 1950s. It was then suggested that the anatomical *Homo sapiens* species was formed by the process of allopatric speciation; that is, when a population of many hominid individuals diverged gradually and together from its ancestral population as a result of geographical isolation which interfered with genetic interchange (see Chardin 1969, p. 210; the original article dates to 1950). In more recent years, mainline Protestant theologian Ian McFarland (2010, pp. 143–4) writes:

> Nor are the principles of evolutionary biology consistent with the descent of all human beings from a single ancestral pair (the theory of human origins known as monogenesis). Instead, the best available evidence suggests that modern humans emerged (in Africa rather than the Mesopotamian setting of Genesis 1 – 3) as a splinter population from pre-existing hominid groups within the last quarter of a million years. These data render contemporary attempts to defend a classical form of monogenesis unpersuasive.

The strongest objection to the existence of Adam comes from studies in population genetics, which indicates that the genetic diversity of the current *Homo sapiens* population requires that this population descended from a population of *Homo sapiens* numbering 8,000 to 10,000, rather than from two individuals (Zhao et al. 2000; Chen and Li 2001; Yang 2002).

A number of bottlenecks at various times for various *Homo sapiens* populations have been postulated. For example, a study published by Li and Durbin (2011) infers that European and Chinese populations experienced a severe bottleneck around 10,000 to 60,000 years ago, whereas African populations experienced a milder bottleneck from which they recovered earlier.

Many think that the mentioned results pose a challenge to the traditional interpretation of the Bible which regards all human beings today as descendants of two people (Adam and Eve) at the beginning of the human race, and of one family (Noah's) after the Flood (I shall consider the case of Noah in the next chapter). In the words of agnostic philosopher Michael Ruse (2017, p. 157):

> According to modern science, there was no unique Adam and Eve. All human ancestors ('hominins') were part of a larger group of conspecifics. Nor is it much help to refer to so-called Mitochondrial Eve, a female ancestor from whom we are supposedly all descended on the basis of shared mitochondrial evidence (Ayala 1995). There is no reason to think that she is the only female from whom we are all descended; she is just the one that we can pin down. The same applies to her male counterpart, Y-chromosomal Adam. He was not the only male around nor even necessarily the only male from whom we are all descended. And in any case, there is no reason to believe that this Eve and this Adam ever knew each other and had offspring. They probably lived thousands of years apart.

Some Christians have objected that studies in population genetics are based on mathematical models that assume a constant rate of mutation, and that divine intervention in the past may have accelerated the rate of mutation.[6] However, scientists have argued that the average population size estimated by population genetics is arrived at through a number of methods, and that not all of them are dependent on the rate of mutation.[7]

---

6. http://www.reasonablefaith.org/defenders-2-podcast/transcript/s10-11. Accessed 7 July 2015. A defender of this approach might suggest that a sort of re-creation by God took place after the flood, and part of this re-creation may be some kind of accelerated mutation among creatures so that they may adapt to this new environment. They might argue that when we compare the genealogies in Genesis 5 and 11, we find that the life span of post-flood humans starts to decrease rapidly in Genesis 11 whereas the pre-flood human life span recorded in Genesis 5 seems to be relatively stable, and this may be an indication of accelerated mutation. Rusbult (2008) notes that some might suggest that God miraculously created these variations for our immune genes so the human race, as a whole, would thus have more adaptive flexibility in our immune system in our responses to diseases, but this argument is weakened if we can ask similar questions for other genes with high diversity but with less of a 'practical functionality'.

7. The other two methods Venema and Falk (2010) note are (1) DNA segments known as *Alu* repeats, which come in various forms ('families') and which can insert themselves at various locations in the genome. For example, members of the *Ya5* have been inserted

5.4 Introducing a God's-Image-Bearer model as a response to the challenge

In this chapter, I propose an alternative way of addressing the issue for the purpose of Task (C), using a God's-Image-Bearer model. This model has similarities to the *Homo divinus* model first suggested by John Stott a few decades ago. Stott (1984, pp. 48–9) calls Adam *Homo divinus* to mark him as 'the first man to whom may be given the Biblical designation "made in the image of God", even though 'several forms of pre-Adamic "hominids" may have existed for thousands of years previously. These hominids began to advance culturally. They made their cave drawings and buried their dead. It is conceivable that God created Adam out of one of them.'[8] Atheist Jason Rosenhouse (2012, p. 231) objects that the statement in Gen. 2.5 that there was no one to till the ground implies that there was no pre-hominid before Adam. However, as noted previously Gavin McGrath (1997) suggests that Gen. 2.5 has a regional focus on the 'earth' of Eden's world, thus the verse does not exclude pre-hominids outside and before the Garden of Eden was set up.

My model would agree with Stott who draws a distinction between those anatomical[9] *Homo* which possessed the image of God (Stott calls these *Homo divinus*, while I call them God's-Image-Bearers [= human beings], Adam being the first of these) and those anatomical *Homo* which did not possess the image of God (call these 'non-human anatomical *Homo*'). It should be noted that my model does not require God's-Image-Bearer to be an anatomical *Homo sapiens*, but, rather, an anatomical *Homo*, for as noted earlier, many scientists nowadays would define a human anatomically as the whole *Homo* genus which emerged around 2.3 million years ago, rather than just the *Homo sapiens* species. The reason I avoid the term *Homo divinus* is that this term has some baggage due to its use by others in the past. On my view, God took a pre-existing anatomical *Homo* species and made

into human chromosomes at 57 mapped locations. 'If all humans descended from a single pair of individuals, all humans would have each of the 57 elements in pretty much the same locations, since individual members of the family almost never move. However, the human population consists of groups of people who share some insertion points but not others . . . this line of evidence also indicates that there were at least several thousand people when the population was at its smallest.' (2) 'Alleles that are *very* close together on chromosomes tend to stay together for many generations before they are "mixed and matched" through a process called recombination. By examining the genetic differences for many people from all over the world, it is possible to tell how many people gave rise to all the prevalent combinations of differences. Nevertheless, a number of Christian biologists continue to challenge their conclusions.' See Gauger, Axe and Luskin (2012, chapter 5).

8. A criss-crossed pattern drawn on stone 73,000 years ago at Blombos Cave, South Africa, may be the oldest drawing yet discovered (Henshilwood et al. 2018).

9. While the term 'anatomical' *Homo sapiens* is standardly used in the literature, it should be noted that the crucial issue concerns genetic structure; in any case, the term 'anatomical' can refer to the parts of an organism, which includes genetic structure.

him to be a God's-Image-Bearer (Adam) through the creation of a human soul, or, if Monism is true, through the creation of certain unique biological materials (see further, later). Using the God's-Image-Bearer model, I shall show later that all the humans today could have a common ancestor even though they descended from a large population of anatomical *Homo* as indicated by population genetics, and that a contradiction between modern science and biblical doctrine does not follow if non-human anatomical *Homo* contributed to the genetic diversity.

As explained in Chapter 1, one must be careful to note the distinction between Tasks (A) 'interpreting the Bible', (B) 'showing that the Biblical account is true' and (C) 'showing that there is no incompatibility between evolution and the Bible'. For the purpose of this chapter (i.e. to accomplish Task C), one does not need to provide positive biblical or scientific evidence to prove that the proposed evolutionary scenario is what the biblical authors had in mind or that it is actual (though it could, indeed, be so!). Rather, all that is required is to show that the proposed evolutionary scenario is a possible model and that it is not contradictory to scientific or biblical evidences. Those who think that evolution is not compatible with the Bible would need to bear the burden of proof to exclude the possible scenario proposed here.

5.5 The image of God

My model proposes that Adam and Eve were the first human beings, but this does not require Adam to be the first anatomical *Homo sapiens*. The key issue is how 'human beings' are defined. What is essential to human being has always been controversial: Plato affirms a tripartite theory of the soul, while Aristotle's view undermines Plato's dualism; Upanishadic Hinduism claims that the essential self of a human being is radically connected to all beings, while Buddhism asserts that a person is made up of five *skandhas* ('aggregates' of the material form and mental aspects such as sensations, mental discriminations, mental formations and consciousness) without any permanent underlying being or self; Marx thinks that the real essence of man is the totality of social relations – 'humans are products of society'; existentialists such as Sartre think that freedom is the key; socio-biologists conceive of humans as products of evolution, with biologically determined species-specific patterns of behaviour (Stevenson and Haberman 2009, pp. 3, 31–2, 56–7, 80, 93). Contemporary philosophers have continued to debate various views concerning personal ontology such as animalism (we are *Homo sapiens* animals), constitutionalism (we are selves constituted by *Homo sapiens* organisms),[10]

---

10. Concerning the difference between animalism and constitutionalism, Loose et al (2018, p. 8) notes that constitutionalists would argue that 'persons and living human bodies have different persistence conditions. Being a person requires having intentional states and a first-person perspective which some living human beings lack, so while persons depend

dualism (we are souls), bundle view (we are made up of mental states and events), nihilism (the view that we do not exist), etc. (Olson 2007).

Most theologians would affirm the need for divine revelation to help us determine what humanity is. Various Scriptural passages affirm that human beings exist as creatures of God. Humans are dependent on God (Neh. 9.6; Acts 17.25, 28); they are beings who can be addressed by God, who can make decisions, who are ultimately responsible to God as their Creator and Ruler, and who possess the image of God (Gen. 1.26-2, 5.1-3, 9.6) (Hoekema 1986, pp. 5, 11–19, 64–9).

Earlier theologians had thought of the image of God as consisting of the capacities for:

(i) rational powers, which reflects God's reason;
(ii) moral sensitivity, which reflects something of the moral nature of God;
(iii) fellowshipping with God, which reflects the fellowship that Father, Son, and Holy Spirit have with each other;
(iv) sense of beauty, which reflects God who scatters beauty profusely in creation;
(v) language, which reflects God who speaks (Hoekema 1986, pp. 21, 70–5).

However, some of these capacities (e.g. rational powers) have been challenged in the recent literature by other authors, who emphasize that certain animals have these capacities too (see Moritz 2013, Levering 2017, Rosenberg ed. 2018 and the discussion that follows).

In his important study on the Imago Dei, Richard Middleton (2006, pp. 24–7 and n.32) explains that understood in its Jewish and ANE context, *tselem*, the Hebrew word for 'image' should be understood as a localized, visible, corporeal representation of the divine.[11] A virtual consensus among contemporary Old Testament scholars concerning the meaning of the Imago Dei in Genesis sees the image of God as the royal function or office of human beings as God's representatives and agents in the world, given authorized power to share in God's rule over the earth's resources and creatures (see also Ps. 8.5-6 and Harris 2018). Middleton argues that such a rule involves imitating God's creativity and mediating divine blessings to the non-human world in love (pp. 89, 278).

Middleton (2006, pp. 24–7 and n.32) notes that the point the author of Genesis is making is not that the image of God consists in a bodily resemblance between God and humanity. (From the perspective of Christian theology, given that God is a spirit [John 4.24], the image of God in humanity should not be understood as a bodily resemblance.) Nevertheless, it can be argued that a certain resemblance in capacities between God and humanity would have been required for humans

---

on living human bodies, a human can persist when a person does not. As a statue may be constituted by, yet not identical with, a piece of marble, so a person is constituted by, but not identical with, a living human body.'

11. For example, the word *tselem* is also used for statues of idols (Num. 33.52; Ezek. 7.20) or pictorial representations (Ezek. 23.14) (van Huyssteen 2005, p. 120).

to carry out the function of representing God. Old Testament scholar John Collins notes that, while the 'resemblance (in capacities)' view was once the most common interpretation, the 'representative' view (defended by Middleton and others) and the 'relational' view (see later) are more popular today. Collins also observes that, while it is common to treat these categories as mutually exclusive, this is surely mistaken. A resemblance in capacities to God would have been required

> to enable them to represent God as benevolent rulers, and to find their fulfillment in their relationships with each other and with God . . . anyone who is convinced of the representative or relational view must also recognize that these views presuppose some distinctive human capacities that make the ruling and relationships possible. (Collins 2010, pp. 155–6)

Commenting on Gen. 1.26-8, Old Testament scholar Richard Hess observes that one of the ways to understand 'to rule' and 'to exercise dominion' is by looking at what the man does in Genesis 2: working and taking care of the Garden so that it would fulfil its purpose and bear fruit (2.15), naming the animals and discerning their purpose and function (2.19-20) (Hess 2009, pp. 95–6). These activities presuppose the capacities to perform them. God's command to human beings to subdue the earth and have dominion over the fish of the sea and over the birds of the heavens and over every living thing that moves on the earth (Gen. 1.28; Ps. 8.6-8) can be understood as a command to actualize the capacity for this kind of dominion, and the nature of the command implies the capacity for a sense of personal responsibility for it.

The notion of personal responsibility and personhood – which is understood to be related to agency, self-awareness and moral status – has been highlighted by some philosophers as the key element distinguishing humans from animals. For example, Immanuel Kant famously states that 'The fact that the human being can have the representation "I" raises him infinitely above all the other beings on earth. By this he is a person . . . that is, a being altogether different in rank and dignity from things, such as irrational animals' (Kant 2010, p. 239).

Christine Korsgaard claims that humans 'uniquely' face the problem of normativity because of the reflective capacities of human consciousness, which allow us to step back from our impulses and determine whether to act on them. She writes:

> A lower animal's attention is fixed on the world. Its perceptions are its beliefs and its desires are its will. It is engaged in conscious activities, but it is not conscious *of* them. That is, they are not the objects of its attention. But we human animals turn our attention on to our perceptions and desires themselves, on to our own mental activities, and we are conscious *of* them. That is why we can think *about* them. . . . And this sets us a problem that no other animal has. It is the problem of the normative. . . . The reflective mind cannot settle for perception and desire, not just as such. It needs a reason. (Korsgaard 1996, p. 93)

Other philosophers, however, have objected by arguing that some animals (e.g. the Great Apes) possessed personhood as well (Gruen 2017). Nevertheless, there is no evidence that such animals possessed the capacity for a unique kind of dominion that could extend to the whole world and over all kinds of creatures, and the capacity for a sense of personal responsibility *towards God the Creator* for this kind of dominion. A possible scenario, therefore, is to understand these capacities and the associated functions as aspects of the uniqueness of human beings.

This does not imply that every human being would have the ability to exercise this capacity in this life – indeed, it has often been objected that those who are born mentally handicapped, or suffered from brain injury or cognitive disorders such as Alzheimer's disease do not have the rational, self-reflective capacities associated with personhood (Gruen 2017). Rather, my proposal here is that the capacity would be found among Adam and his descendants who would be fruitful and multiply, filling the earth and subduing it. (Therefore, from the perspective of Christian theology, the mentally handicapped, etc. should still be regarded as fully human, since they are Adam's descendants; see further the discussion on Acts 17.26 later in Section 5.8.1. A substance dualist (see Section 5.6 that follows) might also argue that this capacity resides in the soul, and that its manifestation in the lives of those who are born mentally handicapped, or suffered from brain injury or cognitive disorders, etc. is impaired by an inadequate physical system just as the manifestation of the informational capacities of a software can be hampered by an inadequate hardware. The Pauline epistles affirm that those who are redeemed would receive a glorious resurrected body at the Eschaton (Rom. 8.23; 1 Cor. 15). Hence, from a Christian theological perspective, those redeemed who are born mentally handicapped and others suchlike would be able to exercise their function as God's-Image-Bearers through an 'enhanced hardware' and reign with Christ in the future kingdom (Rev. 5.10)).

Moritz (2011b) has objected that the Imago Dei should not be understood as ontological uniqueness, but should be understood as God's election of humans for the role of royal representatives, instead.

In response, I agree that human uniqueness *includes* God's election of humans (i.e. of Adam and his descendants) as a group for the role of royal representatives, but I think the ontological uniqueness of this group cannot be excluded as well. Citing Old Testament scholar Phyllis Bird, Moritz (2013) argues that the biblical context of the designation, 'image and likeness of God', makes it plain that its theological significance is in the *place* it gives to humans within the created order, and not in any physical or moral attributes of the species, in either its present or 'original' state. In response, I agree with the theological significance concerning the place given to humans within the created order, but I do not think that the Old Testament authors exclude attributes of human beings as part of their uniqueness. As argued previously, to show that evolution is compatible with biblical doctrines, all that is required is to come up with a possible scenario, not necessarily one which the Old Testament authors had in mind, and it is a possible scenario that God gave human beings certain unique capacities so that they could fulfil their unique role which they have been elected for. Having ontological capacities is clearly a necessary condition; plants, for example, could not have dominion over the fish of the sea and over the birds of the heavens. It is unreasonable to think that God could just have elected any other creatures (e.g. banana slugs) as Imago Dei; rather, God's election is related to capacities in humans which would enable them to freely fulfil the responsibility to benevolently exercise dominion (Barrett and Greenway 2017), and which is fitting for the Incarnation – an Incarnation that would result in a personal account of salvation that others could know and attest, and a Word incarnate that could intentionally teach, pray, heal and forgive sins (Fergusson 2017, pp. 245–6). Those whom God elects for a certain role, God gives them the necessary capacities. Exod. 31.6 is one example in the Old Testament in which God gave certain people certain unique capacities to fulfil what He called them to do. Against those (e.g. Clough 2009) who object that the difference between human beings and other creatures is of degree only, it can be argued that it is this unique combination of election and capacities which sets humans apart.

Moritz is concerned by the arguments that empirical studies have not clearly shown that non-human animals lack all of the human capacities and characteristics, that empirical investigations have shown that various non-human animals have capacities and behaviours once thought to be uniquely human and vindicated Darwin's views on human–animal continuity, that remaining empirical gaps might be closed through future scientific research (Moritz 2013). While van Huyssteen (2005) has claimed the significance of cave art, which he regards as 'the remarkable expression of something that is quintessentially human, something that sets us apart from other animals, and even from our closest prehuman ancestors' (p. 212), Moritz argues that the early hominids such as *Homo erectus*, *Homo neanderthalensis* and *Homo floresiensis* were like *Homo sapiens* in virtually every conceivable respect, and yet members of distinct species. On the last point he observes:

> While we know little about the daily lives of individuals from these distinct human-like species, we are nevertheless able to ascertain from their material remains and artifacts that they were accomplished bearers of culture, technology, art, jewelry, and music, that they created and used sophisticated tools such as scrapers, knives, hand axes, and in some cases composite throwing spears; that they mastered the use of fire; that they constructed shelters with hearths; and that they at times built boats for the purpose of seafaring. There is clear evidence that at least one of these non-human species ritually buried their dead, and many paleoanthropologists have argued that all of these hominids used a type of language akin to that of their human cousins. In addition to this, the respective cranial volumes of these extinct hominids place all but one of them within the cranial volume range of 90% of modern humans. (Moritz 2013)

Moritz's concerns are well taken. Nevertheless, there are two alternative ways to respond to these concerns.

First, while Moritz states that *Homo erectus*, *Homo neanderthalensis*, *Homo floresiensis* and *Homo sapiens* are members of distinct species, from a biological point of view they could all be regarded as humans. As noted earlier, many scientists nowadays would define an anatomical human as the whole *Homo* genus which emerged around 2.3 million years ago, rather than just the *Homo sapiens* species, and my model does not require God's-Image-Bearer to be an anatomical *Homo sapiens*; rather, I define God's-Image-Bearer as 'anatomical *Homo* which possessed the image of God'. Moreover, the claim that *Homo erectus*, *Homo neanderthalensis*, *Homo floresiensis* and *Homo sapiens* are all different species has been challenged. Ancient DNA studies indicate that various *Homo* species have split, moved on, remixed and interbred and then moved on again far back into the past (Reich 2018). For example, there is evidence that Neanderthals and modern humans interbreed as recently as 54,000–49,000 ya, and Denisovans and modern humans interbreed as recent as 49,000–44,000 ya (Reich 2018, p. 51). There is evidence of Neanderthal DNA in modern humans, and while some have claimed that there is also genetic evidence of modern human DNA in a Neanderthal individual (Kuhlwilm et al. 2016), others have disputed this finding based on more detailed analysis (Hajdinjak et al. 2018). Nevertheless, the possibility of gene flow from anatomical *Homo sapiens* to Neanderthals remains open. Reich (2018, p. 56) observes that

> There has long been contention as to whether Neanderthals constitute a species separate from modern humans, with some experts designating Neanderthals as a distinct species of the genus Homo (*Homo neanderthalensis*), and others as a subgroup of modern humans (*Homo sapiens neanderthalensis*). The designation of two living groups as distinct species is often based on the supposition that the two do not in practice interbreed. But we now know Neanderthals interbred successfully with modern humans and in fact did so on multiple occasions seems to undermine the argument that they are distinct species.

Reich goes on to note that 'decisions about whether extinct populations are distinct enough to merit designation as different species are traditionally made based on the shapes of skeletons' (2018, p. 56). From an anatomical perspective, scientists talk about other kinds of hominins being humans, as in 'early humans'; but when they talk about 'anatomically modern humans' they mean something more specific with reference to features of their foreheads, chins, retracted and reduced faces and linear body build. Thus *Homo erectus*, Neanderthals, Denisovans, etc. could loosely be called human, but not anatomically modern human.[12] Nevertheless, for the purpose of my model, minor differences in shapes of skeletons do not matter, and if it turns out that *Homo erectus*, *Homo neanderthalensis* and *Homo floresiensis* were like *Homo sapiens* in virtually every

---

12. I thank a reviewer for highlighting this point.

conceivable respect as Moritz states, then they could all possibly be regarded by my model as human.

Second, even if one rejects the claim that *Homo erectus*, *Homo neanderthalensis* and *Homo floresiensis* could possibly be regarded as human, there is an alternative way to respond to Moritz's concerns. As explained previously, for the purpose of this chapter, one only has to suggest a possible scenario. Thus, one does not have to provide positive empirical evidence that clearly shows that non-human animals lack all of the human capacities and characteristics, but only that the possible scenario has not been excluded. As for the empirical investigations which Moritz thinks have shown that various non-human animals (e.g. dolphins) have capacities and behaviours once thought to be uniquely human (2013, n.35), the capacities and behaviours revealed by these investigations are rather rudimentary in comparison with those of the early hominids noted earlier. The latter exhibited far more advanced capacities such as the ability to use sophisticated tools and ritually buried their dead,[13] but even these fall short of indicating a dominion that could extend to the whole world and over all kinds of creatures, *and a sense of responsibility towards God the Creator for this kind of dominion*.

It may be, as Darwin stated and Moritz noted, that viewed from a certain perspective 'the difference . . . between man and the higher animals, great as it is, certainly is one of degree and not of kind' (2013, p. 313). However, difference in degree *is* an ontological difference, and one can suggest a possible scenario in which the uniqueness of human beings lies in the fact that only they have the degree of capacity to demonstrate the kind of unique dominion and responsibility to God explained earlier *and* are elected by God for the role of royal representatives.

Opponents of this possible scenario may speculate that, had the other hominid species been given more time, they may also have developed sufficiently to demonstrate the kind of unique dominion and responsibility to God explained previously. In response, it is consistent with this speculation to suggest that, had the other hominid species developed sufficiently to demonstrate this, they would be considered as God's-Image-Bearers as well. Alternatively, one might argue for another possible scenario in which they would not be considered as God's-Image-Bearers, because they are not elected by God for the role of royal representatives. In any case, to exclude the possible scenario I am suggesting speculations are not enough; one needs positive evidence. Likewise, speculations about whether the remaining empirical gaps might be closed through future scientific research are not enough. It should also be noted that denying other hominids the status of God's-image-bearing human beings does not mean that they are not loved or valued by God. On the contrary, it may be argued that God loves all creatures, that they may be comforted by God's presence in their suffering, and in the afterlife they may have a chance to flourish and share in the glories of those creatures whom they had contributed (Sollereder 2016, p. 104–7).

---

13. It should be noted that there have been some debates about the details, see, for example, Bar-Yosef and Bordes (2010).

Other scholars have suggested that the ontological difference lies in the unique *combination* of capacities humans have, which sets them apart from other creatures. Barrett and Greenway (2017, pp. 73–4) notes that, while traditionally arguments focusing on the *Imago Dei* attempt to identify a single capacity that separates humanity from other animals, a biblical focus on dominion as a significant part of the *Imago Dei* (Gen. 1.26-28) requires a number of capacities that work together. The breadth and gravity of the responsibility to benevolently exercise dominion and subdue the earth would require a number of capacities that only humans possess. These include the capacity to

- cooperate and coordinate activities including division of labour – this would require some kind of signalling or communication, and would be enhanced by the use of symbolic language
- create and use tools
- represent God responsibly, which requires the ability to comprehend God's will and understand the thoughts of God in some respect
- plan and foresee potential problems in the future; this requires meta-representation – forming thoughts about thoughts – which allows the individual to represent various possible realities
- care for creation: this requires a certain amount of self-control and the ability to delay gratification (Barrett and Greenway) (2017, pp. 73–4).

Among the above-mentioned capacities, the use of symbolic language has been highlighted as a significant element by many scholars. For example, David Christian observes that, for the beginnings of human history, we should look for evidence for the existence of humans that not only looked like modern humans but also behaved and communicated with each other like modern humans (p. 176). He argues that the most significant aspect of human evolution was the appearance of symbolic language (p. 171). Even though we are extremely close to the chimps genetically, physically, socially and intellectually, our history is utterly different, and we have no evidence that their technologies have changed greatly during the past 100,000 years (pp. 142–3). The critical difference is due to the evolution of symbolic human language, which allows more precise and efficient transmission of knowledge, coupled with pre-adaptations such as sociability, pre-existing linguistic skills, bipedalism and dexterous hands, meat eating and hunting, a long period of childhood learning and large forebrains (pp. 146, 152–3). Likewise, van Huyssteen (2005) argues for origin of ability for symbolic human language and metaphysical thinking as well as the ability to represent both theoretically and practically the sense of God as crucial elements of the image of God.

Christian observes that symbolic thinking, which requires shifting attention from the concrete to the abstract, requires a lot of computing power, and this helps explain why it is apparently confined to human beings with their exceptionally large brains (2011, pp. 172–3).

Christian notes that

The modern human brain is arguably the most complex single object we know.... Each human brain contains perhaps 100 billion nerve cells, as many cells as there are stars in an average galaxy. These connect up with each other (on average, each neuron may be connected to 100 other neurons) to form networks of astonishing complexity that may contain 60,000 miles of linkages. Such a structure can compute in parallel. That means that although each computation may be slower than that of a modern computer, the total number of computations being carried out in a particular moment is much, much greater (p. 165).

With regard to capacity for religious thought, there are evidences that *Homo sapiens* engaged in religious activities about 50,000 years ago (Scarre 1996), although it should be noted that the evidences concerning how the earliest humans lived is still vastly incomplete (see next chapter), as the result of which many conclusions have been drastically revised due to further discoveries. (For example, the Neolithic archaeological site *Göbekli Tepe* in modern day Turkey (dated between c. 9500 and 8000 BC) has been described as the world's first temple, but more recent findings have challenged this conclusion [Clare 2020].)

On the basis of modern studies of small-group religions, historian David Christian thinks that early human communities thought of the entire cosmos as bound into webs of kinship, with the supernatural world seen as 'a distinct but accessible realm – almost like a separate tribal territory, with whose occupants one could negotiate, fight, or intermarry' (p. 189). Beliefs in afterlife were present, as well as practices of sacrifice of animals to please or pacify the gods, modelling gift-giving relationships with other humans (p. 189). The religions and cosmologies of the *Palaeolithic* world were attached to particular places, lacking the distinctive modern concern with universality and generality; 'such places were the source of everything that mattered' (p. 190). However, it is questionable how accurately modern studies of small-group religions reflect the beginning of religion in human history, especially given that the evidences concerning how the earliest humans lived is still vastly incomplete (see next chapter). In relation to this point, Van Baaren (2018) notes that 'there is no valid reason to assume, for example, that monotheism is a later development in the history of religions than polytheism. There exists no historical material to prove that one system of belief is older than the other.' On the other hand, while Gen. 4.26 indicates the beginning of public worship of YHWH, this does not exclude the possibility that there might have been earlier religious rites by other hominids in worship of idols.

A number of scholars have argued that the human capacity to think religiously emerged naturally in the course of the evolution of human cognitive systems (van Huyssteen 2005, p. 261). Various theories of how religion evolved have been suggested by cognitive anthropologists and psychologists. For example, Scott Atran (2006) argues that religion is a by-product of human evolution just as the cognitive intervention, cultural selection and historical survival of religion is an accommodation of certain existential and moral elements that have evolved in the human condition. Israeli historian Yuval Noah Harari, author of the bestsellers *Sapiens: A Brief History of Humankind* (2015a) and *Homo Deus: A Brief History of*

Tomorrow (2017), claims that humans are able to succeed more than other animals because humans are able to invent fictional things like God and afterlife and get other humans to believe these myths and thereby unite together to cooperate on complex tasks (Harari 2015b; 2017, chapter 5). One might ask why he thinks that God and afterlife are fictional. Harari seems to assume that only things that can be detected by our physical senses exist. For example, he says that human rights is only a fiction: cut open a human being and one does not see human rights. Now one does not see human value and morality either; are these also fictions? Harari says that the Holocaust is horrible; would he say that it is not morally wrong for Hitler to kill 6 million Jews – a conclusion which follows if human rights and morality are only fictions? On the other hand, why think that only things that can be detected by our physical senses exist? Harari provides no evidence or reason to justify this assumption. Moreover, where did physical entities come from? I argue in Loke (2009; 2017a; 2017b; 2020a;2021; 2022a) that there are good reasons and evidences to think that the physical universe came from a Divine First Cause who resurrected Jesus from the dead, thereby showing that there is a God and afterlife. Thus, instead of saying that humans are able to succeed more than other animals because humans are able to invent fictional things like God and afterlife, one might argue that there is a God who created the universe and gave humans the ability to think about God, afterlife and morality, and thus also be able to succeed in having dominion over the earth (Gen. 1.28). This does not exclude the possibility that God could have allowed natural and gradual processes (such as some of those suggested by Atran) to bring about many aspects of humankind's capacity to think religiously.

Barrett and Greenway (2017, p. 74) conclude that, while many of the capacities they listed may not be unique to the human species, it is the unique combination of these capacities that matters for humans possessing the image of God and having the ability to exercise dominion.

Going back to the biblical data, it should be noted that, even if there is no evidence to show that Old Testament authors had attributes of human beings in mind when they talked about human uniqueness, the New Testament authors may have hinted at this when they talked about the image of God in relation to Jesus Christ as the perfect image of God (2 Cor. 4.4; Col. 1.15). In this case the possession of the image by humankind can be understood as the capacity to be made to become conformed to the image of His Son (Rom. 8.29), in particular to be Christ-like in their attitudes (Phil. 2.5).

While earlier theologians affirm that the image of God is to be found primarily in humans' structural capacities, a number of recent theologians have affirmed that it is the functioning of humans (their worshipping, serving, loving, ruling, etc.) which constitutes the essence of the image. In response to this, Hoekema argues that the most balanced view would be to hold that the image of God involves both function and structure (Hoekema 1986, pp. 5, 11–19, 64–9).[14]

---

14. See also Emil Brunner's distinction between formal and material aspects of the image of God: he understands the formal aspect as consisting of a formal likeness to God in

Others have argued that the functional Imago Dei requires and is based on unique cognitive features (Levering 2017) and that this view is defensible in the context of cognitive evolution (Visala 2018). In addition to being structural (substantive) and functional, the image of God, van Huyssteen (2005) observes, has also been understood as relational and eschatological (see also Burdett 2018). The possible scenario I am proposing encompasses all these aspects: the property of having the above-mentioned capacities would be the substantive aspect, the exercise of these capacities in relation to creatures and in obedience to God would be the functional and relational aspects, and the actualization of these capacities over time and in the future kingdom (Rev. 5.10) would be the eschatological aspect.

Much more can be said about the image of God, but it is beyond the scope of this chapter to discuss this further. For our present purposes here, one may agree with Averbeck (2020) that the biblical texts on the image of God 'clearly focus[es] on our vocation or function within the rest of creation. . . . There is no mention here of the metaphysical "capacities" on which the structuralist view focuses its attention. . . . This does not deny the fact that God gave us the capacities to function the way he intended.' In other words, the Scriptural portrayal of the image of God is primarily functional, but it does not exclude the substantive aspect; on the contrary, the functional aspect has implications concerning human capacities. I will be using both of these for my possible model; that is, I will be using the definition of the image of God as functional with the associated capacities. To elaborate, according to the possible scenario I am proposing, (i) the election by God for the role (function) of royal representatives, and having the capacity for this function, that is, for (ii) a unique kind of dominion that could extend to the whole world and over all kinds of creatures (iii) a sense of responsibility towards the Creator God and other creatures for this kind of dominion, and (iv) becoming conformed to Christ would be some of the properties that differentiate human beings as a group from animals which do not have the image of God. It could be the case that these properties were created by God on a pre-existing member of the hominid species. This results in a new, originally sinless person (Adam), who would be the first anatomical *Homo* to possess the image of God. Hence, Adam would be the first 'human being'. The possession of the image of God is what made human beings special, even though their bodies do not appear to be special in comparison with other animals.

It should be noted that I am not simply defining human beings as creatures which possess certain capacities. It is logically possible that an alien or an angel possesses these capacities as well, but it is unlikely that the biblical authors

---

being 'subject', being 'person', and having a (limited) freedom that allows him to respond to God and be responsible to him. This aspect is what differentiates man from lower creation, and it cannot be lost as a result of sinful misuse of freedom. The material aspect refers to the realization of this God-given quality – that is, that man should really give the answer which the Creator intends, and that he should reflect Christ, the primal image (Brunner 1952, pp. 56–8).

would call them human if that were the case. The standard lexicons and concordances list 'humankind' as one of the definitions of 'ādām (consider, for example, the adjectival use of 'ādām in Lev. 5.3 to refer to human uncleanness), and Walton (2015, p. 59) states that 'ādām refers to human beings as a species in Gen. 1.27. While ancient biblical authors did not have a carefully worked out scientific understanding of 'species', they nevertheless were able to recognize the differences between the anatomy of a human compared with that of (say) a cat, a dog, etc. Thus anatomical features cannot be totally disregarded when considering the biblical definition of human, which includes these features in addition to possessing the image of God which (as explained earlier) is to be understood as God's election of humans for the role of royal representatives and the capacities for this role. Additionally, there is also no evidence that God elected angels or aliens for this role, even if they may possess the capacities for this role, and thus it would not be appropriate to say that they possess the image of God.

In the possible scenario I am suggesting, it is not true that Adam and Eve were 'among about ten million other human beings on earth at that time', as Grudem (2009) alleges. At the time of Adam's creation there were perhaps other 'anatomical *Homo sapiens*'. Nevertheless, these other 'anatomical *Homo sapiens*' did not possess the image of God and hence were not truly human beings. While between them and God's-Image-Bearers, there would be many similarities, both physical and behavioural, there would be differences in their election by God and/or capacities relating to the image of God. The capacities which are possessed by God's-Image-Bearers but not by other 'anatomical *Homo sapiens*' might include (as explained earlier) the capacity for a unique kind of dominion that could extend to the whole world and over all kinds of plants and animals, the capacity for a sense of responsibility towards God the Creator for this kind of dominion and the capacity to be made to become conformed to Christ. As noted earlier, Christian (2011) also makes the important distinction between the existence of humans that merely looked like modern humans and those that behaved and communicated with each other like modern humans (p. 176).

Since the model I am proposing does not require Adam to be the first anatomical *Homo sapiens*, my model has no problems with the claims that there was genetic mixing between early anatomical *Homo sapiens* and late surviving Neanderthals (Green et al 2010), nor with the claims that anatomical *Homo sapiens* originated in Africa and moved out in waves across the rest of the world (Cole-Turner 2016, pp. 98–9), regardless of whether these claims are true or not. McFarland (2010, p. 143) raises the concern that the best available evidence suggests that modern humans emerged in Africa, rather than the Mesopotamian setting of Genesis 1–3. My model shows that, while anatomical *Homo sapiens* may have emerged and moved out from Africa into Mesopotamia and elsewhere, it could be the case that the first God's-Image-Bearer was created from one of the anatomical *Homo sapiens* in Mesopotamia.

5.6 The generation of humans after Adam and Eve: Traducianist and Creationist Perspectives

Concerning the generation of human persons after Adam and Eve, in the early church there were three competing views: Traducianism, Creationism and Pre-existence. All of these views are based on the assumption of substance dualism which – contrary to physicalists – affirms that humans have immaterial souls which cannot be reduced to their material bodies. In more recent years various forms of Christian physicalism such as animalism (van Inwagen 2007), constitutionalism (Baker 2013; Corcoran 2006) and non-reductive physicalism/emergent monism (Murphy 2006) have been proposed.

The consistency of substance dualism with Darwinian evolution has been argued for in the recent literature (e.g. Visala 2014). Moreover, a number of recent academic publications (Farris 2016b; Varghese ed. 2012, Moreland 2009) such as the comprehensive *Blackwell Companion to Substance Dualism* (Loose ed. 2018) have defended substance dualism against various objections and argued for its superiority over alternative views. For example, it has been argued that substance dualism offers a more compelling account for the fact that our distinct conscious experiences at a particular time (e.g. looking at this sentence while listening to music) seem to be tied together and unified in some sort of deep way.[15] This sort of unity possessed by consciousness arguably cannot be located or otherwise explained given a physicalist ontology, according to which all wholes above the level of atomic simples are mereological aggregates of separable parts that stand in external relations to each other (Moreland 2018, pp. 184–7). Moreland states that

> a physicalist may claim that such a unified awareness of the entire room by means of one's visual field consists in a number of different physical parts of the brain each terminating a different wavelength, each of which is aware only of part – not the whole – of the complex fact (the entire room). But this cannot account for the single, unitary awareness of the entire visual field. (Moreland 2018, p. 189)

Moreland replies to various objections and concludes that 'only a single, uncomposed mental substance, that is, a substantial soul can adequately account for the unity of consciousness' (Moreland 2018, p. 190). This conclusion does not deny that the regular operations of consciousness in corporeal beings are dependent upon the workings of the brain and can be disrupted by physiological events; rather, the point here is that there is evidence of a living embodied mind that has a property which exceeds material causality without being free of the conditions of corporeal life (Hart 2013, pp. 198–9).

---

15. Other arguments include the failure of physicalism and other alternative views to provide a plausible account of intentionality, what it is like to have an experience, first-person perspective and personal identity across time. See the sources cited earlier.

Koons and Bealer (2010) argue that the current lack of popularity of substance dualism among philosophers is explicable by a materialistic prejudice which is insufficiently motivated. While it has often been objected that the relationship between immaterial souls and material bodies is inexplicable, our lack of understanding of a relation is not a good reason to reject the existence of the relation. As Koons and Bealer point out, physics itself admits lawful relationships among physical entities that are extraordinarily diverse in nature and, in turn, admits relations of causal influence and law-grounded explanation among these entities. Physics allows, moreover, that some of these lawful relationships are brute facts having no further explanations. Likewise, the relationship between mind and body could well be a brute fact having no further explanation (Koons and Bealer 2010, xviii).

New Testament scholar Craig Keener observes that most Jews during biblical times accepted this distinction between soul and body, and believed that the soul remained immortal after death (Keener 2003, pp. 538, 553–54). This dualism is also implied by biblical texts which indicate the possibility of human existence outside the body (e.g. 2 Cor. 12.2), and fits with a coherent understanding of the Incarnation (Loke 2014). The dualism indicated by biblical texts is a holistic one which should be distinguished from Greek dualism; the former does not entail the sundering of the unity of human life, a sundering which would result in evils such as the neglect of the material dimensions of human existence (Cooper 2001, 2009; cf. Green 2008).

According to Traducianism, God uses parents to create the souls of children, while according to Creationism the souls of children are directly created by God either at or soon after biological conception. Pre-existence is the doctrine that God has a 'stock of souls from eternity and allocates them as needed' (Baker 2005, p. 370). Pre-existence is widely regarded as unorthodox, while theologians have been divided on Traducianism and Creationism (Crisp 2006), with Augustine famously acknowledging in his *Retractationes* (1.1.3) that he does not know which position is the correct one.[16] Creationism has been the dominant position in Reformed Theology and the Catholic Church since the time of Peter Lombard (*c.* 1100–60), though never subject to formal definition by the Magisterium, while Traducianism has been the dominant position in Lutheran Theology (following Luther himself; see *Die Promotionsdisputation von Petrus Hegemon* [1541]) (McFarland et al. 2011,

---

16. In Loke (2018), I propose a possible way in which Traducianism and Creationism may be combined such that the merits of both can be retained: Utilizing a modified hylomorphic theory of human souls, I propose that, while the soulish potentialities are passed down from parents to children in accordance with Traducianism, the particular restrictions on the form of soul-stuffs are created by God so as to bring into existence particular individuals. This proposal provides a metaphysical explanation for the counterfactuals of human freedom that is required by the Middle Knowledge account of divine predestination, an account which is arguably superior to Dort's (Loke 2013). However, the model defended in this book is not dependent on the success of this proposal.

pp. 123, 514). Traducianism has also been affirmed by theologians from a variety of Christian traditions and eras, including Tertulian (*On the Soul*, 27.5; 100.27), Gregory of Nyssa (*Making of Man*, 29), Jerome (*Letter to Marcellinus*, 1.1), William Shedd (*Dogmatic Theology*), Millard Erickson (*Christian Theology*) and Norman Geisler (*Systematic Theology*).

One of the arguments which has been offered for Traducianism is that it offers a basis for how the image of God (see Gen. 5.3) and corruption of human nature could be passed down from Adam to his descendants, the latter in accordance with a particular interpretation of the doctrine of Original Sin (see later). In this way, Traducianism does an excellent job of affirming the unity of the human race (McFarland et al 2011, p. 514). Hoekema (1986) observes that the Scripture affirms that after Adam's sin in Genesis 3 (the Fall), his descendants still bear the image of God, for according to Gen. 9.6 the reason no human being may shed another human's blood is that a human has a unique value, a value that is not to be attributed to any other of God's creatures – namely that he/she is an image-bearer of God. And it is precisely because he/she *is* such an image-bearer (not was one in the past or might be one in the future) that it is so great a sin to kill him/her. The view that humans still retain the image after the Fall also fits better with Ps. 8, which affirms humans' dominion over the rest of creation (pp. 17–18), and also with Jam. 3.9, which forbids the cursing of humans because they are creatures who have been made in the likeness of God (pp. 13–22). Nevertheless, a number of New Testament passages (Rom. 8.29; 2 Cor. 3.18; Col. 3.9-10; Eph. 4.22-24) teach that the image of God must be restored in humans, which implies that there is a sense in which the image has been distorted after the Fall (p. 28).

Another argument for Traducianism is based on the interpretation of Scriptural passages such as Gen. 25.23, according to which the nations that descended from Esau and Jacob are described as within their ancestors, and Heb. 7.10 which states that Levi was within the loins of his ancestor Abraham before he was born. While Creationists have cited scriptural texts which affirm that God is the originator of souls (e.g. Eccl. 12.7; Isa. 57.16; Zech. 12.1) to support their position, these texts are not conclusive for Creationism because God could work through secondary causes such as using ancestors as Traducianists affirm (Grudem 1994, p. 484). In favour of Creationism, Reformed theologian Francis Turretin (1623-87) argues that the unity of the human race required that all human beings must share the ontology of Adam, and given that God created Adam by directly infusing a soul into pre-existing matter (Gen. 2.7), Adam's descendants must have been formed in like manner (*Institutes of Elenctic Theology* 5.13.3) (McFarland et al 2011, p. 123). However, a Traducianist may reply that the method of formation of the soul is not an essential property of human or Adam's ontology.

Opponents of Traducianism object that the notion that the soul could be transmitted through the bodily act of sexual intercourse seems to be promoting a materialistic understanding of the soul (McFarland et al 2011, p. 514). Some forms of Traducianism which affirm that the soul of the child is a separated fragment of the father's soul ('literally a chip off the old block!') seem to be beset with this problem (as pointed out in Swinburne 1997, p. 199). It has been argued that, because souls do not have separable parts, they do not seem to be the sorts of things from which pieces can be taken (Moreland and Rae 2000, p. 221). However, other forms of Traducianism have been proposed. For example, on the assumption that ensoulment begins at conception, a possible mechanism is that human gametes are 'carriers' of DNA and soulish potentialities which, when syngamy takes place, generate a new immaterial, as well as material, substance (Moreland and Rae 2000, p. 221; they elaborate on p. 304: '*What we may be on the verge* of discovering with the advances in human *cloning* is that virtually any cells, not just the sex cells in sperm and eggs, have these soulish potentialities. When the proper physical reproductive conditions exist for cloning – that is, when the cloned cells are placed in the enucleated egg and it begins to develop – the soulish potentialities are actualized to form a new soul.') If God can cause unified souls directly as Creationism proposes, God can also cause eggs and sperms to be 'carriers' of soulish potentialities such that, during the event of fertilization, these potentials are actualized and bring about unified souls. There is no materialistic understanding given that the immaterial and the material remain distinct on this proposal.

It should be noted that, even though Traducianism is my preferred view, my model is compatible with Creationism as well, as explained later at the end of Section 5.7. Additionally, even though substance dualism is my preferred view, my model is compatible with Monism as well, as explained later at the end of Section 5.7. Thus, for the purpose of this monograph I do not have to prove that the Monists are wrong. (As noted earlier there has been debate about personal ontology among Christian theologians and philosophers, in particular between dualists and various forms of Christian Monism such as animalism, constitutionalism and non-reductive physicalism; see Loose et al. 2018.)

There is a range of views among theologians concerning the distinction and the relationship between

- Original Sin: All human beings except, at most, four (i.e. Adam, Eve, Jesus and, according to Roman Catholics, Mary) suffer from a kind of corruption that makes it very likely or inevitable that they will fall into sin, and this corruption is a consequence of the first sin of the first man, and
- Original Guilt: All human beings (except, at most, four) are guilty from birth in the eyes of God, and this guilt is a consequence of the first sin of the first man. (The definitions are taken from Rea 2007; Rea includes both under Original Sin for convenience of exposition of his article.)

It is beyond the scope of my book to provide a detailed assessment of the different opinions (for discussion, see Rea 2007 and Loke 2022b). Suffice to note that my model is consistent with all of them. The consistency of my model with a broad range of theological traditions and viewpoints is a merit of the model.

5.7 Elaboration of the God's-Image-Bearer GAE model

My proposal affirms that the descendants of Adam[17] would possess the image of God, and this would be the case even when these descendants were produced through mating with anatomical *Homo* that did not have the image of God. According to substance dualism, the capacity for the unique human qualities would be in the soul. As explained in previous chapters, many theologians past and present have recognized that it is consistent with the Scripture to affirm that animals also have souls – though lacking the image-of-God qualities – and thus it could be the case that their gametes were 'carriers' of DNA and soulish potentialities as well. Substance Dualists can propose that God set up a spiritual mechanism for the generation of souls which is independent of the physical laws governing the genetic mechanism, such that God uses parents to create the souls of children. When mating between humans and non-human *Homo* occurred, the unique human capacity in the soul as well as the election of being human would be passed on to the offspring, and the offspring would thus have the full image of God and thus be fully human. This is similar to the above-mentioned mechanism which Moreland and Rae suggest for Traducianism, the only modification being that one gamete from one human parent (rather than from two human parents) would be sufficient for the generation of an individual soul with the image of God when syngamy takes place between a gamete from a human being and one from a non-human anatomical *Homo*.

Note that there is nothing ad hoc about postulating such a spiritual mechanism – it is not postulated just for the sake of responding to the challenge of population genetics. Rather, it merely expounds on what Traducianist theologians have been proposing for centuries. As explained previously, the Traducianist proposal is based on biblical and theological considerations which are understood as evidences for this proposal according to the Christian world view. Unless we beg the question against Christian Theism by assuming physicalism, we should allow for the possibility that God can set up such a spiritual mechanism for the generation of souls which does not follow the laws of genetic inheritance.

Alternatively, if one prefers the Creationism view of the generation of human souls, one might suggest that God keeps track of the human lineage and creates a human soul whenever reproduction involving Adam's descendants and non-human *Homo* occurs.

My model proposes that the image of God is possessed by every human today and is passed down from Adam who was our common ancestor, even though (as population genetics indicate) we descended from a large population of anatomical

---

17. The only descendant of Adam who would not receive his soul via the Traducianist mechanism explained later would be Jesus, who is the Incarnation of the Second Person of the Trinity. Just as the creation of the human soul in the First Adam was special, the creation of the human soul in the last Adam (1 Cor. 15.45) would have been special too (for how the Second Person of the Trinity acquired a human soul, see Loke 2014).

Homo as indicated by population genetics. I first came to realize this while reading geneticist Dennis Venema's explanation of the 'Y-chromosome Adam' and 'Mitochondrial Eve' back in 2015. To elaborate, geneticists have discovered, on the basis of studies on Y-chromosomes and mitochondrial genomes, that all human males living today have a common male ancestor, identified as Y-chromosome Adam, and that all humans today have a common female ancestor, identified as Mitochondrial Eve. While there were other anatomical *Homo sapiens* alive during the time of Y-chromosome Adam, and there were other anatomical *Homo sapiens* alive during the time of Mitochondrial Eve, the genetic information in their Y-chromosome and mitochondrial genomes did not pass down to us. Rather, they passed down other genetic information – with mutations changing it – when descendants of Y-chromosome Adam and Mitochondrial Eve mated with them or their descendants and produced offspring. Venema (2014) has illustrated how this is possible using various pedigrees (family trees). The scientific findings concerning Y-chromosome Adam and Mitochondrial Eve illustrate a case in which, in the words of Venema, 'all humans do share a single man and single woman as common ancestors – but that these ancestors are not our *unique*, or sole, ancestors. Rather, they both come from that population of about 10,000 individuals' (2014).

I would like to emphasize that I am not postulating that the uniqueness of humans resides in Y-chromosomes and mitochondrial genomes, nor am I postulating that the spiritual capacities spread by genes. On the substance dualist view, souls are different from matter and are not reducible to matter, although soulish potentialities can still be passed down from parents to offspring along with matter as Traducianists traditionally propose (see earlier).

There are also multiple disanalogies between the Y-chromosome Adam and Mitochondrial Eve and my model. First, Y-chromosomes and mitochondrial genomes do not transmit reliably, whereas on my model the spiritual mechanism set up by God works reliably such that all the descendants of Adam would possess the image of God and would be fully human. Second, the Y-chromosome Adam and Mitochondrial Eve are calculated for everyone alive right now, not those at some point in the past. So it is not at all clear that, for example, the Y-chromosome Adam and Mitochondrial Eve were the genetic ancestors of every male and female, respectively, 2,000 years ago. Moreover, Y-chromosome Adam and Mitochondrial Eve change identities over time, as more lineages die off. Thus the Y-chromosome Adam and Mitochondrial Eve today would be different from the Y-chromosome Adam and Mitochondrial Eve in the future,[18] whereas according to my model the Scripture implies that Adam was the ancestor of every person 2,000 years ago and has remained so (see later). Third, whereas Y-chromosomes were passed down from 'Y-chromosome Adam' only through sons and mitochondrial genomes were passed down from 'mitochondrial Eve' only through daughters, on my model the image of God would be present in the descendants of Adam regardless of whether the offspring was a son or a daughter. A recent paper by computational biologist

---

18. I thank Joshua Swamidass for the previously mentioned disanalogies.

S. Joshua Swamidass explains that genealogical ancestry works very differently from genetics (Swamidass 2018; 2019), although in certain cases genetic ancestry (e.g. the Y-chromosomes of male humans today came from one male) also implies genealogical ancestry (e.g. of male humans today from this one male through the process of reproduction over many generations). The point remains that in accordance with genealogical ancestry all the humans today could have had Adam as a common ancestor and possess the image of God as proposed by my model, even though their genetic materials came from a sizeable population of anatomical *Homo* (which explains our current human genetic diversity). In fact, the science of genealogical ancestry implies that there are a large number of common ancestors of humans today, and that it is nearly certain that these common ancestors would have existed in the time frames I am thinking of (see Chapter 6 for a discussion of time frame).[19] Given that genealogical (rather than genetic) ancestry is the main issue here and the feature that is essential to my model, my model may be called a Genealogical Adam and Eve (GAE) model.[20]

There are different types of GAE model. Some postulate Adam as the first God's-image-bearer, some do not. Swamidass defends both possibilities in his book, while I defend the first. The fact that there are different possible GAE models implies that, even if one of the possibilities fails, this does not mean that GAE fails. In light of this, consider Madueme's (2020) objection in his review of Swamidass's book that 'the genealogical hypothesis itself is still dissonant with the biblical Adam and Eve. In that latter picture, Adam and Eve are genealogical ancestors of all human beings who have ever lived, not merely the ones alive today'. Madueme fails to note that there are different types of GAE model presented in Swamidass's book, and GAE model per se is not committed to denying that Adam and Eve are genealogical ancestors of all human beings who have ever lived. Given Swamidass's clarification on pages 105 and 149 that he is not committed to the view which Madueme rejects, Madueme's criticism does not affect the main conclusion of the book, namely, evolutionary genetics and the existence of Adam are compatible.

---

19. This point has been verified by scientists – Christians and non-Christians. See the review of Swamidass (2019) by well-known atheist biologist Nathan Lents in *USA Today*: https://www.usatoday.com/story/opinion/2019/10/04/upcoming-book-leaves-scientific-possibility-existence-adam-eve-column/3826195002/.

20. I thank Joshua Swamidass for suggesting this term, which he uses in his work (see Swamidass 2018; 2019; Garvey 2020), and for referring me to Kemp (2011), who has suggested a similar model and which I accessed after finishing this book. In my view Kemp's model is underdeveloped and does not address a variety of objections adequately, for example, the objection in Suarez (2015, p. 66) that Kemp's model 'deviates from the genealogical, cultural and technological context described in the Old and the New Testament'. I address these objections in Chapters 3 and 6 of this book. Moreover, Kemp's discussion of the image of God focuses too much on rational powers which have been criticized in the recent literature, see discussion in Chapter 5.

Contrary to earlier studies which have informed the views of a number of philosophers and theologians such as Ruse (2017, p. 157) and McFarland (2010, pp. 161), two recent major studies of modern humans' Y-chromosomes suggest that Y-chromosome Adam and Mitochondrial Eve may have lived around the same time.[21] Nevertheless, given that the science of genealogical ancestry implies that there are a large number of common ancestors of humans today (see earlier), it would be unlikely that Y-chromosome Adam and Mitochondrial Eve happened to be the biblical Adam and Eve. It is far more likely that the Y-chromosomal Adam and Mitochondrial Eve merely passed down the genetic information in their Y-chromosomes and mitochondrial genomes, while another couple (the biblical Adam and Eve) passed down the image of God in the way I described earlier. In this way, my model can coexist with Y-chromosome Adam and Mitochondrial Eve. However, my model is not dependent on Y-chromosome Adam and Mitochondrial Eve. That is, even if there were not any Y-chromosome Adam or Mitochondrial Eve who passed down the genetic information in their Y-chromosomes and mitochondrial genomes, there could still have been a couple (the biblical Adam and Eve) which passed down the image of God in such a way that all the humans today do share Adam as a common ancestor, even though their genetic materials came from a large population.

Even though substance dualism is my preferred view, my model is compatible with Monism as well, for my model does not exclude the possibility that the capacity for unique human qualities (the image-of-God qualities) has a biological basis, even though my model is not dependent on this possibility. Monists (if they wish) might propose that these qualities resulted from certain biological materials which were passed down from Adam. That is, God's-Image-Bearers and the rest of the anatomical *Homo* were all similar biologically except that God's-Image-Bearers had certain unique biological materials (there are, however, difficulties with this postulation; see later). It is biologically acceptable that members of the same anatomical species might have slightly different biological materials (that explains why some people suffer from genetic disease but others do not, for example). My view is also compatible with emergent substance dualism, according to which souls are generated by or emerge from physical neurological processes.[22] That is, one might argue that God directed the formation of physical neurological processes through an evolutionary process which resulted in the emergence of the first human soul in Adam, and as Adam passed down these neurological properties to his descendants they will possess the human souls as well. On these views there are real physical distinctions (genetically or neurologically) between those anatomical *Homo* with Imago Dei and those without. On the alternative dualist view, the real distinction lies in the differences between the souls of those anatomical *Homo* with Imago Dei and those without.

---

21. http://www.nature.com/news/genetic-adam-and-eve-did-not-live-too-far-apart-in-time-1.13478. Accessed 7 July 2015.

22. Saying this does not imply that I accept emergent substance dualism.

Concerning the Monist view which proposes that the capacity for unique human qualities (the image-of-God qualities) has a biological basis, it should be noted that mitochondrial and Y-chromosome inheritance are exceptions to the laws of Mendelian inheritance. An inheritance involving the autosomes, which constitute 98 per cent of the DNA and which follow the laws of Mendelian inheritance, would not follow the inheritance pattern I propose for the image-of-God qualities. Assuming there were many (e.g. around 10,000) individuals without the allele responsible for the image of God, and that only two individuals (male and female) were homozygous for the allele responsible for 'the image of God'. In that case, their offspring would be homozygous for that allele also. However, if the production of their next generation involved mating with individuals without the allele, the non-carrier individuals would contribute a different allele, such that their offspring would be heterozygous. With further mating with individuals without the allele, half of their offspring would no longer carry the allele at all. And the further this progressed, the 'dilution' would become more and more profound.[23]

Thus, in order for my model to work, the generation of the image of God cannot follow the laws of Mendelian inheritance. This is not a problem for the substance dualist version of my model. As explained previously, one view for the generation of individual souls is that egg and sperm have soulish potentialities that, on the occasion of fertilization, become actualized. This Traducianist view explains how it is that we are all offspring of Adam and Eve, by postulating that our souls came through them via a spiritual mechanism that follows the spiritual laws which God has set, and which are different from the physical laws governing Mendelian inheritance.

The key question is: 'Is this Traducianist view contradicted by population genetics, which indicates that the genetic diversity of the current human population requires that human beings descended from a population of *Homo sapiens* numbering 8,000–10,000 rather than two individuals?' The answer is 'No'. For even though our genes were passed down from a population numbering 8000 to10,000, our souls could still have come through two individuals via the spiritual mechanism that does not follow the laws of Mendelian inheritance, as explained earlier. Thus, the traditional Christian view that regards all human beings as descendants of two people (Adam and Eve) is not threatened by population genetics.

As for the Monist view, it might be argued that, even within genetics itself, there are exceptions to the laws of Mendelian inheritance, such as mitochondrial and Y-chromosome inheritance,[24] and that perhaps some yet undiscovered exceptions might explain the image-of-God qualities and the inheritance of these qualities.

---

23. I thank Dr Francis Collins for raising this issue in personal email correspondence.

24. Another exception to the Mendelian form of inheritance is a 'gene drive', which is now attracting a lot of attention because of its possibility of ending insect-borne diseases like malaria and Zika. I thank Dr Francis Collins for mentioning this in personal email correspondence.

Those who think that Monism is not compatible with my model would need to bear the burden of proof to exclude this possibility.

In summary, I propose that the image of God can be understood as God's election of humans for the functional role of royal representatives and for possession of the associated capacities. If one accepts Traducianism, Monism or emergent substance dualism, these capacities can be understood to have been passed down from Adam to his descendants. If one accepts Creationism, one might suggest that God keeps track of the human lineage and creates a human soul whenever reproduction involving Adam's descendants occurs.[25] In any one of these various possible ways (and perhaps there are other possibilities), all humans today could have a common ancestor.

5.8 Replies to questions and objections

5.8.1 Do all anatomical Homo living today possess the image of God?

One might ask how we can be assured that all anatomical *Homo* living today have, indeed, descended from Adam in the way I described and do, indeed, possess the image of God. This question is related to the issue of racism: could it be that certain 'human races' today do not possess the image of God, and that there are some human beings today who were more fully 'human' than others (Carter and Sanford 2020)?

As explained earlier, the purpose of this chapter is merely to show that there is no incompatibility between evolutionary population genetics and biblical doctrine. My model affirms that all people living today are, indeed, descendants of Adam on the basis of theological premises which is within the power of God to accomplish, based on the traditional interpretation of Acts 17.26: 'From one he made all nations to inhabit the whole earth.' This verse implies that, way before the first century AD when this verse was written, people from different nations who inhabit the whole earth were already descendants of one person. Modern scientific findings are not contradictory to this view given that the possible mechanisms I proposed have not been excluded. In fact, as noted earlier the science of genealogical ancestry implies that there are a large number of common ancestors of humans today. Scientists have calculated that the answer to the question 'how far back in time we must go to find an individual who was the ancestor of all present-day humans' (Most Recent Common Ancestor MRCA) is surprisingly recent (Hein 2004, p. 518). This implies that it would not take a long time for someone to become the common ancestor of all the anatomical *Homo* living at a later period of time. Therefore, my proposal does not imply that for most of human history, humans would have been interacting with non-human (i.e. non-God's-image-bearing) anatomical

---

25. It is beyond the scope of this chapter to settle the debate between these different views.

Homo (see discussion in Chapter 6). My model is not polygenic or racist because it affirms that all anatomical *Homo* today are human beings from a common ancestor (Adam) and are equally valued as God's image bearers.

5.8.2 The issue of 'bestiality'

As explained earlier, my model proposes that when humans mate with a non-human anatomical *Homo*, their offspring would be fully human as well. The mating between human beings and non-humans is not an ad hoc postulation in this case given that on my model God's-Image-Bearers and other anatomical *Homo* share similar biological properties and physical appearances. Nevertheless, some might ask whether this view implies that humans created in the image of God were involved in bestiality at some point with non-human anatomical *Homo*.[26] Against the Genealogical Adam proposal, Houck (2020, pp. 198–9) asks: 'Why didn't God elevate us as a group, if evolution had prepared an entire population for human existence? Similarly, why wouldn't God have created a population of theological human beings large enough for them to avoid widespread interbreeding with non-humans?'

A Christian theologian can reply that God created a single first human rather than a group because his human (Adam) is intended to be 'a type of the one who was to come' (Rom. 5.14), that is, a prefiguration of Christ (see Loke 2022b, Chapter 6). As for interbreeding with non-humans, there are two possible responses with respect to Task (C):

First, it is possible that descendants of Adam mated with non-human anatomical *Homo* (those whom they knew were outside of their community) in disobedience to God. It is observed that the pre-flood sin explicitly mentioned in Gen. 6.1-2 was also sexual in nature. 'When people began to multiply on the face of the ground, and daughters were born to them, the sons of God saw that they were fair; and they took wives for themselves of all that they chose.' One might even wonder whether this passage indicates the mating between God's-Image-Bearers (sons of God) and non-human anatomical *Homo*. However, the interpretation of the 'sons of God' in this text is highly disputed, with a number of commentators arguing that these were angels who incarnated and married against God's will (Wenham 1987; cf. Job 38.7; Jub. 4.22-24; Josephus *Antiquities*, 78),[27] and others (e.g. Walton 2001; Fischer 2008, pp. 60–2) arguing that they were humans.

---

26. The objection concerning bestiality has been raised before with regard to the mating of humans with other hominid species such as Neanderthals. See Wood (2012).

27. Mt. 22.30 portrays that Jesus said that angels do not marry; but one might object that Jesus was only referring to good angels. Ancient Jewish texts affirm that good angels do not marry but bad angels did (see, for example, *1 En*. 15.6-7; Jub. 10.5). Collins (2018, 7C1) argues that 'the simplest way to read the mention of "angels" who sinned in Jude 6 and 2 Peter 2:4 seems to be with reference to Genesis 6:1–4. None of these texts proposes a

Second, it is possible that it was not in disobedience to God because it was not considered as bestiality. Bestiality can be defined as sexual intercourse between humans and animals which are biologically non-human; lusting after 'other flesh' (Jude 1.7) is condemned in the Scripture (for condemnation of bestiality, see also Exod. 22.19; Lev. 18.23; 20.15-16; Deut. 27.21). However, unlike other animals, non-human anatomical *Homo* were similar to human beings biologically – they were all anatomically *Homo* and therefore of the 'same flesh' (as argued in Chapter 6, these anatomical *Homo* may even be persons).

It is possible that this was how Cain got his wife and descendants: he left the God's-Image-Bearer community after killing Abel and mated with other anatomical *Homo*. Likewise, Cain's concern that he would be killed by others (Gen. 4.14, 'whoever finds me will kill me') is consistent with the idea that there were already other anatomical *Homo* around.

Van Kuiken (2015, p. 686) objects by suggesting the alternative interpretation that 'given that Adam's family included other children (Gen 5:4) and that even in Abram's time, marriage to one's (half) sister was practiced (Gen 20:12), Cain's wife and other contemporaries are easily explained as Adam's progeny'. However, Van Kuiken's suggestion is less plausible given that Cain's concern was expressed before Seth was born (Gen. 4.25).

Anti-evolutionist theologian Wayne Grudem (2017, p. 790) objects that Gen. 2.18-20 ('Then the LORD God said, "It is not good that the man should be alone" . . . but for the man there was not found a helper as his partner') implies that there was no other human being around. However, one can reply that the state of loneliness is referring to Adam in the Garden; this does not exclude the possibility of others outside the Garden. In any case Grudem's conclusion is not strictly contradictory to my view given that I distinguish between anatomical *Homo* and God's-Image-Bearers (=human beings). That is, one might agree that there was no other human being around, but point out that there could be anatomical *Homo* outside of the Garden.

One might also suggest (in accordance with substance dualism) that the souls of God's-Image-Bearers and non-human anatomical *Homo* shared many of the same base qualities, with the difference being that the latter did not have those image-of-God properties mentioned earlier. If so, non-human anatomical *Homo* would be a lot more closely related to humans than they were to animals, and hence their sexual relationship with humans need not be considered a form of bestiality, at least not in the traditional sense.

My model raises interesting questions concerning what possible kinds of mental capacities non-human anatomical *Homo* would have possessed. This is particularly significant if Cain's wife was actually a non-human *Homo*. Could a human really enter into a marriage relation with a non-human? Could Cain's wife really play the role of a mother and wife? Could such an 'animal' really be a meaningful wife or

---

biological theory about how these sons of God acquired bodies: anything from possession to actual incarnation would suit the overall biblical picture.'

mother? Could it speak and communicate in human languages?[28] The idea that animals could have many capacities similar to human beings (except the capacity for the unique dominion, responsibility and Christ-likeness mentioned earlier in relation to the image of God) is not contrary to the Scripture given Moritz's (2013) observation that in the Scripture

> Both humans and animals are described as 'living souls/living beings' (*nephesh*), and the word used here implies a certain kinship (for animals, see Gen. 1:20, 1:30, 2:19, 9:4 and for humans, see Gen. 2:7, 9:5, 12:5). The word 'spirit' (*neshama*) is also used in reference to both humans and animals (Gen. 6:17, 7:22). Other biblical Hebrew terms also reflect this similarity between humans and animals. The phrase 'spirit of life' (*ruach hayyim*) is used for both animals and humans without distinction (for animals see Gen. 1:20–24, 2:19, 9:10, 15; for humans, see Gen. 2:7, 9:5). The word 'flesh' (*basar*) includes both humans and animals. The expression 'all flesh' (*kol basar*) literally means 'all living creatures, animal as well as human'.] In Scripture, there is only one designation that humans unequivocally have and that animals do not: humans, unlike animals, are said to be created 'as the image and likeness of God' (Imago Dei).

Given this and the previously mentioned scientific evidences concerning animal capacities, it is plausible to think that Cain's wife could, indeed, enter into a primitive marriage relation, play a primitive role of a mother and wife, speak and communicate in primitive languages like Cain; the only thing she would lack would be one/some or all of the 'image of God' properties mentioned previously, namely, (1) election by God, (2) having the capacity for a unique kind of dominion that could extend to the whole world and over all kinds of creatures (3) having the capacity for a sense of responsibility to God for this kind of dominion and (4) having the capacity to be made to become conformed to Christ (see further, Chapter 6).

On the other hand, Cain's role in marriage and family life and his communicative abilities might have been quite primitive as well; after all, the earlier mentioned capacities had only just begun to be realized. Thus the differences in behaviour between Cain and his wife might not have been very great, though the differences might still have caused difficulties and thus such a relationship would not have been ideal (unlike the case of an ideal helper for Adam, see previous discussion). Their descendants might manifest increasing capabilities as the earlier mentioned capacities gradually became realized over time, but as noted in the next chapter cultural degeneration might also lead to a decreased level of cultural achievements.

In summary, the above arguments for or against the possibility that the mating between humans created in the image of God and non-human anatomical *Homo* was considered as bestiality seem inconclusive. In any case, both are compatible with the model proposed in this book.

---

28. I thank Ray Yeo for raising these questions.

On the other hand, one might argue that there is an additional reason favouring the view that it was not bestiality. For example, one might suggest that God wanted God's-Image-Bearers to interbreed with non-human anatomical *Homo* as a way to address the concern about incest which would be present if Adam's offsprings were to mate only among themselves. Nevertheless, others might reply by suggesting that incest is permitted by God before the giving of the Mosaic Law and was practiced by many ancient cultures such as the Egyptian pharaohs. (There are various possibilities to explore concerning Cain's wife: for example, she could be his sister [this view is found in the ancient pseudoepigraph *The Book of Jubilees* 4.9 and various Jewish and Christian commentators], niece, grandniece etc., although as noted earlier it could also be a non-God's-image-bearing anatomical *Homo*; including the possibility of Neanderthal or other *Homo* species.) Alternatively, one might suggest that God wanted God's-Image-Bearers to interbreed with non-human anatomical *Homo* as a way of helping them spread across the earth. This is biologically more feasible as a way to spread across the earth, explains why God made them biologically compatible for producing offspring, and it also renders the bestiality objection incorrect.[29] Nevertheless, my model does not depend on this point; even if it was bestiality, one can argue that descendants of Adam mated with non-human anatomical *Homo* (those whom they knew were outside of their community) in disobedience to God.

5.8.3 How should Gen. 2.7 and the creation of Eve be understood?

Gen. 2.7: 'Then the LORD God formed the man of dust from the ground and breathed into his nostrils the breath of life, and the man became a living creature' (ESV).

The phrase '. . . of dust from the ground' should be understood in light of Gen. 3.19 'for dust you are and to dust you will return', which is a reference to our mortality.[30] As Walton (2015, 73) observes, 'This association would make sense to an Israelite reader who was well acquainted with the idea of a corpse that was laid out on the slab in the family tomb and deteriorating to merely a pile of bones and the dust of the desiccated flesh within a year.' The phrase indicates that

---

29. I thank Joshua Swamidass for helpful inputs here.

30. Walton (2015, pp. 73–4) argues that God created humans mortal, for immortal humans would not have needed a Tree of Life. This is not inconsistent with Paul's statement that 'death [came] through sin, and in this way death came to all people, because all sinned' (Rom. 5.12), which can be understood as saying that sin caused humans to be cut off from the Tree of Life and so they became trapped in mortality and doomed to die. This does not require taking the effects of the fruit of the Tree literally; rather, the Tree can symbolize a close relationship with God who would sustain humans in bodily life had they not sinned. See further, Section 5.8.4.

humans are made of the material to which they shall return when they are buried in the ground. Dust, after all, are fine particles of matter that come from various sources including the soil. Collins (2018, section 10.A.3) comments that the fact that the human body is made of the common elements of the soil would have been 'simple and obvious to the audience of Genesis, familiar as they were with what happens when people die: not only would Adam "return to dust" (3:19), all people do.' Walton observes that Ps. 103.14 'for he knows how we are formed, he remembers that we are dust' implies that other humans are also formed of dust, yet (obviously) having biological parents. This implies that even though Adam is formed (Hebrew *yatsar*) of dust, he could still have biological parents (Walton 2015, pp. 75–6), as explained previously, according to my model, the 'parents' of Adam were not human beings but were non-human anatomical *Homo*, since they did not have the image of God. 'Formed of dust' does *not* therefore mean formed *directly* from dust.

On the other hand, Moritz observes concerning the Hebrew words *yatsar*, *asah* and the biblical description of the creation of animals and humans and the formation of a human being in the womb (Ps. 139.13-16; Isa. 44.24, 49.5, 44.2) that

> The same Hebrew words (*yatsar* and *asah*) which describe the 9-month-long process of development from two single cells to a fully formed human being are used to describe the earth's creation of the different types of animals in direct response to God's command. In other words, in the emergence of plant and animal life through earth's history, we find the same general trajectory as in the formation of an embryo in the womb: first single cells, then multicellularity, and then more complex organisms . . . the exact same Hebrew words (*asah* and *yatsar*) that describe God's forming of embryos in the womb, and God's forming of plant and animal life, are used to describe God's forming of the human species. The use of these words implies (or at the very least, does not rule out) that God's forming of humankind was a process and not an instantaneous event. (Moritz 2013; cf. Grudem 2017, p. 800)

Grudem (2017, pp. 801–2) also raises the objection that the statements in Gen. 3.19-23 'for out of it you were taken . . . to dust you shall return . . . therefore the LORD God sent him forth from the garden of Eden, to till the ground from which he was taken' imply that Adam was created directly from the earth, but as explained earlier these statements could just mean that humans are made of the material to which they shall return when they are buried in the ground. (Nevertheless, I shall explain later (citing Swamidass) that, even if Grudem is correct, this does not contradict the Genealogical Adam model.)

Thus, according to Gen. 2.7, the use of the word *yatsar* implies that the formation of the body could have taken place over time, that is, a process. (For the purpose of Task A), the text does not imply that it was an evolutionary process, but (for the purpose of Task C) the text does not exclude the possibility that this happened as a result of an evolutionary process either.) Hence, Lamoureux misrepresents me when he states, 'Loke explains that in Genesis 2:7 "the Hebrew word *yatsar* (formed) can literally mean that God's forming of humankind was a process," implying an evolutionary process' (2020, p. 187). Now I did not argue that the process implies an evolutionary process. Rather, what I argued is that the process is not inconsistent with an evolutionary process. Lamoureux fails to grasp the distinction between 'implication' and 'consistency', and fails to understand the distinction between Task (A) 'interpreting the Bible' and Task (C) 'showing that there is no incompatibility between evolution and Bible' which I have explained previously.

Before God breathed into the nostrils, the 'man' referred to in this verse was not a 'living creature', it was perhaps just a 'physical body' which was to become the body of a man. It was only after God breathed into the nostrils that the 'physical body' became a living creature. 'Formed' is consistent with the idea of making an already existing body which was 'made of dust' functional (i.e. with the capacity for possessing the image of God).

The reader should note the subtle distinction between Task (A) and Task (C) which has been explained in Chapter 1. I am not claiming that Gen. 2.7 *is* conveying that God breathed into the already existing body of an anatomically *Homo* body. Rather, what I am arguing is that, for all we know, the 'already existing body' *could be* the body of an anatomical *Homo*. While the phrase 'breathed into his nostrils the breath of life' does not necessarily imply the creation of a human soul in the image of God, it does not exclude that either. (Zech. 12.1 says that God forms the *ruah* [translated as wind or spirit] of man within him.) While the same word *nephesh* is also used of animals, this does not imply that *nephesh* should not be understood as soul; on the contrary, as argued in Chapter 4 there are indications that biblical authors regarded both humans and animals to have souls which can exist beyond death. The creation of human soul is consistent with Pope Pius XII's statement (reiterated by Pope John Paul II in 1996) that

> The teaching authority of the Church does not forbid that, in conformity with the present state of human sciences and sacred theology, research and discussions . . . take place with regard to the doctrine of evolution, in as far as it inquires into the origin of the human body as coming from pre-existent and living matter – [but] the Catholic faith obliges us to hold that souls are immediately created by God. (Pius XII, *Humani Generis* 36)

Many fundamentalist Christians think that embracing evolution would mean accepting that we came from ape-like ancestors, which is objectionable. Evolutionary Creationists can reply that only the physical aspect of humanity came from a biological common ancestor. The spiritual aspect in God's image, however, could be directly created by God (see the quote from Pius XII). Given that God is a spiritual being (John 4.24), the image of God in humanity should not be understood as asserting that our physical body is similar to God. Rather, it should be referring to the spiritual aspect which includes the election and capacities explained earlier (cf. Calvin, *Institutes of the Christian Religion* 1.15.3, who thinks there is no absurdity in holding that humans are called the image of God in respect to the soul). It could be the case that human spiritual properties were directly and specially created by God on a pre-existing physical body of the hominid species, resulting in a new person with the image of God (Adam), who would be the first 'human being'. In this way, human uniqueness compared to animals is affirmed, and whether the physical aspect came via macroevolution or not is of no theological importance.

One might object that Gen. 2.7 states that it is man – rather than his body – that is said to be formed of dust. However, in ancient Jewish thought the man is often identified by the body (even the corpse); see Jacob's identification of himself ('me') be his corpse in Gen. 47.30 'but when I rest with my fathers, carry me out of Egypt and bury me where they are buried'.

Against the idea that God created Adam using an already existing body of a pre-existing anatomical *Homo*, it might also be objected that

> the term rendered 'living creature' means animate being, creature with the breath of life. In itself this predicate does not express anything distinctive of man as compared with other animate beings. The designation is generic and is applied to other creatures (cf. Gen 1:21, 24, 30). . . . If 'man' were previously animate, and the inbreathing constituted him man as distinct from and superior to other animate creatures, then it could not be said that by the inbreathing he became 'living creature'. The inbreathing was not an action superimposed upon an already existing animate being. (Murray 1982, pp. 8–9)

In reply, the 'already existing body' could be the body of an 'anatomical *Homo*' which had just died, and which after God breathed into it became a 'living creature' with the image of God. On this possible model, the 'parents' of Adam were not human beings (cf. the concern raised in Grudem 2009); rather, they were 'anatomical Homo sapiens' since they did not have the image of God. God could have chosen to pick up a handful of dust from the ground as Murray goes on to claim, or God could have chosen to pick up a corpse as I suggested. I don't think any of these possibilities is more ad hoc than the other.

On the other hand, it should be noted that my Genealogical Adam model is also compatible with God picking up a handful of dust from the ground and creating Adam de novo as Murray and Grudem claim. As Swamidass (2019) observes, God could still have created Adam's physical body de novo and made him the common ancestor of all human beings today (even though we would also descend from anatomical *Homo* outside the Garden), and that there is no incompatibility between this alternative possible model and evolutionary science because Adam's offspring 'would have blended with those outside it, biologically identical neighbors from the surrounding area' (p. 10) whom God created using the process of evolution.

Concerning the creation of Eve, the scenario which I am sketching does not require nor exclude the possibility of Eve being miraculously created by God using a part of Adam. As in the case of Adam being formed of dust (de novo) by God,

I see no reason to reject a literal interpretation of this (note that by making this point I am not claiming that a literal interpretation is the best in this case). In both cases the scenario is allowable by a literal reading of the text, as well as a physical understanding of it, and in both cases the scenario is compatible with evolution. (The fact that men and women have the same number of ribs does not contradict this, for the 'surgery' on 'Adam's rib' would not have affected his genetic constitution and hence would not have affected the subsequent generations of males.)

One might object that pre-Adamic sexual differentiation was already present in the anatomical *Homo*, and claim that the miraculous creation of Eve's physical body is inconsistent with the creation of Adam who was anatomically descended from previous anatomical *Homo*. However, these reasons are inadequate for excluding the possibility that God could have chosen to do a miracle in Eve's case to illustrate to her and to Adam that she is intended to be a close and intimate companion by his side.

Walton (2015, pp. 77–8) observes that more than a rib is involved here because Eve is not only called 'bone of his bone' but also 'flesh of his flesh' (Gen. 2.23), and that the Hebrew word ṣēlāʿ can refer to the entire side or to the entire rib cage 'comparable to our English use when we talk about a "side of beef"'. Walton (pp. 78–81) goes on to argue that Adam had a visionary experience rather than a miraculous surgery. However, a mere vision does not seem adequate to ground Adam's statement that 'from a man was she taken' (Gen. 2.23) and the subsequent implication from Gen. 2.24 that 'when Man and Woman become one flesh, they are returning to their original state' (Walton 2015, p. 81). Walton's interpretation is also inconsistent with the New Testament which states that 'man was not made from woman, but woman from man' (1 Cor. 11.8). Paul was implying that this actually happened and was not only a vision (Grudem 2017, p. 804).

Some might object that 'If God created humans to take care of the earth, why create humans after the earth had already existed for such a long time?' In reply, this objection is based on fallacious assumptions. God did not need a gardener to help Him take care of the earth; God could have done it Himself if He wanted, or He could have assigned angels to do it. God assigned humans certain roles (Gen. 1.28, 2.15) not because God needed humans to serve Him (Acts 17.25); rather, this assignment should be understood as an act of grace that allow humans to express their gratitude, love and worship to Him.

5.8.4 Is my model compatible with the gradual evolution of humans?

Some scientists have objected that 'the criteria for "humanness" . . . even if you accept them, must have evolved gradually' (Coyne 2021) and 'biologists are likely to be highly skeptical of the idea that humanness is a binary condition that can be induced by a change in a single pair of ancestors' (Schaffner 2021).

The above objections are based on a scientific criteria of humanness, which is different from the theological criteria of humanness (image of God) which I discussed above. The theological criteria I use does not conflict with the scientific criteria because (1) these two criteria are used in different discourses and they are not referring to exactly the same properties, and (2) on my model, the postulation of the direct creation of spiritual properties (see Section 5.3) does not imply that there was a sudden acquisition of all the properties characteristic of a human being by a pre-existent hominid. Rather, many of these properties (e.g. creativity, ability to use language) could have already been acquired gradually over a long evolutionary process (see further, Sections 5.8.2 and 6.3.2.). As argued previously, God could have used a natural and gradual process to form many aspects of biological species including humankind. The direct creation of spiritual properties could have only conferred what was lacking to make that hominid possess the image of God; for example, it could have involved only election by God to function as God's royal representatives in the world. To assume that God could not have elected royal representatives would be to beg the question against Christian Theism. The postulation of this election for the purpose of Task (C) is not ad hoc given the evidence for Christian Theism (e.g. Loke 2009; 2017a; 2017b; 2020a; 2021a; 2022a) and that this intervention is (arguably) implied by Christian doctrine.

The usage of different criteria of humanness for different discourses (scientific, theological) does not imply the compartmentalization of Science and Christianity, because they still overlap at some points concerning human origins. To illustrate: a student scoring 50 per cent in a university exam might fit the criteria for competence in Country x but not in Country y (which requires 80 per cent). The criteria in these two countries are different and the different criteria have legitimacy in different countries, but there is still overlap (for example) in the types of answers deemed acceptable for the exam. Likewise, a hominid possessing the characteristics of planning depth, innovativeness, abstract thinking and symbolic behaviour (McBrearty and Brooks 2000, p. 492; see further, Section 6.3.2.) might fit the criteria for sufficiency of humanness in a scientific discourse but not in a theological discourse (which requires, for example, the election by God). The criteria in these two discourses are different, and the different criteria have legitimacy in different discourses, but there is still overlap; for example, the election by God to function as God's royal representatives to govern the world would require the capacity for in-depth planning, innovativeness, abstract thinking and symbolic behaviour.

5.8.5 What about the origin of sin and the Fall?

Issues concerning the presence of suffering and death which occurred before Adam have already been addressed in previous chapters. My model affirms that the sin of Adam and Eve was the first sin committed by *human beings*, regardless of whether there were sins committed by creatures before that. There is no passage in the Scripture which claims that the sin of Adam and Eve was the first sin in the universe. On the contrary, Genesis 3 portrays that the serpent sinned prior to Adam and Eve by tempting Eve to eat from the Tree of Knowledge of Good and Evil (for angelic sin and fall, see O'Halloran 2015; Lloyd 2018).

Against a literal interpretation of Adam, it might be objected that, for Adam and the Garden of Eden to have been real, then there 'really' was a tree in it which would have permitted Adam and Eve to live forever if they had just eaten from it. But that is biologically nonsense: no food can make you immortal, just as no food can give you the knowledge of good and evil.[31]

In reply, it is over-simplistic to think that a literal interpretation of Adam entails a literal interpretation of the effects of the fruits of the Trees. Rather, each detail in the narrative should be considered on the basis of the hermeneutical principles I explained earlier, namely, considering the genre, context, historical background, etc. I have explained earlier the historical background of the text, namely, that the ANE genealogical lists found so far have included only real people. 'Consequently there would be no precedent for thinking of the biblical genealogies differently from others in the ancient world. By putting Adam in ancestor lists, the authors of Scripture are treating him as a historical person' (Walton 2015, p. 102). One should also note the context of the text concerning the Tree of Knowledge of Good and Evil. Tremper Longman (2017) observes that, as a result of receiving God's command not to eat from the Tree, Adam and Eve already knew what was good and what was evil prior to eating from the Tree. In particular, they knew that they should not eat from the Tree. Moreover, according to the narrative, prior to eating from the Tree Adam already had the knowledge to cultivate and maintain a garden (2:15), to name the animals (2:19-20), etc. Thus the eating of the fruit did not give them intellectual knowledge, and neither did God's command to them not to eat from that tree imply that God did not want them to have true knowledge and wisdom (Prov. 3.13-18 comments that Wisdom is a Tree of Life to those who take hold of her; those who hold her fast will be blessed (v.18)). Rather, the eating of the fruit of the Tree of Knowledge of Good and Evil signifies the human decision to reject God and to decide for oneself what is good and evil. As Lewis (1980, p. 49) writes,

> What Satan put into the heads of our remote ancestors was the idea that they could 'be like gods' – could set up on their own as if they had created themselves – be their own masters – invent some sort of happiness for themselves outside God, apart from God. And out of that hopeless attempt has come nearly all that we call human history – money, poverty, ambition, war, prostitution, classes, empires, slavery – the long terrible story of man trying to find something other than God which will make him happy.

Hence, when Genesis portrays the LORD God said, 'See, the man has become like one of us, knowing good and evil' (Gen. 3.22a), what this intends to convey is that the man has become like God in the sense that he decides for himself what is good and evil. Therefore there are exegetical considerations for thinking that the biblical authors intended Adam as a historical person and intended the Tree of Knowledge

---

31. I thank a reviewer for suggesting this objection.

of Good and Evil – and likewise the Tree of Life – to be symbolic. The Tree of Life symbolizes a right relationship with God who would sustain humans in bodily life had they not sinned. As explained previously, according to my scenario all 'anatomical *Homo* who have the image of God' are the descendants of Adam and Eve, and that it was through Adam's disobedience that sin entered into the human race (Rom. 5.12-21). The cursing of the ground by God because of Adam's sin can be understood in functional terms, that is, the ground was cursed with respect to Adam. As suggested (following Gavin McGrath) in previous chapters, after his creation Adam was placed in a divinely protected environment (Eden) which occupied a limited geographical area on the earth. However, after he sinned the ground on which he lived was cursed in the sense that it no longer had that divine protection.

Concerning the historicity of the biblical account, Blocher (2009, pp. 169–70) wisely observes that the lack of remains from an Edenic state should not surprise and embarrass believers, for 'even if that state was enjoyed for some time (years and not hours as some have thought), the chances of finding convincing traces are practically nil. The absence of proof is no proof of absence.'

5.9 Conclusion

Many scholars from a wide variety of world views including Atheists, Agnostics, Roman Catholics, Mainline Protestants, and Evangelicals have argued that evolutionary population genetics, which indicates that the genetic diversity of the current *Homo sapiens* population requires that this population descended from a population of *Homo sapiens* numbering 8000 to 10,000, poses an insurmountable challenge to the traditional interpretation of Scripture which regards all human beings as descendants of two people. I have shown that a contradiction does not follow. Beginning with the identity of human beings, I have argued that we should consider evidence for the existence of creatures that not only looked like modern humans but also behaved and communicated with each other like modern humans. Various Scriptural passages affirm that human beings exist as dependent creatures of God and possess the image of God. The image of God should be regarded as (i) election by God to function as God's royal representatives in the world and given authorized power to share in God's rule over the earth, and having the associated capacities (ii) for a unique kind of dominion that could extend to the whole world and over all kinds of creatures, (iii) for a sense of responsibility to God for this kind of dominion, and (iv) to be made to become conformed to Christ.

While there is a range of views among Christians concerning the Scriptural affirmation of Adam, a weighty exegetical consideration is offered by Walton who notes that the ANE genealogical lists found so far have included only real people, 'consequently there would be no precedent for thinking of the biblical genealogies differently from others in the ancient world. By putting Adam in ancestor lists, the authors of Scripture are treating him as a historical person' (Walton 2015, p. 102).

Concerning Task (C), I have shown that the existence of Adam is compatible with modern science by developing a model which distinguishes between anatomical *Homo* possessing the image of God (God's-Image-Bearers=human beings) and anatomical *Homo* which did not possess this. In my model, God took a pre-existing anatomical *Homo* or created one de novo and made him (Adam) to be a God's-Image-Bearer. I defended the possibility that the image of God was passed down from him to his descendants, and that all humans today could have him as their common ancestor even though they descended from a large population of anatomical *Homo* as indicated by population genetics. Some descendants of Adam could have mated with non-human anatomical *Homo* which contributed to the genetic diversity, but their descendants were nevertheless fully human. This proposal is consistent with the Scriptural account and with the findings of science; indeed, its central idea that all humans today could have a man as their common ancestor even though they descended from a large population is plausible given scientific studies concerning the MRCA (Rohde, Olson and Chang 2004; Hein 2004). I shall elaborate on this point in the next chapter.

Chapter 6

THE TIME FRAME OF OUR COMMON ANCESTOR

6.1 Introduction

In previous chapters, I have argued that, contrary to widespread opinion, evolutionary population genetics does not contradict the traditional interpretation of the Bible which regards all human beings today as descendants of Adam, for all humans today could have a common ancestor even though they descended from a large population of anatomical *Homo* as indicated by population genetics. But if this common ancestor did exist, when did he live? Moreover, does evolutionary population genetics contradict the biblical account that all human beings today are descendants of one family (Noah's) after the Flood? The size of one family is obviously way below the population of 8,000–10,000 indicated by recent population genetics. How would my model address this apparent conflict?

Some might try to avoid this conflict by interpreting the biblical flood symbolically or typologically, noting that the New Testament writers sometimes read the Old Testament symbolically or typologically (Hays 2016). However, the New Testament writers evidently interpreted some details in the Old Testament as historical. For example, the Gospel of Matthew portrays Jesus as saying,

> For as the days of Noah were, so will be the coming of the Son of Man. For as in those days before the flood they were eating and drinking, marrying and giving in marriage, until the day Noah entered the ark, and they knew nothing until the flood came and swept them all away, so too will be the coming of the Son of Man. (Mt. 24.37-39)

Just as the Matthean Jesus evidently regarded the coming of the Son of Man as a real event that would happen in the future, the Matthean Jesus evidently regarded the biblical flood as a real event and Noah as a historical person. Among contemporary Christians, those who agree with this view include not only Evangelicals but also many Eastern Orthodox Christians who accept the traditional interpretations of early church fathers such as Justin Martyr (*Dialogue with Trypho* 138), Gregory of Nazianzus (*Second Theological Oration* 18) and John Chrysostom (*Homily 8 on First Thessalonians*). Even though some of the details were interpreted symbolically,[1] these early church fathers evidently regarded that the event happened (a real event can have symbolic significance). Likewise, many Roman Catholics accept the *Catechism of the Catholic Church* (nos. 58, 71, 845, 1094, 1219, etc.), which refers to Noah as a historical person and the covenant made with him after the Flood as a historical event. While there are other scholars who read the Flood in a symbolic or typological manner, the contribution of my book lies in showing that – even when read in a more literal manner – there is no incompatibility with population genetics. In the following sections, I shall discuss the different interpretations concerning the extent of the Flood, followed by a discussion of the issue concerning the dating of human common ancestors.

6.2 The extent of the Flood

To begin with the Flood, a literal interpretation of the account in Genesis does not require the Flood to be interpreted as what we understand to be a global phenomenon. While YECs influenced by John Whitcomb's and Henry Morris's influential *The Genesis Flood* (1961) have insisted that it must be interpreted as a global phenomenon, many scholars have argued that the Flood can be interpreted quite literally as a localized phenomenon.[2] As will be explained later, I propose that it is plausible to interpret it as localized to the extent sufficient for wiping out God's-image-Bearers as well as their possessions (including animals within their area of dominion), leaving Noah and his family. If this is the case, then in accordance with Task C (see Chapter 1) one can postulate a model in which many other animals around the globe – including many anatomical *Homo sapiens* who did not possess the image of God – would have survived the Flood. It is possible that a number of Noah's descendants (God's-Image-Bearers) mated with non-human anatomical *Homo* after the Flood, thus accounting for the genetic diversity we observe today.

Objections against the local flood interpretation can be answered. For example, Seely (2007, p. 39) objects that Gen. 7.19 states that the rain waters covered 'all of the high mountains under all the heavens', and argues that the phrase 'under all the heavens' necessarily includes the country of Ararat since that country is part of the context (Gen. 8.4), and thus the phrase, 'all the high mountains' would have included the high mountains of Ararat, not just the foothills. If the ark came to rest on the Ararat foothills, the tops of the mountains in the vicinity would have been

---

1. For example, Justin interpreted the number of persons who survived the flood (Noah, his wife, his three sons and their wives), that is, 'eight in number, were a symbol of the eighth day, wherein Christ appeared when He rose from the dead' (*Dialogue with Trypho* 138).

2. Scholars who defended the local flood have replied to difficult questions such as the exegesis of Genesis 6–8, why there was still a need for Noah to keep the animals in the Ark, etc. For an overview, see http://www.asa3.org/ASA/education/origins/flood.htm. Accessed 7 July 2015. Cf. Morris 2005.

visible before the waters began to recede, and not as a result of ten more weeks of the waters receding (Gen. 8.15).

In reply, it has been observed by Walton (2003, pp. 321–2) that, when Gen. 7.19 refers to mountains being covered, it uses the *Pual* form of the verb *ksh* in which, when water is the subject, the covering can refer to drenching (Job 38.34; Jer. 46.8; Mal. 2.13) rather than to a total submergence under water, and in Gen. 7.20 the text may only suggest that the water reached 15 cubits upwards from the plain. As for the tops of the mountains becoming visible (Gen. 8.3-5), Walton argues that the Israelites would not include the tall Ararat mountains which they regarded as fringe mountains on which the sky rested. He explains further that

> Noah's ark could be understood as having come to rest against (Heb *'al*) the mountains of Ararat, and from there Noah would have watched the tops of the mountains in the inhabitable world become visible. The logic of not including the fringe mountains would be that they were believed to support the heavens, and the waters would not be seen as encroaching on or encountering the heavens. (2003, p. 322)

Ross (2007, p. 48) also notes that the Hebrew terminology for the 'whole earth' of Genesis 6–9 does not necessarily refer to the entire globe but could refer to the greater Near East, as Gen. 9.19 and Genesis 10 show (Seely 2007, p. 41). With regard to passages that mention 'all' (e.g. Gen. 6.12): 'all flesh had corrupted their way'; 'all flesh died that moved on the earth' (Gen. 7.21), Walton (2003, p. 321) points out that passages such as Gen. 41.57 and Deut. 2.25 indicate that when the text uses the word 'all', it is not always in an absolute sense. He notes similar relative uses in Akkadian texts, and argues that it was perfectly acceptable to use the word 'all' in reference to a relatively delineated area.

In the New Testament, 2 Pet. 3.6 states that 'By these waters also the world of that time was deluged and destroyed'. The Greek word translated as world, *kosmos*, can mean the human race; that is, the flood was sufficient for wiping out the God's-Image-Bearer group as well as their possessions, leaving Noah and his family. That was the main 'function' of the Flood, and as Walton (2006) has argued, the ancient Hebrews were generally more concerned about function than ontology. Scholars have noted that the Flood is portrayed as a reversal of creation; while Genesis 1 portrays creation as a series of separations and distinctions, Gen. 6.9–7.24 portrays the annihilation of these distinctions (Arnold 2009, p. 103). If (as argued in Chapter 3) creation in Genesis is plausibly understood in functional terms with respect to making a localized and suitable habitat for God's-Image-Bearers, then a reversal of creation would imply that the Flood is plausibly understood in functional terms with respect to the destruction of a localized and suitable habitat for God's-Image-Bearers (see further, Longman and Walton 2018).

Ross (2017, p. 85) observes that when 2 Pet. 2.5 states that 'the world of the ungodly' was flooded, this focuses on the ungodly people rather than the land, and it is reasonable to infer that the flood's extent was determined by how far these people had spread, and there is no indication in the biblical text that they had spread over the entire earth by the time of the flood. Wenham (1987) observes that there is a certain parallelism between Genesis 8–9 and Genesis 1–2; in Genesis 8–9, the earth was in chaos again, and God sent His *ruah* (translated as wind or Spirit) over the earth, and the waters receded (Gen. 8.1). There is a functional re-creation similar to that of Genesis 1.

On the other hand, Ross argues that early commentaries on the waters on Creation Day 3 of Genesis found in Psalm 104 ('You set a boundary they cannot cross; never again will they cover the earth') imply that Noah's flood should not be understood as covering the entire globe (Ross also cites Job 38.8-11; Ps. 33.7-9 and Prov. 8.23-29) (Ross 2007, p. 48. Note that Ross cannot justifiably be accused of Concordism here, given that he is arguing on the basis of ancient Jewish writings just as Walton (2017) does when he argues that the earliest commentaries of Genesis are found in Psalms 8 and 104 and these affirm ordered functions). It has also been argued that the existence of 'the Nephilim' before and after the Flood (Gen. 6.4; Num. 13.33) indicates that the Flood was local and that there were survivors outside the area affected by the Flood (Fischer 2008; if this interpretation holds, with respect to Task C these Nephilims may be regarded as gigantic anatomical *Homo* survivors in accordance with my model). Others, however, have claimed that the use of 'the Nephilim' is 'simply for oratorical effect, much as "Huns" was used to designate Germans during the two world wars' (Sarna 1989, p. 46). In any case, even if the Scripture does not indicate that the Flood was local, it does not rule out a local flood either.

With respect to Task (C), Ross (2007, p. 48) argues that Gen. 7.19 is based on what appears to Noah's limited perspective, and the floodwaters' slow (nearly year-long) recession may have been caused by the addition of run-off and snowmelt from the surrounding hills and mountains.

One might ask 'why would the Scripture portray God as saying after the Flood "I will remember my covenant that is between me and you and every living creature of all flesh; and the waters shall never again become a flood to destroy all flesh" (Gen. 9.15) if it were only a local flood? This does not make sense since local floods are quite common.'

One might reply that, while local floods have been common, a local flood that destroyed all human beings, that is, all God's-Image-Bearers (except one family, that is, Noah's) has happened only once. Gen. 9.15 can be understood as indicating that God will no longer destroy all human beings and all living creatures associated with them ('all flesh' understood functionally and phenomenologically with respect to humans) using flood water, and, indeed, no local floods had done that since the time of Noah.

With regard to scientific evidences, those who argue that Noah's flood is global claim that there is evidence of rapid burial of living organisms, as indicated by the preservation of soft tissues in fossil records. However, evidence of rapid burial only indicates that catastrophic events did occur in the earth's history, which no one would deny; it does not prove that there was one catastrophic event in the form of a global flood which covered the earth. While YECs have repeatedly asked why marine fossils would exist on Mount Everest if there was no global flood, the answer is that the Himalayas were once the sea floor crumpled by the tectonic collision between the Indian subcontinent and Asia (Ross 2017, p. 53). On the other hand, desert dunes and other desert deposits do not form under roaring flood waters. These require not only time but also dry land. A global flood supplies neither.[3] Moreover, Haarsma (2017, pp. 58–9) points out that continental rock layers are not a uniform layer over an entire continent as predicted by the global-flood model; rather, the rock is found in many overlapping sections, showing that it formed in multiple periods. The billions of living things buried in rocks are not mixed together as would be expected from the violence of a global flood. Rather, rock formations like the Grand Canyon show discrete layers, each containing organisms only from a particular ecosystem (some only from land, some only from rivers, etc.).

6.3 Dating of Adam and Noah

6.3.1 Introduction to issues

Where Task (C) is concerned, the following objection might be raised against my model. Many evolutionists now accept the hypothesis that anatomical *Homo sapiens* moved out of Africa 55,000 years ago, and that the humans we observe today are of pure African origin, with the total replacement of non-African genes (Stringer 2011, pp. 259–61). It is assumed that, if Adam and Eve are, indeed, at the headwaters of all humans today, they must have existed before such events as the arrival of anatomical *Homo sapiens* in Australia, which means before about 40,000 BC (Collins 2011, p. 117). However, a number of scholars have dated the Flood to around 2650 BC, and Adam to the Neolithic era (see further, in what follows). To many people this seems too recent for Adam to be the ancestor of all humans today, and it seems that such a recent Flood (assuming that it was local) could not have wiped out the God's-Image-Bearer community before it spread across the earth (e.g. before humans arrived in Australia at around 40,000 BC).

Scholars have responded to this perceived problem in various ways. For example, Henri Blocher (2009, pp. 170–2) thought that the problem with the Neolithic Adam proposal is that it requires abandoning Adam's fatherhood of all present humans. However, the genealogies in the biblical texts consistently go back to Adam (Genesis 5; 1 Chro. 1; Luke 3.38), and Acts 17.26 states that 'From one he made all nations to inhabit the whole earth, and he allotted the times of their existence and the boundaries of the places where they would live'. Thus, Blocher argued against a Neolithic (Recent) Adam view and defended an Ancient Adam view.

On the other hand, a number of scholars (e.g. Walton 2015; Alexander 2014; Suarez 2015; Fischer 2008) have defended a Recent Adam view and denied that

---

3. https://ncse.com/cej/1/1/fatal-flaws-flood-geology.

he was the ancestor of all human beings today. For example, in his chapter 'It Is Not Essential That All People Descended from Adam and Eve', Walton (2015, pp. 186–7) suggests the possibility that Acts 17.26 is not talking about biology or about human origins, but about national origins and that God's 'making' (*poieō*) of a nation is not a material act but an organizational one. This is communicated in the so-called Table of Nations in Genesis 10, which traces the lineage of the seventy known countries to Noah's three sons. Walton argues that, if human origins were the point, we might expect Paul to use the basic *anthrōpōn* rather than making the nations the focus. Furthermore, the concept of national identity fits better in connection with historical periods and territorial boundaries. Thus, he interprets Acts 17.26 as affirming the work of God's formation of multiple national identities from the three sons of Noah.

However, the reason Paul makes nations the focus is compatible with the view that Paul is emphasizing that all nations of people – whether Greeks or Jews – were descended from one man. Van Kuiken (2015, p. 687) notes that, instead of echoing Gen. 10.32, Acts 17.26

> may equally well echo Deuteronomy 4 and 32, which, like Acts 17:16–31, contrast the one true God with idols (4:15–31; 16–17, 37–39) and speak of God's determining the portions and boundaries of the nations (Deut 4:19; 32:8–9; cf. Acts 17:26b). In this case, Acts 17:26a's 'one ancestor' may link to Deut 4:32's 'the day that God created human beings' and so refer to Adam, not Noah.

On the other hand, Keener (2014) notes that 'An Adam allusion seems consistent with the contrast in 17:29 between being God's offspring and human-made images and so may have more support from the context'. Paul was, of course, not stating 'from one' (Acts 17.26) for the purpose of arguing against a wider range of genetic sources for humanity (polygenism; cf. Walton 2015, pp. 186–7); rather, he was stating it to make the point that we are God's offspring through one (Acts 17.28).

While Paul's emphasis is on the common humanity of his hearers (cf. Alexander 2014), the basis of that common humanity is that they came from one. Van Kuiken notes that other Second Temple Jewish texts also understood Adam to be the 'first-formed' human and the progenitor of all others (Wis. 7.1, 10.1[4]; Tob. 8.6[5]). 'Since Paul concludes by speaking of all people's judgment by one man, Christ (Acts 17.31), taking "one ancestor" as referring to Adam fits Paul's usual Adam–Christ

---

4. 'I also am mortal, like everyone else, a descendant of the first-formed child of earth; and in the womb of a mother I was molded into flesh' (Wis. 7.1). 'Wisdom protected the first-formed father of the world, when he alone had been created; she delivered him from his transgression' (Wis. 10.1). The claim that 'everyone else' (Wis. 7.1) descended from this first-formed male of earth (Wis. 7.1, 10.1) is contrary to the idea that there were other male or female humans prior to him.
5. 'You made Adam, and for him you made his wife Eve as a helper and support. From the two of them the human race has sprung.'

correlation. Nowhere else does Paul mention Noah' (2015, p. 686). Additionally, the interpretation that Adam is not the ancestor of every other human cannot be found in the earliest commentaries of the relevant texts.[6]

It can also be argued that 1 Cor. 15.45,[7] 11.8 and Mt. 19.4-6 imply that Adam was the first God's-Image-Bearer. In any case, it is plausible to think that the biblical authors affirm that (at least from their time onwards) all nations of people were descended from Adam. In what follows, I shall argue that – where Task C is concerned – both the Recent Adam view and the Ancient Adam view are defensible against objections.

6.3.2 Recent Adam view

As noted earlier, the objection against a Recent Adam view is based on the assumption that Adam and Noah must have existed before such events as the arrival of anatomical *Homo sapiens* in Australia (i.e. before about 40,000 BC) in order to be the ancestors of all human beings today. However, this assumption has been challenged. Scientists have calculated that the answer to the question 'how far back in time we must go to find an individual who was the ancestor of all present-day humans' (Most Recent Common Ancestor MRCA) is surprisingly recent (Hein 2004, p. 518).[8] Rohde, Olson and Chang (2004, pp. 562–6) have shown that all human beings today could have had very recent common ancestors (say, around 2300 years ago) even if substantial forms of population subdivision existed with a very low rate of migration. They note the caveat that, 'if a group of humans were completely isolated, then no mixing could occur between that group and others, and the MRCA would have to have lived before the start of the isolation' (p. 565). However, complete reproductive isolation of a group of humans over an extended period of time is difficult to prove. It should be noted that genealogical ancestry is distinct from genetic ancestry; 'being somebody's great-great-great-great grandparent is no guarantee of genetic relatedness' (Hein 2004, pp. 518–19). Because of the dilution effect explained in the previous chapter, many of our ancestors are 'simultaneously (i) genealogical ancestors of each of the individuals at the present, and (ii) genetic ancestors to none of the individuals at the present'

---

6. There is an interesting ancient tale called the myth of Lilith, which reads Genesis 1 and 2 sequentially. It claims that Eve (Genesis 2) was not the first woman, and that there was another woman Lilith who was created alongside Adam in Genesis 1 prior to the creation of Eve. However, this myth originated much later after the New Testament was already written; the earliest extant text was *The Tales of Ben Sira* which dates to tenth century AD. Moreover, even this myth affirms Adam as the first human being alongside Lilith. Thus in no way does the myth of Lilith support the interpretation that there were human beings prior to Adam.

7. See Loke 2020b.

8. Compare with the view of Jerry Coyne here: https://newrepublic.com/article/115759/adam-eve-theologians-try-reconcile-science-and-fail.

(Gravel and Steel 2015, p. 47). It is difficult to trace genealogical ancestry beyond fifteen generations using genetic data (Kelleher et al. 2016, pp. 9–10). As explained in Chapter 5, my model requires only genealogical ancestry; it does not require genetic ancestry.

On the other hand, 'even populations on isolated Pacific islands have experienced occasional infusions of newcomers' (Rohde, Olson and Chang 2004, p. 565). Other factors such as the existence of (yet undiscovered) intercontinental migration routes, the large-scale movement and mixing of populations and marked individual differences in fertility could have reduced the time to the MRCA (2004). With regard to water barriers, multiple land bridges (e.g. between Australia and Tasmania) allowing for easy migrations still existed in the early Neolithic period before being submerged by rising waters later. In any case, recent discoveries suggest that ancient *Homo sapiens* were far more capable of crossing large water barriers than previously thought.[9] Moreover,

> Even if rates of migration between some adjoining populations are very low, the time to the MRCA tends not to change substantially. For example, with a migration rate across the Bering Strait of just one person in each direction every ten generations, rather than the ten per generation in the more conservative simulation described earlier, T_n only increases from 3,415 years to 3,668 years. (2004).

Given the uncertainties about migration rates and mating patterns, the date of the MRCA cannot be identified with great precision (2004). Nevertheless, the results suggest that 'the most recent common ancestor for the world's current population lived in the relatively recent past – perhaps within the last few thousand years' (2004; for further discussion, see Swamidass 2018; 2019). My model does not require Adam or Noah to be the MRCA; it only requires Adam and Noah to be common ancestors of all human beings (not necessarily the most recent ones). Nevertheless, an MRCA existing a few thousand years ago is consistent with my model. Given the above-mentioned considerations, a Recent Adam who was also the common ancestor of all human beings has not been ruled out.

One might object that, by the time a Neolithic Adam appeared, there would have been anatomical *Homo sapiens* with a quite advanced culture which included participation in religious activities. Would it not be problematic to deny that these were also human beings? Venema thinks that

> If only those who descend from Adam and Eve have the Imago Dei . . . then there are a few hundred thousand years of human history where everyone else is not made in God's image – and they only become made in God's image once they interbreed with Adam's descendants. Not to put too fine a point on it, but I

---

9. https://news.nationalgeographic.com/news/2010/02/100217-crete-primitive-humans-mariners-seafarers-mediterranean-sea/.

find this idea horrific. Humans are widely dispersed on the planet at 6,000 years ago – in the Americas, in Australia and Tasmania, and so on. Do we really want a theology that names them all as subhuman animals until their lineage happens to encounter and interbreed with Adam's (Eurasian) offspring? God forbid.[10]

In reply, on the one hand, Venema's use of the term 'human' presupposes that anatomical *Homo sapiens* are human beings, which begs the question because this is the point being disputed here. His phrase 'happens to encounter' ignores divine providence. Saying that it is 'horrific' is just an emotional response, reminiscent of the emotional response of YEC against evolution. Venema does not say what he bases his theology on when he exclaims 'God forbid'.

On the other hand, as explained in Chapter 5, there are different definitions of human, and they have legitimacy in different fields and discourses. Many scientists would regard the abilities for abstract thinking, cave art drawing, etc. as characteristics that distinguish human behaviours from those of non-human animals. For example, anthropologists Sally McBrearty and Alison Brooks list four characteristics of modern human behaviour:

1. Abstract thinking, the ability to act with reference to abstract concepts not limited in time or space;
2. Planning depth, the ability to formulate strategies based on past experience and to act upon them in a group context;
3. Behavioral, economic, and technological innovativeness;
4. Symbolic behavior, the ability to represent objects, people, and abstract concepts with arbitrary symbols, vocal or visual, and to reify such symbols in cultural practice. (McBrearty and Brooks 2000, p. 492)

However, these scientists do not consider whether the capacity to have a right relationship with God the Creator should be regarded as essential to the definition of humanity. These scientists are adopting a secular perspective without taking into account theological considerations. The latter considerations, however, take priority in Christian discourse. As noted in Chapter 5, what is essential to human beings has always been controversial, and most theologians would affirm the need for divine revelation (the revelation from our Creator) to help us answer this question. According to the Christian Scripture, human beings should be defined in relation to God the Creator, regardless of whether human beings recognize this or not (e.g. atheists would reject this, but from the Christian theological perspective they would still be regarded as humans since they are regarded as the descendants of Adam with the properties listed in what follows). As explained in detail in Chapter 5, from the Christian theological perspective, what differentiates human beings from other animals would be the possession of the image of God, which should be regarded as having properties (i), (ii), (iii) and (iv): (i) election by God

---

10. http://henrycenter.tiu.edu/2017/07/response-to-the-symposium-part-1/.

to function as God's royal representatives in the world and given authorized power to share in God's rule over the earth, and having the associated capacities (ii) for a unique kind of dominion that could extend to the whole world and over all kinds of creatures, (iii) for a sense of responsibility to God for this kind of dominion, and (iv) to be made to become conformed to Christ.

Concerning the ability for abstract thinking, cave art drawing, freedom of will, etc., one can regard these as characteristics of persons but not sufficient conditions for being theological humans. The Christian tradition affirms that being a person is not equivalent to being a human; angels, for example, are persons but not humans. Some philosophers have argued that some animals (e.g. the Great Apes) possess personhood as well (Gruen 2017). Recent scientific studies have shown that there are glimmers of both free will and moral awareness in the other members of the animal kingdom (Enns, McGrath and Schloss 2011). On the other hand, commenting on Gen. 6.12's 'all flesh had corrupted their way', biblical scholars have observed that throughout the Flood narrative 'all flesh' refers to humans and animals (Wenham 1987; Hamilton 1990), and thus 'all flesh had corrupted their way' implies that animals had sinned. Since sinning is widely regarded as a property of persons, this would imply that animals are persons (concerning the possibility of animals freely choosing evil, see the discussion in Loke 2022b, Section 4.8). Thus Christian theologians should be open to the possibility of non-human animal persons. It has been argued in Chapter 5 that the Scripture leads us to expect that animals should have many capacities similar to human beings (except perhaps the election and capacity for the unique dominion, responsibility, and Christ-likeness mentioned in Scripture in relation to the image of God).

Hence, while one might argue that having rationality is sufficient for personhood, being a person is not equivalent to having the image of God. As explained in Chapter 5, the Scriptural usage of the term 'image of God' is associated with election and certain functions, which being a person per se may or may not entail. Thus, people outside the Garden of Eden may not be theologically human (even though they may be regarded as scientifically human, or human of a different type.[11] See further my engagement with Craig 2021 in Loke forthcoming.) I have also explained in Chapter 5 that my model is not polygenic or racist because it affirms that all anatomical *Homo* today have a common ancestor (Adam) and are equally valued as God's-image Bearers.

In my model, the first anatomical *Homo* to possess all of the previously mentioned properties would be Adam. There might have been other anatomical *Homo* with a quite advanced culture by the time Adam appeared, and they might even have possessed one of the previously mentioned properties, such as property (ii). Nevertheless, they might still have fallen short of having all the earlier mentioned properties (e.g. they might still lack property (i), (iii), and/or (iv)). Even participation in religious activities would not have been adequate apart from the previously mentioned function and capacities (note that religious activities

---

11. I thank Joshua Swamidass for his helpful discussion on this point.

may be idolatrous in nature; they do not by themselves entail the capacity to have a right relationship with God *the Creator*). This does not mean that those non-God's-image-bearing anatomical *Homo* are not loved or valued by God. On the contrary, it may be argued that God loves all creatures, that they may be comforted by God's presence in their suffering, and in the afterlife they may have a chance to flourish and share in the glories of those creatures whom they had contributed (Sollereder 2016, pp. 104-7). For all we know, the eternal destiny of those anatomical *Homo* may be similar to those humans who died in infancy and, even though they did not hear the Gospel before they died, may nevertheless still be accepted by God into His kingdom on the basis of Christ's meritorious sacrifice which is sufficient to reconcile all things to himself (Col. 1.20).[12] Only those creatures who hate and reject the truth would be condemned (cf. John 3.19-20; 2 Thess. 2.10).[13]

In Chapter 5, it was noted that according to Gen. 9.6 the reason no human being may shed another human's blood is that a human has a unique value, a value that is not to be attributed to other animals – namely that he/she is an image-bearer of God (Hoekema 1986). Would this imply that killing a non-God's-image-bearing anatomical *Homo* would be acceptable?[14] In reply, as explained in Chapter 5, according to my model, non-human anatomical *Homo* were similar to human beings biologically, and their souls shared many of the same base qualities, such that their sexual relationship with humans need not be considered a form of bestiality. Given this, there would be grounds for thinking that these non-human anatomical *Homo* would also share many rights which God's-Image-Bearers had, rights which were not shared by other animals.

Rosenhouse (2012, p. 231) objects that, if God desires a special relationship with creatures and decides to bestow on them a rational soul, it would be unjust of him to provide this gift to only a couple (Adam and Eve) but not provide it to others. In reply, it may be argued that God loves all creatures (Sollereder 2016),that different creatures are able to experience God's blessings to their fullest satisfaction in accordance with their different capacities, and that there is no injustice if God arranges for that to happen (say, in the afterlife) in his providence, without having to give every creature the exact same capacities. Rosenhouse (2012, p. 231) also notes that God cursed the ground for everyone because of the sin of this couple, and reasons that, if God had given more creatures the gift of the rational soul, some would have made better use of it than the couple. In reply, it is also possible that, if God had given more creatures the gift of the rational soul, some would have

---

12. Plantinga suggests it might be the case that every creaturely essence does, in fact, suffer from transworld depravity and would freely choose to sin (Plantinga 1974, pp. 186, 189), therefore these creatures need the atonement by Christ. I discuss these issues and the doctrine of Original Sin further in Loke (2022b).

13. For a range of views among Christian theologians concerning the fate of the un-evangelized, including the possibility of post-mortem salvation, see Sanders (1995); Tiessen (2004); Walls (2012).

14. I thank Joshua Swamidass for raising this question.

made worse use of it than the couple. One might propose that only an omniscient God with Middle Knowledge (i.e. knowledge of what any particular free creature would freely do in any circumstance; see Loke 2013; 2018c) would know how to arrange the circumstances in order to obtain the optimal balance of good and bad choices for all the free creatures He intended to create on earth in the long run, and He did just that. In order for Rosenhouse to justify his objection, he has to bear the burden of proof to exclude this proposal, which he cannot do given that he lacks divine omniscience.

6.3.3 Ancient Adam view

On the other hand, an Ancient Adam is defensible against objections as well. Consider, for example, the objections by Seely (2007). Seely argues that, according to Genesis, the pre-Flood culture 'had agriculture, domesticated cattle, and cities, it had "implements of bronze and iron"' (Gen. 4.22). He thinks that the culture described is late Neolithic or Chalcolithic (*c.* 4500 BC), whereas the culture of humans 35,000 years ago is *Palaeolithic*, having neither domesticated crops nor domesticated cattle (pp. 38–40). With regard to the use of metals, David Christian states that the earliest available evidence of working with soft metals such as gold, silver and copper in Mesopotamia comes from *c.* 5500 BC; working with hard metals such as iron (which is hardest if combined with some carbon) and alloys such as bronze (made from copper and tin or sometimes arsenic), which could be used for making weapons or tools, was a later development, because their manufacture required higher temperatures and more efficient ovens (2011, p. 258). The skills needed to work with hard metals were similar to those needed to fire pottery (2011, p. 258). Bronze was first produced in Sumer in the fourth millennium BC, while hard irons were produced in the Caucasus in the middle of the second millennium BC (2011, p. 258). The first true steels were probably produced in the Roman Empire (2011, p. 259).

Seely (2007, pp. 38–40) also argues that, shortly after the Flood, Noah planted a vineyard (Gen. 9.20), yet domesticated grapes do not show up in the archaeological record until *c.* 4000 BC, thus again dating the Flood to late Neolithic times. Seely (2007, pp. 40–1) adds:

> Because of its location in Shinar (southern Mesopotamia) and the mention of the top of the tower rising into heaven (Gen 11:2, 4), which was typically said of ziggurats, most scholars have identified the Tower of Babel as a ziggurat. When do ziggurats first appear in the archaeological record? Not before *c.* 3500 BC. And building a city with a ziggurat that would bring fame, as was the goal of the builders in Gen. 11:4, indicates the beginning of monumental architecture, which also did not begin until *c.* 3500 BC. Similarly, although there are archaeological sites throughout the Near East which from around 10,000 BC on contain the remains of buildings made of sun-dried brick, buildings made of baked brick, as specified in Gen. 11:3, do not appear in the archaeological record until *c.* 3500 BC. Mortar of various kinds is also used with the earlier sun-dried

bricks, but asphalt for mortar, as specified in Gen. 11:3, does not appear until *c.* 3500 BC.

The problems mentioned by Seely are problems not only for those Evolutionary Creationists who hold to Ancient Adam but also for Old Earth Creationists who hold this view. In reply to Seely, Old Earth Creationist Hugh Ross (2007, p. 47) argues that the kind of plant and animal domestication practised by Abel and Cain would not have been of sufficient scale to be detected by current scientific methods, and that 'the taming of wild mammal herds and the cultivation and processing of wild cereal grains is consistent with the statement, for example, in Genesis 4 that "Abel kept flocks and Cain worked the soil"'. Ross adds that nothing in Genesis 4 demands Cain's city to be large or constructed of materials capable of surviving 40,000-plus years of natural erosion and human exploitation (2007, p. 47).

One should also be wary that some of the terms found in the Bible might not have the same meanings that we have today. David Christian (2011) uses a modern understanding of the word 'city' when he writes that, while evidences of systematic and well-planned building, 'villages' and burials dating more than 20,000 years ago have been found (p. 196), the first cities appeared in Mesopotamia in the fourth millennium BC. This presupposes productivity levels such that rural populations can support themselves and a small surplus population of non-farmers, and a complex division of labour (p. 267). Christian describes the division of labour as follows:

> A complex division of labor within cities and towns, and between cities and their rural hinterlands. Hierarchies of officials, judges, and rulers headed by kings. Armies, controlled by rulers, that provide protection from other tribute takers and also enable the rulers to exact tributes by coercion from their own subjects or from neighboring regions. Literate bureaucracies that keep track of and manage resources. Networks of exchange, through which states and cities procure resources that cannot be secured through naked force. Systems of religion and ideology, often managed by the state, that legitimate state structures and often give rise to monumental architecture and high levels of artistic achievement. Wider hinterlands, which are not directly under their control, whose resources are nevertheless vital for their successful functioning. These hinterlands may lie in other regions of agrarian civilization, or may be settled by independent farmers or pastoralists or foragers. (p. 289)

However, it is not clear that Gen. 4.17 states that Cain built a city in this sense. The biblical portrayal does not include the complex division of labour described by Christian. The Brown-Driver-Briggs Hebrew lexicon notes that the Hebrew word translated as city, namely, *iyr* can also mean an apparently fortified place of any size. Commenting on Gen. 4.17, Keil (1891) notes that *iyr* does not necessarily presuppose a large town, but simply an enclosed space with fortified dwellings, in contradistinction to the isolated tents of shepherds; and lastly, the words 'he was building' merely indicate the commencement and progress of the building, but not its termination.

With regard to the use of bronze and iron, Ross (2007, p. 47) notes that 'archaeology demonstrates that ancient nations frequently gained and lost metallurgy as a consequence of invasion and genocide ... the reported wickedness of these same peoples would likely have destroyed such advance, as well as any evidence of it'.

Regarding the use of 'baked brick' and 'asphalt for mortar' and the Tower of Babel, Ross (2007, pp. 48–9) argues that

> The Hebrew text is unclear as to exactly what kind of brick-making and bricklaying technology is implied. In any case, a lack of evidence does not constitute proof. There is no basis for determining whether anyone attempted to build such structures. Moreover, the biblical text does not specify the size of either the city or the tower, the latter of which was never completed. The text says only that the building project had begun. Given the effects of erosion, the limitations of archaeological research, and the common practice among ancient peoples of exploiting building materials from ruins, the lack of evidence cannot be claimed as proof of conflict between the text and science.

In assessment of the Seely–Ross debate with respect to Task C, it seems that the dating of Adam to Noah (if these existed) is not as straightforward as Seely seems to think. A number of other scholars such as Blocher have also suggested that Adam could be placed well before the Neolithic period (perhaps even before 100,000 years ago), arguing that the low level of cultural achievements during the many subsequent millennia prior to the Neolithic can be interpreted as the effect of degeneracy (Blocher 2009, pp. 170–2). Likewise, Gavin McGrath (1997), who also dates Adam way before the Neolithic period, proposes

> the existence of civilizations that collapsed and were followed by uncivilized societies. For example, the Myan [sic] civilizations of ancient Central America collapsed, and from their ruins came some uncivilized people encountered by the Spanish Conquistadors; or the white man found only tribal Africans living near the collapsed Zimbabwe civilization.

Seely (2007, p. 38) objects that this suggested model seems ad hoc in that no evidence of a Neolithic culture preceding the Palaeolithic has ever been found.

In reply, Seely's accusation of ad hoc-ness is invalid against Task (C) given the following reasons concerning the burden of proof, considerations based on biblical texts, the vast incompleteness of available evidence and independent considerations in support of degeneration.[15]

---

15. Seely (2007, p. 38)'s other complaint is based on the assumption that Lamech and Noah lived around c. 5000 BC, but as argued in what follows, this assumption is unjustified.

As explained in Chapter 1, to show that the biblical account is compatible with science (Task C) is different from showing that the biblical account is true. For the latter, one would have to provide positive evidences, but for the former it is sufficient to suggest a possible (not necessarily actual) evolutionary scenario and then say, 'for all we know, this is how it could have happened'. The 'in-compatibilists' would then need to bear the burden of proof to exclude the possible scenario that I am suggesting here in order to conclude that the biblical account is incompatible with science.

For the 'compatibilists' case, it can be argued that, possibly, the periods of more advanced culture prior to the Neolithic were relatively too short and limited in scope to have left traces in the archaeological record. As Rusbult (2008) observes,

> maybe the agriculture and technology of Genesis 4 occurred much earlier than 9,000 BC, but (especially if it was localized on a small scale) it didn't produce a large amount of evidence, and it hasn't been discovered by archaeologists; due to this possibility, an *absence of evidence* (for the culture and technology existing in their ancient culture) isn't a clear *evidence of absence.*

Moreover, the evidence that we do have concerning how the earliest humans lived are still vastly incomplete, and hence the possibility suggested here cannot be ruled out. In this case, the absence of proof is not proof of absence.

The vastly incomplete nature of the evidence is noted by David Christian who writes, 'Anyone trying to determine how the earliest humans lived must depend on a lot of guesswork' (2011, p. 185). He observes that experts disagree on the question of when human language first appeared (p. 171), citing Henry Plotkin (1997, p. 248) who writes, 'Some put it as recently as 100,000 years ago or less, a few put it back beyond two million years from the present, and the majority go for somewhere in the region of 200,000 to 250,000 years ago.' (Where Task C is concerned, some may regard this point relevant to Gen. 11¹ where it is stated that 'the whole earth used the same language' when they attempted to build the Tower of Babel. However, Walton [2001, pp. 371–2] cautions that 'the Hebrew word translated as "earth" also often means "land" and is more narrowly defined'.)[16] Moreover, scholars used to think that archaeological evidences such as

---

16. Observing that the Babel episode is narrated *after* the Table of Nations in Genesis 10 which mentions various languages being spoken (v.20), Middleton suggests that this episode does not allude to the origination of various languages from an original human language. Rather, the use of the same language in the region was due to the imposition of a powerful civilization (Middleton 2006, pp. 221–8; he identifies it as the ancient Mesopotamian civilization, and reads Genesis 11 as an 'ideology critique' of the abuse of power by the descendants of Adam). Walton (2001, p. 371), however, notes that it is also consistent with the narrative style of Genesis that the narrator is moving back in time in Genesis 11 to narrate an episode which occurred before the various languages mentioned in Genesis 10.

ecological adaptations, new technologies such as precisely made and standardized blades, greater social and economic organization, artistic activity that distinctively evidences modern human behaviours, involving the use of human language, appear about 50,000 years ago, and that this 'revolution of the Upper Palaeolithic' marks the true beginning of human history (p. 178). However, within the last few decades this picture has changed. On the basis of a close analysis of the archaeological evidence from Africa, palaeontologists McBrearty and Brooks (2000) have proposed that evidence of fully human behaviour can be found perhaps from as early as 250,000 years ago. It appears piecemeal and gradually, at different rates and at different times and places (pp. 178–9). Evidence for the use of small-blade tools, grindstones and pigments appears very early, while evidence for other innovative technologies – including fishing, forms of mining, long-distance exchanges of goods, the use of bone tools, and migrations into new environments – also can be seen earlier than in Eurasia. Other scholars have also argued that the 'human revolution' happened tens of thousands of years earlier than previously thought, and in sub-Saharan Africa rather than Europe (Mellars, Boyle, Bar-Yosef and Stringer eds. 2007). Because of the vastly incomplete nature of the evidence in this particular field of study, many conclusions have been drastically revised as the result of further discoveries. For example, weaving and pottery were once thought to have appeared first in the Neolithic era. However, sites discovered later from the Moravian lowlands, dated to between 28,000 and 24,000 years ago, indicate the use of fired clay and also of weaving, probably to make nets and baskets, as well as simple forms of clothing (Christian 2011, p. 195).

Palaeontologist Chris Stringer (2011, pp. 237–8) notes the importance of climate and population densities for technological advancement and the potential to express and accumulate 'signals of modernity'. In line with this observation, one might suggest the possibility that long periods of harsh climate during the Last Glacial Period (110,000 to 10,000 years ago) and/or decrease in population densities due to catastrophic events caused the degeneracy suggested by Blocher et al. Early humans might have forsaken agriculture and herding, returning to more mobile foraging means due to the cold weather. Christian observes that

> we can no longer assume that communities of foragers were bound to adopt agriculture once they learned about it. Indeed, we are no longer so confident that the appearance of agriculture can automatically be regarded as a sign of progress. To be sure, agriculture can support larger populations than foraging lifeways, and thus in the long run agricultural communities are likely to outcompete foraging communities when the two life-ways come into conflict. But it is also clear that many foraging communities have resisted adopting agricultural practices even when they knew about them. As members of a foraging community in the Kalahari Desert told a modern researcher, why would one want to work as a farmer when there are so many mongongo nuts available to eat? (p. 223)

Christian goes on to observe that evidence from skeletal remains and genetic comparisons shows that early agriculture and domestication bred new forms of disease and new forms of stress; for example, disease bacteria spread from herd animals such as cattle, chickens and pigs to humans (p. 223).

On the other hand, there are independent considerations in support of the degeneration proposed by Blocher et al. The model explains David Christian's observation that agriculture did not spread from a single centre, but apparently appeared independently in many different regions of the world. He notes that it is probably no accident that agriculture appeared first within the largest and oldest world zone, that of Afro-Eurasia, and that it occurred in the corridor linking two very different regions, for 'hub' regions of this kind were clearing houses for ecological information accumulated over huge areas. He observes that 'another hub region, in Mesoamerica, linked North and South America; and here, too, agriculture appeared early' (p. 220). He mentions a few factors which might have led to the emergence of agriculture in several widely separated parts of the world. The warming climate increased the availability of both plant and animal foods. Population growth created pressure for technological advancement in agriculture, and exchanges of valued goods between foraging communities may have encouraged settlement at the hubs of regional networks of exchange (pp. 231–3). Nevertheless, he asks: 'How can we explain the near-simultaneity of these changes in parts of the world that seem to have had no contact with each other?' (2011, p. 223), citing Mark Cohen who stressed, 'The most striking fact about early agriculture . . . is precisely that it is such a universal event.' In reply, if the degeneration suggested by Blocher et al. is correct, the descendants of Cain and Abel would already have possessed the capacity for agriculture, and they restarted agriculture in different parts of the world when the weather conditions improved, for example, after the end of the last Ice Age.

I would like to clarify that the degeneration model mentioned previously is not essential to the GAE model defended in this book. The degeneration model belongs to the Ancient Adam view, which is one of the two possible variants of the GAE model of this book, the other being the Recent Adam view which does not postulate a degeneration. More importantly, the degeneration I mentioned is very different from the degeneration model proposed by the duke of Argyll in the 1870s, which has been refuted by scientists.

To elaborate, the duke proposed a model which denied human evolution and rejected the conclusion that foraging was the ancestral condition of humankind (Gillespie 1977). By contrast, the degeneration model described here affirms human evolution and agrees with the scientific evidences that foraging was, indeed, the ancestral condition of pre-Adamic anatomical *Homo sapiens*. It suggests the possibility that later a small subgroup of anatomical *Homo sapiens* emerged (call them Adam and his early descendants). They acquired the capacity for agriculture which they practised on a small scale (due to their small population size) and which very soon degenerated as a result of harsh conditions, hence leaving no trace in the archaeological record. Subsequently, their descendants increased and spread to different parts of the world, and later slowly restarted agriculture in different parts of the world when the weather conditions improved. Therefore, I do not reject the archaeological evidence for the origin and spread of food production. On the contrary, I have explained how my suggestion might explain the archaeological evidence that agriculture did not spread from a single centre, but apparently appeared independently in many different regions of the world. My suggestion therefore agrees with the archaeological evidences that people domesticated plants and animals over a long period of time, in different places, by hard work, and that people made maize in places far away from Eden, in Central America and over a period of thousands of years.[17]

Barrett and Greenway (2017, p. 74) note that the cluster of capacities associated with the Imago Dei (see previous chapter) have been present in humans for a long time, likely more than 100,000 years, and possibly more than 200,000. This indicates that humans could, indeed, have been *Imago Dei* for that long. Nevertheless, they suggest the alternative possibility that 'maybe the Genesis account points to a much more recent occurrence: the domestication of animals'. They state that the earliest available evidence for any domestication is for the dog at 13,000 to 17,000 years ago. More recent evidence suggests that dog domestication occurred between 27,000 and 40,000 years ago.[18] In any case, their alternative hypothesis is insufficiently motivated. While their interpretation is consistent with the Genesis account and domestication does, indeed, exemplify the cluster of capacities associated with the Imago Dei, there is no necessity that the Genesis must be interpreted in the way they suggested. Neither is domestication necessary for the possession of the Imago Dei which, as argued in the previous chapter, can be understood as a capacity which does not necessarily have to be manifested immediately in the form of domestication.

On the other hand, if the degeneracy model is correct, the descendants of Cain and Abel would already have had the capacity for domestication, and they would have started domestication just as they restarted agriculture in different parts of the world when the weather improved. This would explain the apparent independent emergence of domestication in various parts of the world, just as it would explain the apparent independent emergence of agriculture in various parts of the world. It should be noted that this explanatory power of the degeneration model does not prove that it is correct and thereby rules out the Recent Adam view, for there could be other yet undiscovered alternative hypotheses (e.g. yet undiscovered migration routes?) which might somehow explain the apparent independent emergence of agriculture and domestication. Nevertheless, until such an alternative hypothesis is developed, this explanatory power of the degeneration model stands as a consideration in its favour.

Alexander (2014, p. 299) is concerned that a model which postulates an Ancient Adam would have to forsake the Near Eastern culture and religious context of the Genesis account in order to retell the theological story in a completely different place and time. Other scholars have argued for a Neolithic dating of the Flood on

---

17. I thank a reviewer for mentioning these evidences.
18. https://www.scientificamerican.com/article/dog-domestication-much-older-than-previously-known/.

the basis of the pre-Flood account in Genesis 4, which mentions Jabal as 'the father of such as dwell in tents, and of such as have cattle', Jubal as 'the father of all such as handle the harp and pipe' and Tubal-Cain as 'an instructor of every craftsman in bronze and iron' (Gen. 4.19-22). They relate these to the ANE culture and to the Bronze Age which is known to have begun in the fourth millennium BC. They also observe similar flood stories in the Sumerian '*Gilgamesh Epic*' and 'King List', and they note the mentioning of Gilgamesh (widely regarded as a real person who reigned in Mesopotamia around 2650 BC) who is said to have reigned following the great flood (Hill 2001).

In reply, while the author of Genesis' account may have utilized the language and expressions (e.g. to rear cattle, to 'handle the harp and pipe', to be 'an instructor of every craftsman in bronze and iron') of his contemporary surrounding ANE culture, this does not imply that he intended the story he was telling to refer to the period around that time.

On the other hand, as mentioned earlier, palaeontologist Chris Stringer (2011, pp. 237-8) has noted the importance of climate and population densities for technological advancement and the potential to express and accumulate 'signals of modernity'. It could be that long periods of harsh climate during the Last Glacial Period (110,000 to 10,000 years ago) and/or decrease in population densities due to catastrophic events or tribal wars[19] caused a degeneracy of culture, and that there were brief scattered periods of more advanced culture similar to that described in Genesis and involving a few individuals (the Genesis texts refer to a few individuals – not vast numbers of people – having this culture) that were relatively too short and limited in scope to have left traces in the archaeological record, which at present is still vastly incomplete.

Alternatively, it is possible that the author was using expressions that were more familiar to his first readers (cf. the notion of accommodation defended in Chapter 2), and thus these expressions should be understood as approximations rather than as precise literal descriptions.

Collins (2011a, p. 113) has gone further to suggest that certain descriptions (e.g. of farming and the use of bronze and iron) in Genesis are not literal but anachronistic, describing aspects of older times in terms of what the writer and his audience were familiar with. Harlow (2010, p. 181) objects that anachronistic notions would have been inconceivable to the ancient author(s) and audience(s) of Genesis. In reply, Collins (2011b, p. 11) notes that many Old Testament scholars have observed the way in which the Garden of Eden becomes a pattern for

---

19. Hugh Ross suggests that, 'For example, often a nomadic tribe would conquer a city-state and its accompanying farming communities. In their conquest the tribe would kill all the inhabitants and destroy the city and culture. Consequently, the advanced technology developed by the city-state would be lost, requiring reinvention. Thus, there may have been many cycles of Stone-to-Copper-to-Bronze-to Iron Ages and a return to the Stone Age.' http://www.reasons.org/articles/q-a-does-tubal-cain-predate-the-bronze-and-iron-ages. Accessed 12 August 2015.

describing the Israelite sanctuary and the land of Israel. The portrayal of Adam in Genesis could have similar goals; 'he is "like" an Israelite, so that each member of God's people will see himself or herself as God's "renewed Adam" in the world' (2011b, p. 11). These considerations indicate that the biblical author may have used such devices as anachronisms if they served the purpose of communicating the message he wished to affirm. Thus, Gen. 4.17-22 may be understood as describing the trailblazers of the skills of city building, ranching, musical instruments, and metalworking that eventually led to the crafts the audience would be familiar with, and that the Hebrew terms 'father' and 'forger' can be read with these nuances (Collins 2018, section 6C).

In summary, there is no passage in the Scripture which explicitly identifies the era in which Adam lived to be the Neolithic era; those who argue for this conclusion base it on their interpretation of the scientific data and attempt to correlate it with the Scriptures. However, their attempts fail to consider the various hermeneutical issues raised by Collins et al., and thus they have failed to prove their case.

As for the mentioning of flood stories in the Sumerian '*Gilgamesh Epic*' and 'King List', there are significant differences in details between their flood hero and Noah. For example, unlike Noah, their flood hero Utnapishtim was said to have been given eternal life, and Gilgamesh was said to have searched for him in order to obtain immortality. Concerning the relationship between the Sumerian '*Gilgamesh Epic*' and the Genesis account, Old Testament scholar Tremper Longman III observes that

> The relationship between these texts is debated, some believing that the biblical text is simply a rewrite of the Babylonian original. However, it may also be suggested that the Babylonian and the biblical versions descend from a common tradition. For those who accept a biblical worldview, it may be hypothesized that the Babylonian version got corrupted to conform to the polytheistic religions of its people. (Longman III and Dillard 2006, p. 52)

Thus, the Sumerian version's mentioning of Gilgamesh who is said to have reigned following the great flood does not prove that 'Noah's Flood' happened right before Gilgamesh. Rather, it could be the case that the Sumerian version conflated and adapted the stories of Gilgamesh and earlier versions of 'Noah's Flood' (the date of origin of which is unknown), or borrowed details from earlier versions of 'Noah's Flood' for their own flood hero, to give their account the impression of antiquity and credibility.

6.4 Noah's descendants

Is the biblical account concerning Noah's descendants compatible with the results of evolutionary population genetics? The Scriptures say that 'the sons of Noah who went out of the ark were Shem, Ham, and Japheth . . . and from these the whole earth was peopled' (Gen. 9.18-19). Of course, this verse does not exclude the fact that their wives were also involved in the propagation of the human race; it only states that the human beings can trace their ancestry to these three and back to Noah. As explained previously, where Task (C) is concerned, the scientific evidence is compatible with the view that all humans share a small number of humans as their common ancestors – but that these ancestors are not our *unique*, or sole, ancestors. Rather, biologically speaking, they could have come from a population of about 10,000 anatomical *Homo sapiens* of which the God's-Image-Bearer group was a subset. Non-human anatomical *Homo* could have contributed to the genetic diversity; in particular, a portion of Noah's descendants could have mated with non-human anatomical *Homo* who were not killed by the Flood which can be interpreted as a local flood (see earlier), but their descendants were nevertheless fully human (see previous chapter).

One might ask: given that Canaan was an immediate descendant of Ham and that the firstborn of Canaan is Sidon, which was the name of a city that was founded fairly recently, does that not imply that Noah could not have existed earlier than 2000 BC?

In reply, the use of the name Sidon may have meant an ancient ancestor of the Sidonians. As Walton (2001, pp. 368–9) explains regarding the list of names in the so-called Table of Nations in Genesis 10,

> Not all of the seventy are names of individuals. A number of them clearly name people groups (e.g. 10:15-17). Others are well-known as city names (e.g. Sidon) or geographic designations (e.g. Mizraim, Tarshish, Sheba), but possibly the list considers these to be the patronymic ancestors of those places. In Hammurabi's genealogy a number of the names are tribal or geographical names, so this is not unusual in an ancient document. . . . Nevertheless, kinship language is sometimes used in the Bible to reflect political associations (cf. 1 Kgs 9.13). As a vertical genealogy, this list is simply trying to establish relationships of various sorts.

With regard to the observation that there is no discussion in the genealogy of any group of people outside the known world of ANE (Fischer 2008, pp. 172–3), Walton explains that the text seeks to account only for many of the groups the ancient Israelites were aware of and how these were related to the sons of Noah, without attempting to provide a comprehensive list of all the people(s) who were descended from the sons of Noah (Walton 2001, pp. 368–9).

6.5 Conclusion

In this chapter, I have shown that my model can be used to demonstrate the compatibility between population genetics and the biblical account that all human beings today are descendants of one family (Noah's) after the Flood. While there are scholars who read the Flood in a symbolic or typological manner, the contribution of my book lies in showing that – even when read in a literal manner – there is no incompatibility with population genetics. Many scholars have previously argued that the Flood can be interpreted quite literally as a localized phenomenon, and I have shown that it is possible to interpret it as localized to the extent sufficient for wiping out the God's-Image-Bearer group as well as their possessions (including animals within their areas of dominion), leaving Noah and his family. That was the main 'function' of the Flood, and as Walton (2009) has argued, the ancient Hebrews were generally more concerned about function than ontology. I have responded to various objections and pointed out with respect to Task (C) that, if the Flood was local, then many other animals around the globe, including many anatomical *Homo*, would have survived, and it is possible that a number of Noah's descendants mated with non-human anatomical *Homo* after the Flood, thus accounting for the genetic diversity we observe today.

I argued that – where Task (C) is concerned – my model is compatible with the Recent Adam view and the Ancient Adam view. With regard to the Recent Adam view, I noted that scientists have calculated that the answer to the question 'how far back in time we must go to find an individual who was the ancestor of all present-day humans' (Most Recent Common Ancestor MRCA) is surprisingly recent (Hein 2004, p. 518). Given the uncertainties about migration rates and mating patterns, the date of the MRCA cannot be identified with great precision (Rohde, Olson and Chang) (2004, p. 565). Nevertheless, the results suggest that 'the most recent common ancestor for the world's current population lived in the relatively recent past – perhaps within the last few thousand years' (2004, p. 565). My model does not require Adam or Noah to be an MRCA; it only requires Adam and Noah to be a common ancestor of all human beings (not necessarily the most recent one). Nevertheless, an MRCA existing a few thousand years ago is compatible with my model, and I showed that this conclusion is defensible against objections.

On the other hand, following Blocher (2009), Collins (2018) and others, I have argued that Adam and Noah could also be placed well before the Neolithic period. I note that some of the terms found in the Bible might not have the same meanings that we have today (e.g. the Hebrew word *iyr* translated as 'city' in Gen. 4.17 can mean an apparently fortified place of any size). The biblical authors may have used expressions that were more familiar to their first readers (cf. the notion of accommodation defended in Chapter 2), and thus these expressions may be understood as approximations or anachronistic literary devices (Collins 2018, section 6C) rather than as precise literal descriptions. There are also significant differences between the flood stories in the Sumerian '*Gilgamesh Epic*' and the Genesis account, and it is possible that the Babylonian and the biblical versions descended from a common tradition, and that the Babylonian version became corrupted to conform to the polytheistic religions of its people (Tremper Longman III 2006, p. 52). It could be the case that the Sumerian version conflated and adapted the stories of Gilgamesh and earlier versions of 'Noah's Flood' (the date of origin of which is unknown), or borrowed details from earlier versions of 'Noah's Flood' for their own flood hero, so as to give their account the impression of antiquity and credibility.

In conclusion, evolutionary population genetics does not contradict the biblical account that all human beings today are descendants of one family (Noah's) after the Flood, for all humans today could have members of this family as common ancestors even though they descended from a large population of anatomical *Homo* as indicated by population genetics. This conclusion is compatible with either a Recent Adam view or an Ancient Adam view. My book is not committed to either one of these views. Therefore, even if one of these views were to be refuted one day, it would not constitute a refutation of the Genealogical Adam model which I propose in this book.[20]

---

20. While I have defended the possibility of both the Recent and Ancient Adam views, I am slightly less comfortable with the Recent Adam view. For even though I have argued that drawing cave art is not necessarily characteristic of the image-of-God function (and the associated capacity) as indicated in the Scripture but, rather, could be regarded as characteristic of personhood (and I have argued for the need to consider the possibility of animal persons), nevertheless I think that there is a likelihood that those ancient persons who were able to draw those works of cave art may well had the capacity and function for dominion and responsibility towards the Creator (i.e. the image of God). Although the latter has not been confirmed yet, I would not be surprised if it is confirmed one day.

Chapter 7

CONCLUSIONS AND IMPLICATIONS

Where did we come from? Why are we here? Issues concerning the origins of humanity have significant implications for how we live our lives. Science and religion are two of the most significant influences shaping people's views on these issues, and recent debates concerning human evolution and Scriptural texts have involved scholars from a wide variety of world views, including Atheists, Agnostics, Judaists, Roman Catholics, Eastern Orthodox Christians, Mainline Protestants, and Evangelical Christians, and generated significant global public interest.

In his book *The Atheist's Guide to Reality*, atheist philosopher Alex Rosenberg (2011) claims that science is the only way to understand the nature of reality, that we are not the creations of God but are the products of an evolutionary process, that the universe does not exist with a purpose and that there is no meaning of life. He also concludes that there is no moral difference between right and wrong – a deeply troubling consequence for those who think that there is a moral difference between an Adolf Hitler and a Mother Teresa and who aspire to live a life like the latter.

Against such a reductionist view, I have argued elsewhere (Loke 2017a, 2022a) that – contrary to Rosenberg – science is not the only way to understand the nature of reality. I demonstrate that philosophical arguments are capable of yielding knowledge about reality that are more epistemically certain than scientific discoveries, and that by using such arguments together with science, it can be shown that there are good reasons for thinking that the universe was created by a Divine First Cause. The conclusion that there is a Creator should not hinder scientists from discovering how creation works and thereby progressing in their understanding of the natural world.

In this book, I have developed my anti-reductionist and transdisciplinary approach and argued that, while many people think of creation and evolution as mutually exclusive, evolution can be regarded as the process by which God created various life forms – including humankind. This conclusion implies the possibility of discovering evidence for *both* creation *and* evolution. I have proposed a new model which shows that science and Scripture are compatible with each other with regard to the origin of humanity and connected different strands of arguments together with this model in a way that no other book has done before. While making an original defence of the traditional theological view of Traducianism in the context of engagement with evolution, I have also explained that my model is compatible with alternative views (Creationism and Monism) as well. The flexibility of my model is another significant contribution of this present book.

Previous attempts to establish compatibility between science and Scripture have often been accused of Concordism (twisting Scriptural teachings to make them fit science or rejecting or distorting scientific findings to make them fit the Scripture). I have avoided this problem by interpreting scientific findings in ways that are consistent with proper scientific methodology and the views of recognized, mainstream scientists, and by interpreting Scripture according to proper hermeneutical principles, paying attention to genre, context, word meaning, grammar, historical and cultural background, etc. These hermeneutical principles are the criteria I adopted for determining which particular details of the biblical texts are to be understood as historical and which are to be understood as metaphorical, allegorical, etc. I have also explained that Task (A) 'interpreting the Bible' is distinct from Task (B) 'showing that the biblical account is true' and Task (C) 'showing that there is no incompatibility between human evolution and Bible'. For (A), one would ask for evidences to show what the human biblical author had in mind, but for (C) it is perfectly legitimate to suggest a possible and plausible model (e.g. one which involves evolution) which the biblical authors may not have thought of, as long as the possibility is not contradictory to what the biblical authors expressed. The Christian doctrine of Divine Inspiration of Scripture does not require God to reveal to the human biblical authors an exhaustive knowledge of everything, and it can be argued that the reason evolution does not feature in the Bible is not because the human biblical authors rejected evolution but because they did not think about evolution at all. In this book, I have discussed both Task (A) and Task (C), keeping them distinct and applying the hermeneutical principles mentioned earlier rigorously, and cited biblical scholars in support for the purpose of Task (A), while mentioning modern scientific knowledge for the purpose of Task (C) when appropriate.

After explaining that Divine Accommodation does not necessarily entail the affirmation of what we now know are scientific errors in Chapter 2, I proceeded to explain and defend my model in Chapters 3 to 6. To briefly summarize some of the main points: First, following Old Testament scholars Walton, Collins and others, and using the proper hermeneutical principles explained previously, I have argued that the Genesis account can be plausibly construed as a description of the process through which God refashions the creation as a Cosmic Temple. Moreover, the story of Adam and the subsequent Fall can be understood as localized events, not global ones. Given these and other interpretations, there is no contradiction between the Scripture and the standard scientific picture of cosmic origins. Second, using proper hermeneutical principles in accordance with Task (A), I have argued that, by 'humans beings', the biblical authors refer to beings created in the image of God. For the purpose of Task (C), one can draw a distinction between 'anatomical *Homo* which possessed the image of God' (God's-Image-Bearer, Adam being the first of these) and anatomical *Homo* which did not possess the image of God. Furthermore, by associating the image of God with Divine election for royal function and the associated capacities, I proposed that God could have chosen an anatomical *Homo* and made that organism a human being (i.e. possessing the image of God) in a specific environment (the Garden of Eden). After the Fall, the descendants of Adam procreated with non-imago-Dei-*Homo* such that all *Homo sapiens* today possess the image of God and have Adam as a common ancestor even though they descended from a large population of anatomical *Homo*. My GAE model is consistent with a gradual evolutionary process (see my engagement with Coyne 2021 and Schaffner 2021 in Chapter 5), with evolutionary population genetics and with the science of genealogical ancestry which has indicated the plausibility of common ancestors for the current world population (Rohde, Olson and Chang 2004; Hein 2004).

Concerning the relationship between the scientific and Scriptural accounts of human origin, Alexander points out that 'We really don't know the precise answer. There are simply too many unknowns in both the evolutionary account, and in our own interpretation of Scripture, to be dogmatic on this issue' (Alexander 2008, p. 234). While it has been noted in Chapter 1 that many scientific theories are well established, many details of many scientific theories (e.g. of evolution) are still uncertain. Is it possible that the possible scenario I suggested might be falsified by future scientific discoveries? Of course. However, a falsification of my model would not necessarily imply the falsification of Scripture. There is no adequate reason for thinking that there could not be other scenarios which would be consistent with such discoveries and with plausible interpretations of Scripture, and hence no adequate reason for thinking that such discoveries would be inconsistent with Scripture. Relating my model to the wider science-and-religion discourse concerning the distinctions between doctrine and theory and between central and non-central doctrines (van den Toren 2018), one should note that my model is a theory concerning a non-central but important doctrine of Christianity (see Craig 2021, Chapter 1) it is not 'an article of faith by which the church stands or falls' (Mahlmann 2007). Nevertheless, my model is valuable in showing the falsity of the widespread belief that current evolutionary science is contradictory to what the Scripture says about human origins.

One might object that the reason I have made a plausible case is that my claims are very weak: to claim that two sets of beliefs are logically consistent is only to say that they are not contradictory. However, a logically modest claim does not imply that the significance of the contribution is only modest. There are many scholars today from a wide variety of world views including Atheists, Agnostics, Judaists, Roman Catholics, Eastern Orthodox Christians, and Protestants who claim that science has definitely proven that the Scriptural account of human origins is false. Therefore, even though my claim is logically modest, the contribution of my book is highly significant because it shows that these scholars are wrong, and because resolving this area of perceived conflict would greatly benefit both scientific and religious communities and contribute to the spiritual quest of humankind in the following ways.

First, perceived conflicts between science and Scripture have had detrimental effects on both scientific and religious communities. For the scientific community, such perceived conflicts have resulted in bright religious students staying away from scientific research leading to loss of talent, and/or joining fundamentalist groups and contributing to the public misunderstanding of science. For religious communities, such perceived conflicts have resulted in people leaving or choosing to stay away from these communities. One major area of perceived conflict concerns the issue of human origins, and the resolution of this area of perceived conflict in my book would greatly benefit both communities.

Second, my book has shown that, instead of resulting in a real conflict, the progress of science has – similar to what happened during the Galileo incident – led to a better understanding of various Scriptural passages. I have previously explained that the Scripture should be interpreted according to proper hermeneutical principles and that science should be done according to proper scientific methodology without mutual interference. This is compatible with the view that the results of modern science (say, evolutionary population genetics) have challenged modern readers to re-examine long-held hermeneutical assumptions, to look more closely at the textual and historical (ancient Jewish) contexts of Scriptural passages and to be more sensitive to their sometimes accommodative, phenomenological, and/or functional ways of expressions. (Sadly, some Christians have refused to learn from the mistakes of Galileo's persecutors and have insisted on saying that certain scientific theories are incompatible with the Scripture when, in fact, this is unproven; it is also a pity that many people have been too quick to say that there are conflicts without carefully exploring other options and considering how they might be developed.)

Third, my book has demonstrated how the Charybdis of Young Earth Creationism and the Scylla of biblical minimalism can be avoided, which is another significant contribution to scholarship. Unlike some recent models (such as those which, by denying that Adam was the ancestor of all human beings, have been accused of Pelagianism; see Waters 2017), my model has no problem with the essential points of the doctrine of creation, humanity and Original Sin as understood in religious traditions based on their understanding of the Scriptural account of human origins (for an in-depth discussion of the issue of Original Sin and theodicy, see [Loke 2022b]). Even though these doctrines were derived from Scriptural passages that were written thousands of years ago, they have been shown to be remarkably resilient despite the apparent challenges of modern science (such a resilience is not found in (say, for example) Babylonian creation stories or the views of Aristotle when they are interpreted according to proper hermeneutical methods; see the discussion on an example of his scientific error in Section 2.2). This is likewise the conclusion of Harris' (2013, p. 194) in-depth study of the relationship between Bible and science:

> we have discovered that the biblical texts are remarkably resilient to the imperialistic tendencies of science. They have consistently pointed to a reality beyond that revealed by modern science, and to a creation faith that is not constrained by scientific discoveries, but is in many ways enriched by them. This is a message clearly at odds with the popular conception that science has disproved the Bible.

The remarkable resilience of biblical doctrines can be regarded as yet another indication of their divine origins (in addition to other evidences for Christian Theism which I discussed in Loke 2017a, 2017b, 2020a, 2021a, 2022a).

Finally, resolving the apparent conflicts between science and religion concerning the origin of humanity allows for both to work together to provide a richer view of reality (McGrath 2016). While science is very useful for discovering how the universe works, it cannot provide any answers concerning meaning and morality on its own, as Rosenberg (2011) realized. Religion, however, can offer its *own resources and insights* concerning meaning, morality and the human condition. For example, the Christian doctrine that humans are created in the image of God implies ethical responsibilities towards God, fellow humans, other creatures and the Earth itself. Yet, as Fergusson (2017, p. 237) notes, 'there is also a shadow side to our existence; our lives are entangled in violence, sin, misfortune, and suffering.' This shadow side to our existence is affirmed by the doctrine of Original Sin. It is also recognized by atheist historian Yuval Harari, who ended his bestseller *Sapiens: A Brief History of Humankind* (2015a, pp. 465–6) with deeply troubling words about the future of humanity, which highlighted the underlying problems of uncertainty about purpose and morality, lack of accountability and constant dissatisfaction:

> In the last few decades we have at last made some real progress as far as the human condition is concerned, with the reduction of famine, plague and war. Yet the situation of other animals is deteriorating more rapidly than ever before, and the improvement in the lot of humanity is too recent and fragile to be certain of. Moreover, despite the astonishing things that humans are capable of doing, we remain unsure of our goals and we seem to be as discontented as ever. We have advanced from canoes to galleys to steamships to space shuttles – but nobody knows where we're going. We are more powerful than ever before, but have very little idea what to do with all that power. Worse still, humans seem to be more irresponsible than ever. Self-made gods with only the laws of physics to keep us company, we are accountable to no one. We are consequently wreaking havoc on our fellow animals and on the surrounding ecosystem, seeking little more than our own comfort and amusement, yet never finding satisfaction. Is there anything more dangerous than dissatisfied and irresponsible gods who don't know what they want?

Christian Theism would reply that it is not true that we are self-made gods with only the laws of physics to keep us company, nor is it true that we are accountable to no one. Belief in God is not based on ignorance; on the contrary there are reasons for thinking that the laws of physics came from a Lawgiver – the Divine First Cause (God) who created the universe (Loke 2017a, 2022a), and who has revealed himself in Jesus Christ (Loke 2014; 2017b; 2020a; 2021a). Humans are accountable to him who will judge the world in righteousness (Acts 17.31), and who has accomplished salvation for all humankind through his death and resurrection (Luke 24.46-47). By believing in the Lord Jesus they will be saved

(Acts 16:31) and reconciled to God (Rom. 5.10), in whom they will find ultimate purpose and satisfaction. Therein lies the solution to our human predicament.

Christian Theism can therefore offer an additional dimension to our understanding of reality which science cannot offer: an account of the ultimate origin and foundation of physical and moral laws, a diagnosis of the fundamental problem of our human condition and the provision of grace, forgiveness and hope. In these troubling times in which humans face a deeply uncertain future as a result of scientific and technological progress, the resources of religion are needed more than ever. By reconciling one of the major areas of perceived conflict between science and religion, it is hoped that both can work closer together for the good of humanity.

BIBLIOGRAPHY

Alexander, Denis. *Creation or Evolution: Do We Have to Choose?* Oxford: Monarch Books, 2008.

Alexander, Denis. *Creation or Evolution: Do We Have to Choose?* 2nd edn. Oxford: Monarch Books, 2014.

Alexander, Denis. 'Adam and the Genome: Some Thoughts from Denis Alexander'. 2017a. Available at http://biologos.org/blogs/jim-stump-faith-and-science-seeking-understanding/adam-and-the-genome-some-thoughts-from-denis-alexander (Accessed 17 August 2017).

Alexander, Denis. 'The Various Meanings of Concordism'. 2017b. Available at http://biologos.org/blogs/guest/the-various-meanings-of-concordism (Accessed 17 August 2017).

Arnold, Bill. *Genesis*. Cambridge: Cambridge University Press, 2009.

Arnold, Bill. 'The Genesis Narratives'. In *Ancient Israel's History: An Introduction to Issues and Sources*, edited by Bill Arnold and Richard Hess, 23–45. Grand Rapids: Baker Academic, 2014.

Arnold, Bill and Richard Hess. *Ancient Israel's History: An Introduction to Issues and Sources*. Grand Rapids: Baker Academic, 2014.

Astley, Jeff. 'Evolution and Evil: The Difference Darwinism Makes in Theology and Spirituality'. In *Reading Genesis after Darwin*, edited by Stephen Barton and David Wilkinson, 163–80. Oxford: Oxford University Press, 2009.

Atran, Scott. *In Gods We Trust: The Evolutionary Landscape of Religion*. Oxford: Oxford University Press, 2006.

Averbeck, Richard. 'A Literary Day, Inter-Textual and Contextual Reading of Genesis 1–2'. In *Reading Genesis 1–2: An Evangelical Conversation*, edited by J. Daryl Charles. Peabody, MA: Hendrickson Publishers, 2013.

Averbeck, Richard. 'A Review of Joshua Swamidass's *The Genealogical Adam and Eve*'. *Sapientia*, 2020. https://henrycenter.tiu.edu/2020/08/let-scripture-speak-clearly/

Baker, Lynne Rudder. 'Death and the AFTERLIFE'. In *The Oxford Handbook of Philosophy of Religion*, edited by William J. Wainwright. Oxford: Oxford University Press, 2005.

Baker, Lynne Rudder. *Naturalism and the First-Person Perspective*. Oxford: Oxford University Press, 2013.

Balserak, Jon. *Divinity Compromised: A Study of Divine Accommodation in the Thought of John Calvin*. Dordrecht: Springer, 2006.

Barr, James. 'One Man, or All Humanity? A Question in the Anthropology of Genesis 1'. In *Recycling Biblical Figures*, edited by A. Brenner and J. van Henten. Leiden: Deo, 1999.

Barrett, Justin and Tyler Greenway. 'Imago Dei and Animal Domestication'. In *Human Origins and the Image of God: Essays in Honor of J. Wentzel van Huyssteen*, edited by Christopher Lilley and Daniel Pederson. Grand Rapids: Eerdmans, 2017.

Barton, Stephen and David Wilkinson, eds. *Reading Genesis after Darwin*. Oxford: Oxford University Press, 2009.

Barrett, Michael and Ardel B. Caneday, eds. *Four Views on the Historical Adam*. Grand Rapids: Zondervan, 2013.

Bar-Yosef, O. and J. -G. Bordes. 'Who Were the Makers of the Châtelperronian Culture?' *Journal of Human Evolution* 59 (2010): 586–93.

Bauks, Michaela. *Die Welt am Anfang: Zum Verhältnis von Vorwelt und Weltentstehung in Gen 1 und in der altorientalischen Literatur*. Wissenschaftliche Monogarphien zum Alten und Neuen Testament, Band 74. Neukirchen-Vluyn: Neukirchener Verlag, 1997.

Beale, Greg. *The Book of Revelation: A Commentary on the Greek Text*. Grand Rapids: Eerdmans, 1999.

Beale, Greg. *The Erosion of Inerrancy in Evangelicalism: Responding to New Challenges to Biblical Authority*. Wheaton, IL: Crossway, 2008.

Beale, Greg. *Handbook on the New Testament Use of the Old Testament: Exegesis and Interpretation*. Grand Rapids: Baker Academic, 2012.

Behe, M. *The Edge of Evolution*. New York: Free Press, 2008.

Berezow, Alex and James Hannam. 'Coyne's Twisted History of Science & Religion'. 2013. Available at http://www.realclearscience.com/articles/2013/10/21/twisted_history_jerry_coyne_on_science__religion_106729.html (Accessed 30 August 2016).

Betty, Stafford. 'The Growing Evidence for Demonic Possession'. *Journal of Religion and Health* 44 (2005): 13–30.

Blocher, Henri. *In the Beginning: The Opening Chapters of Genesis*. Leicester, England: IVP, 1984.

Blocher, Henri. 'The Theology of the Fall and the Origins of Evil'. In *Darwin, Creation and the Fall: Theological Challenges*, edited by R. J. Berry and Thomas Noble, 170–2. Nottingham: Apollos, 2009.

Bockmuehl, M. 'Creatio ex nihilo in Palestinian Judaism and Early Christianity'. *Scottish Journal of Theology* 65, no. 3 (2012): 253–70.

Brown, Andrew. *The Days of Creation: A History of Christian Interpretation of Genesis 1:1–2:3*. Blandford Forum, UK: Deo, 2014.

Brown, William. *The Seven Pillars of Creation: The Bible, Science, and the Ecology of Wonder*. Oxford: Oxford University Press, 2010.

Brunner, Emil. *The Christian Doctrine of Creation and Redemption*. London: Lutterworth, 1952.

Burdett, Michael. 'Part I: The Image of God and Evolution'. In *Finding Ourselves after Darwin: Conversations on the Image of God, Original Sin, and the Problem of Evil*, edited by Stanley Rosenberg. Grand Rapids: Baker Academic, 2018.

Burkhardt, Frederick, ed. *The Correspondence of Charles Darwin*. Vol. 7. Cambridge: Cambridge University Press, 1991.

Butler, J. 'Mirages are Light Benders'. *Journal of the American Scientific Affiliation* 3 (1951): 1–19. Available at https://www.asa3.org/ASA/PSCF/1951/JASA12-51Butler.html (Accessed 13 May 2018).

Calvin, John. *Commentaries on the First Book of Moses Called Genesis*. Edited and translated by John King. 1847. Reprint, Grand Rapids: Baker, 1981.

Carter, Robert and John Sanford. 'A "Genealogical" Adam and Eve?'. 2020. Available at https://creation.com/review-swamidass-the-genealogical-adam-and-eve .

Cavanaugh, William and James Smith, eds. *Evolution and the Fall*. Grand Rapids: Eerdmans, 2017.

Chavalas, Mark. 'Genealogical History as "Charter": A Study of Old Babylonian Period Historiography and the Old Testament'. In *Faith, Tradition and History: Old Testament*

Historiography in Its Near Eastern Context, edited by A. R. Millard, James K. Hoffmeier and David W. Baker. Winona Lake, IN: Eisenbrauns, 1994.

Chen, C. and W. H. Li. 'Genomic Divergences between Humans and Other Hominoids and the Effective Population Size of the Common Ancestor of Humans and Chimpanzees'. *American Journal of Human Genetics* 68 (2001): 444–56.

Charles, J. Daryl, ed. *Reading Genesis 1-2: An Evangelical Conversation*. Peabody, MA: Hendrickson Publishers, 2013.

Childs, B. *Introduction to the Old Testament as Scripture*. London: SCM Press, 1979.

Christian, David. *Maps of Time: An Introduction to Big History*. Berkeley: University of California Press, 2011.

Clare, Lee. 'Göbekli Tepe, Turkey. A Brief Summary of Research at a New World Heritage Site (2015-2019)'. *E-Forschungsberichte*. Deutsches Archäologisches Institut 2 (2020): 81–8.

Clough, David. 'All God's Creatures: Reading Genesis on Human and Nonhuman Animals'. In *Reading Genesis after Darwin*, edited by Stephen Barton and David Wilkinson. Oxford: Oxford University Press, 2009.

Coats, G. W. *Genesis with an Introduction to Narrative Literature*. Grand Rapids: Eerdmans, 1983.

Cole-Turner, Ron. *The End of Adam and Eve: Theology and the Science of Human Origins*. Pittsburgh, PA: Theology Plus Publishing, 2016.

Cole-Turner, Ron. 'New Perspectives on Human Origins: Three Challenges for Christian Theology'. *Theology and Science*, 2020. DOI: 10.1080/14746700.2020.1825187

Collins, C. John. *Genesis 1-4: A Linguistic, Literary, and Theological Commentary*. Phillipsburg, NJ: P&R, 2006.

Collins, C. John. 'Adam and Eve as Historical People, and Why It Matters'. *Perspectives on Science and Christian Faith* 62 (2010): 147–65.

Collins, C. John. *Did Adam and Eve Really Exist?* Wheaton: Crossway, 2011a.

Collins, C. John. 'Adam and Eve in the Old Testament'. *Southern Baptist Journal of Theology* 15 (2011b): 4–25.

Collins, C. John. 'Reading Genesis 1-2 with the Grain: Analogical Days'. In *Reading Genesis 1-2: An Evangelical Conversation*, edited by J. Daryl Charles. Peabody, MA: Hendrickson Publishers, 2013c.

Collins, C. John. 'Recent Inerrancy Studies and the Old Testament'. *Evangelical Theological Society Annual Conference*, 2017.

Collins, C. John. *Reading Genesis Well: Navigating History, Science, Poetry, and Truth in Genesis 1-11*. Grand Rapids: Zondervan, 2018.

Collins, Francis. *The Language of God: A Scientist Presents Evidence for Belief*. New York: Free Press, 2006.

Collins, Robin. 'The Connection Building Theodicy'. In *The Blackwell Companion to the Problem of Evil*, edited by Dan Howard-Snyder and Justin McBrayer. Oxford: Blackwell, 2013a.

Collins, Robin. 'The Fine-Tuning Evidence is Convincing'. In *Debating Christian Theism*, edited by J. P. Moreland, Chad Meister and Khaldoun A. Sweis. Oxford: Oxford University Press, 2013b.

Corcoran, Kevin. *Rethinking Human Nature: A Christian Materialist Alternative to the Soul*. Grand Rapids, MI: Baker Academic, 2006.

Conway Morris, Simon. *Life's Solution: Inevitable Humans in a Lonely Universe*. Cambridge: Cambridge University Press, 2008.

Conway Morris, Simon. *The Runes of Evolution: How the Universe Became Self-Aware*. West Conshohocken, PA: Templeton Press, 2015.

Cooper, J. *Body, Soul and Life Everlasting: Biblical Anthropology and the Monism-Dualism Debate*. Leicester: Apollos, 2001.

Cooper, J. 'Exaggerated Rumors of Dualism's Demise'. *Philosophia Christi* 11, no. 2 (2009): 453–64.

Cowan, Steven and Terry Wilder, eds. *In Defense of the Bible: A Comprehensive Apologetic for the Authority of Scripture*. Nashville: B&H Academic, 2013.

Copan, Paul and Willian Lane Craig. *Creation Out of Nothing: A Biblical, Philosophical and Scientific Exploration*. Leicester: Apollos, 2004.

Coyne, Jerry. 'Adam and Eve: The Ultimate Standoff Between Science and Faith'. 2011 Available at https://whyevolutionistrue.wordpress.com/2011/06/02/adam-and-eve-the-ultimate-standoff-between-science-and-faith-and-a-contest/.

Coyne, Jerry. *William Lane Craig's New Book on Adam and Eve Given Semi-Laudatory Review—in Science!* 2021. https://whyevolutionistrue.com/2021/10/08/william-lane-craigs-new-book-on-adam-and-eve-given-semi-laudatory-review-in-science/.

Craig, William Lane. 'What Price Biblical Errancy?'. 2007. Available at https://www.reasonablefaith.org/question-answer/P20/what-price-biblical-errancy (Accessed 5 Febuary 2018).

Craig, William Lane. 'Scepticism about the Neo-Darwinian Paradigm'. 2008. Available at http://www.reasonablefaith.org/scepticism-about-the-neo-darwinian-paradigm (Accessed 17 August 2017).

Craig, William Lane. 'Animal Pain and the Ethical Treatment of Animals'. 2011. Available at http://www.reasonablefaith.org/animal-pain-and-the-ethical-treatment-of-animals#ixzz4uOvBw9fO (Accessed 12 October 2017).

Craig, William Lane. *In Quest of the Historical Adam: A Biblical and Scientific Exploration*. Grand Rapids: Eerdmans, 2021.

Craig, William Lane, and J. P. Moreland, eds. *The Blackwell Companion to Natural Theology*. Chichester: Wiley-Blackwell, 2009.

Creegan, Nicola Hoggard. *Animal Suffering and the Problem of Evil*. Oxford: Oxford University Press, 2013.

Crisp, Oliver D. 'Pulling Traducianism out of the Shedd'. *Ars Disputandi* 6 (2006): 265–87.

Currid, John. 'Theistic Evolution Is Incompatible with the Teachings of the Old Testament'. In *Theistic Evolution: A Scientific, Philosophical, and Theological Critique*, edited by J. P. Moreland, et al. Wheaton, IL: Crossway, 2017.

Dalley, Stephanie. *Myths from Mesopotamia*. Oxford: Oxford University Press, 2000.

Darwin, Charles. *On the Origin of Species*. Norwalk: The Heritage Press, 1963.

Darwin, Charles. *The Correspondence of Charles Darwin, vi. 1856–1857*. Cambridge: Cambridge University Press, 1990.

Darwin, Charles. *The Correspondence of Charles Darwin, viii. 1860*. Cambridge: Cambridge University Press, 1993.

Davis, Ted. 'Science and the Bible: Concordism, Part 1'. 2012. Available at http://biologos.org/blogs/ted-davis-reading-the-book-of-nature/science-and-the-bible-concordism-part-1 (Accessed 17 August 2017).

Dawkins, Richard. *The Blind Watchmaker*. New York: Norton, 1985.

Dawkins, Richard. *River Out of Eden*. New York: Basic Books, 1996.

Dawkins, Richard. *The God Delusion*. London: Bantam Press, 2006.

Dawkins, Richard. *The Greatest Show on Earth*. New York: Free Press, 2010.

Day, John. *From Creation to Babel: Studies in Genesis 1–11*. London: Bloomsbury, 2013.

De Chardin, Pierre Teilhard. *Christianity and Evolution*. New York: Harcourt Brace Jovanovich, 1969.

Deane-Drummond, Celia. *Christ and Evolution: Wonder and Wisdom*. Minneapolis: Fortress Press, 2009.

Deane-Drummond, Celia. 'Moral Origins and Evolutionary Ethics'. In *Human Origins and the Image of God: Essays in Honor of J. Wentzel van Huyssteen*, edited by Christopher Lilley and Daniel Pederson. Grand Rapids: Eerdmans, 2017.

Dembski, William and Michael Ruse, eds. *Debating Design: From Darwin to DNA*. New York: Cambridge University Press, 2007.

Détroit, F., et al. 'A New Species of Homo from the Late Pleistocene of the Philippines'. *Nature* 568 (2019): 181–6.

Dirks, P. H., et al. 'The Age of Homo Naledi and Associated Sediments in the Rising Star Cave, South Africa'. *eLife* 6 (2017): e24231.

Donald, Alistair. 'Evolution and the Church'. In *Should Christians Embrace Evolution?: Biblical and Scientific Responses*, edited by Norman Nevin, 15–19. Nottingham: Inter-Varsity Press, 2009.

Draper, Paul. 'Darwin's Argument From Evil'. In *Scientific Approaches to Philosophy of Religion*, edited by Yujin Nagasawa. London: Palgrave-Macmillan, 2011.

Ecklund, Elaine. *Science vs Religion: What Scientists Really Think*. Oxford: Oxford University Press, 2010.

Ellis, George. 'Issues in the Philosophy of Cosmology'. In *Philosophy of Physics*, edited by J Butterfield and J. Earman. Amsterdam: Elsevier, 2007.

Enns, P. *Inspiration and Incarnation: Evangelicals and the Problem of the Old Testament*. Grand Rapids, MI: Baker Academic, 2005.

Enns, Peter. *The Evolution of Adam: What the Bible Does and Doesn't Say about Human Origins*. Grand Rapids: Brazos Press, 2012.

Enns, Peter, Alister McGrath and Jeff Schloss. 'At What Point in the Evolutionary Process Did Humans Attain the "Image of God"?' *The BioLogos Forum*. 2011. Available at http://biologos.org/questions/image-of-god (Accessed 7 September 2017).

Farris, Joshua. 'Originating Souls and Original Sin: An Initial Exploration of Dualism, Anthropology, and Sins Transmission'. *Neue Zeitschrift für Systematische Theologie und Religionsphilosophie* 58 (2016a): 39–56.

Farris, Joshua. *The Soul of Theological Anthropology: A Cartesian Exploration*. London: Routledge, 2016b.

Fergusson, David. 'Are We Alone? And Does It Matter? The Narrative of Human Particularity'. In *Human Origins and the Image of God: Essays in Honor of J. Wentzel van Huyssteen*, edited by Christopher Lilley and Daniel Pederson. Grand Rapids: Eerdmans, 2017.

Finlay, Graeme. *Human Evolution: Genes, Genealogies and Phylogenies*. Cambridge: Cambridge University Press, 2013.

Fischer, Richard. *Historical Genesis: From Adam to Abraham*. Lanham: University Press of America, 2008.

France, R. T. *The Gospel of Matthew*. Grand Rapids: Eerdmans, 2007.

Franke, John. 'Recasting Inerrancy: The Bible as Witness to Missional Plurality'. In *Five Views on Biblical Inerrancy*, edited by J. Merrick and Stephen Garrett. Grand Rapids: Zondervan, 2013.

Gallup, G. G. Jr. 'Chimpanzees: Self-Recognition'. *Science* 167, no. 3914 (1970): 86–7.

Garraghan, Gilbert J. and J. Delanglez. *A Guide to Historical Method*. Westport, CT: Greenwood Press, 1973.

Garvey, Jon. *The Generations of Heaven and Earth: Adam, the Ancient World, and Biblical Theology*. Eugene, OR: Cascade, 2020.
Gauger, Ann, Douglas Axe and Casey Luskin. *Science and Human Origins*. Seattle: Discovery Institute, 2012.
Giberson, Karl and Mariano Artigas. *Oracles of Science: Celebrity Scientists versus God and Religion*. Oxford: Oxford University Press, 2007.
Gillespie, Neal. 'The Duke of Argyll, Evolutionary Anthropology, and the Art of Scientific Controversy'. *Isis* 68 (1977): 40–54.
Gingerich, Owen. *God's Universe*. Cambridge, MA: Harvard University Press, 2006.
Gingerich, Owen. *God's Planet*. Cambridge, MA: Harvard University Press, 2014.
Gordon, B. L. 'Scandal of the Evangelical Mind: A Biblical and Scientific Critique of Young-Earth Creationism'. *Science, Religion and Culture* 1, no. 3 (2014): 144–73.
Gould, S. J. *Rock of Ages*. New York: Ballantine Books, 2002.
Gravel, S. and M. Steel. 'The Existence and Abundance of Ghost Ancestors in Biparental Populations'. *Theoretical Population Biology* 101 (2015): 47–53.
Green, J. *Body, Soul, and Human Life: The Nature of Humanity in the Bible*. Grand Rapids: Baker Academic, 2008.
Green, Richard E., Johannes Krause, Adrian W. Briggs, Tomislav Maricic, Udo Stenzel, Martin Kircher and Nick Patterson, et al. 'A Draft Sequence of the Neandertal Genome'. *Science* 328, no. 5979 (2010): 710–22.
Green, William. 'Primeval Chronology'. *Bibliotheca Sacra* 47 (1890): 285–303.
Greenwood, Kyle. *Scripture and Cosmology*. Downer's Grove: InterVarsity Press, 2015.
Grudem, Wayne. *Systematic Theology*. Grand Rapids: Zondervan, 1994.
Grudem, Wayne. 'Foreword'. In *Should Christians Embrace Evolution?: Biblical and Scientific Responses*, edited by Norman Nevin. Nottingham: Inter-Varsity Press, 2009.
Grudem, Wayne. 'Theistic Evolution Undermines Twelve Creation Events and Several Crucial Christian Doctrines'. In *Theistic Evolution: A Scientific, Philosophical, and Theological Critique*, edited by J. P. Moreland, et al. Wheaton, IL: Crossway, 2017.
Gruen, Lori. 'The Moral Status of Animals'. In *The Stanford Encyclopedia of Philosophy (Fall 2017 Edition)*, edited by Edward N. Zalta, 2017. Available at https://plato.stanford.edu/archives/fall2017/entries/moral-animal/ (Accessed 12 October 2017).
Guessoum, N. *Islam's Quantum Question: Reconciling Muslim Tradition and Modern Science*. London: I. B. Tauris, 2011.
Gunkel, H. *Genesis*. GAT. Göttingen: Vandenhoeck & Ruprecht, 1901; 1902; 1910.
Haarsma, Deborah. 'Evolutionary Creationism'. In *Four Views on Creation, Evolution, and Intelligent Design*, edited by Jim Stump. Grand Rapids: Zondervan, 2017.
Haarsma, Deborah and Loren D. Haarsma. *Origins: Christian Perspectives on Creation, Evolution, and Intelligent Design*. Grand Rapids, MI: Faith Alive, 2011.
Habermas, Gary. *The Risen Jesus & Future Hope*. Lanham: Rowman & Littlefield Pub, 2003.
Hajdinjak, M., et al. 'Reconstructing the Genetic History of Late Neanderthals'. *Nature* 555 (2018): 652–6.
Halton, Charles, ed. *Genesis: History, Fiction, or Neither?: Three Views on the Bible's Earliest Chapters*. Grand Rapids: Zondervan, 2015.
Ham, Ken. *The New Answers Book*. Colorado Springs: Master Books, 2007.
Ham, Ken. 'Young Earth Creationism'. In *Four Views on Creation, Evolution, and Intelligent Design*, edited by Jim Stump. Grand Rapids: Zondervan, 2017.
Ham, Steve. 'The Lost World of Adam and Eve: A Response'. 2015. Available at https://answersingenesis.org/reviews/books/lost-world-adam-and-eve-response/ (Accessed 4 February 2018).

Hamilton, Victor. *The Book of Genesis Chapters 1-17 (NICOT)*. Grand Rapids: Eerdmans, 1990.
Hanson, R. P. and A. T. Hanson. *The Bible without Illusions*. London: SCM Press, 1989.
Harari, Yuval. *Sapiens: A Brief History of Humankind*. New York: Harper, 2015a.
Harari, Yuval. 'Why Humans Run the World'. *TED Talk*. 2015b. Available at https://www.youtube.com/watch?v=nzj7Wg4DAbs&feature=youtu.be (Accessed 3 February 2018).
Harari, Yuval. *Homo Deus: A Brief History of Tomorrow*. New York: Harper, 2017.
Harlow, Daniel. 'After Adam: Reading Genesis in an Age of Evolutionary Science'. *Perspectives on Science and Christian Faith* 62 (2010): 179-95.
Harrison, Peter. *The Bible, Protestantism, and the Rise of Natural Science*. Cambridge: Cambridge University Press, 1998.
Harris, Mark. *The Nature of Creation: Examining the Bible and Science*. London: Routledge, 2013.
Harris, Mark. 'The Biblical Text and a Functional Account of the *Imago Dei*'. In *Finding Ourselves after Darwin: Conversations on the Image of God, Original Sin, and the Problem of Evil*, edited by Stanley Rosenberg. Grand Rapids: Baker Academic, 2018.
Hart, David Bentley. *The Experience of God: Being, Consciousness, Bliss*. New Haven: Yale University Press, 2013.
Haught, John F. *God and New Atheism: A Critical Response to Dawkins, Harris, and Hitchens*. Louisville: Westminster John Knox Press, 2008.
Hays, Richard. *Echoes of Scripture in the Gospels*. Waco, TX: Baylor University Press, 2016.
Hein, Jotun. 'Pedigrees for All Humanity'. *Nature* 431, no. 7008 (2004): 518-19.
Hendel, Ronald. 'Adam'. In *Eerdmans Dictionary of the Bible*, edited by David Noel Freedman. Grand Rapids: Eerdmans, 2000.
Henry, John. 'Religion and the Scientific Revolution'. In *The Cambridge Companion to Science and Religion*, edited by Peter Harrison. Cambridge: Cambridge University Press, 2010.
Henshilwood, Christopher, et al. 'An Abstract Drawing from the 73,000-Year-Old Levels at Blombos Cave, South Africa'. *Nature* 562 (2018): 115-18.
Hess, Richard. 'God and Origins: Interpreting the Early Chapters of Genesis'. In *Darwin, Creation and the Fall: Theological Challenges*, edited by R. J. Berry and Thomas Noble. Nottingham: Apollos, 2009.
Hess, Richard. 'The Meaning of Mîn in the Hebrew Old Testament'. 2012. Available at http://biologos.org/blog/the-meaning-of-min-part-1; http://biologos.org/blogs/guest/the-meaning-of-mîn-in-the-hebrew-old-testament-part-2 (Accessed 30 August 2017).
Hill, Carol. 'A Time and a Place for Noah'. *Perspectives on Science and Christian Faith* 53 (2001): 24-40.
Hoekema, Anthony. *Created in God's Image*. Grand Rapids: Eerdmans, 1986.
Hublin, J., et al. 'New Fossils from Jebel Irhoud, Morocco and the Pan-African Origin of Homo Sapiens'. *Nature* 546 (2017): 289-92.
Humphreys, D. Russell. *Starlight & Time*. Green Forest: Master Books, 1994.
Hurtado, L. *Lord Jesus Christ: Devotion to Jesus in Earliest Christianity*. Grand Rapids: Eerdmans, 2003.
Holding, James. 'The Legendary Flat-Earth Bible'. *Christian Research Journal* 36, no. 3 (2013). https://www.equip.org/article/legendary-flat-earth-bible/
Houck, Daniel. *Aquinas, Original Sin, and the Challenge of Evolution*. Cambridge: Cambridge University Press, 2020.

Houldcroft, Charlotte and Simon Underdown. 'Neanderthal Genomics Suggests a Pleistocene Time Frame for the First Epidemiologic Transition'. *American Journal of Physical Anthropology* 160 (2016): 379–88.

Jablonka, E. and M. J. Lamb. *Evolution in Four Dimensions: Genetic, Epigenetic, Behavioral, and Symbolic Variation in the History of Life*. Cambridge, MA: MIT Press, 2005.

Kant, Immanuel. 'Anthropology from a Pragmatic Point of View (1798)'. In *Anthropology, History, and Education (Cambridge Edition of the Works of Immanuel Kant)*, edited and translated by Robert Louden and Gunter Zoller, 227–429. Cambridge: Cambridge University Press, 2010.

Keel, Othmar. *The Symbolism of the Biblical World: Ancient Near Eastern Iconography and the Book of Psalms*. New York: Seabury Press, 1978.

Keener, C. *The Gospel of John: A Commentary*. Peabody: Hendrickson, 2003.

Keener, C. *Acts: An Exegetical Commentary. Vol. 3. 15:1–23:35*. Grand Rapids: Baker, 2014.

Keil, C. F. *Commentary on the Old Testament – Volume 1: The Pentateuch*. Edinburgh: T. & T. Clark, 1891.

Kelleher, J., A. M. Etheridge, A. Veber and N. H. Barton. 'Spread of Pedigree Versus Genetic Ancestry in Spatially Distributed Populations'. *Theoretical Population Biology* 108 (2016): 1–12.

Kemp, K. W. 'Science, Theology, and Monogenesis'. *American Catholic Philosophical Quarterly* 85 (2011): 217–36.

Kepler, Johannes. *New Astronomy*. Translated by William H. Donahue. Cambridge: Cambridge University Press, 1992.

Kepler, Johannes. *Optics: Paralipomena to Witela and Optical Part of Astronomy*. Translated by William H. Donahue. Santa Fe, NM: Green Lion Press, 2000.

Kidner, Derek. *Psalms 73–150*. London: Inter-Varsity Press, 1973.

Kingsley, Charles. *The Natural Theology of the Future*. London: Macmillan, 1874.

Kitchen, Kenneth. *Ancient Orient and Old Testament*. London: Inter-Varsity Press, 1966.

Kitcher, P. 'A Plea for Science Studies'. In *A House Built on Sand: Exposing Postmodernist Myths About Science*, edited by Noretta Koertge. New York: Oxford University Press, 1998.

Klein, William W., Craig L. Blomberg and Robert L. Hubbard. *Introduction to Biblical Interpretation*. Grand Rapids: Zondervan, 2017.

Kojonen, Rope. 'Tensions in Intelligent Design's Critique of Theistic Evolutionism'. *Zygon* 48 (2013): 251–73.

Kojonen, Rope. *The Compatibility of Evolution and Design*. Palgrave Frontiers in Philosophy of Religion Series. Cham: Springer Nature, 2021.

Koons, Robert and George Bealer, eds. *The Waning of Materialism*. Oxford: Oxford University Press, 2010.

Korsgaard, Christine. *The Sources of Normativity*. Cambridge: Cambridge University Press, 1996.

Korsgaard, Christine. 'Fellow Creatures: Kantian Ethics and Our Duties to Animals'. In *The Tanner Lectures on Human Values, 25/26*, edited by Grethe B. Peterson, Salt Lake City: University of Utah Press, 2004.

Korsgaard, Christine. 'Facing the Animal You See in the Mirror'. *Harvard Review of Philosophy* 16, no. 1 (2007): 4–9. doi:10.5840/harvardreview20091611

Köstenberger, Andreas. 'John'. In *Commentary on the New Testament use of the Old Testament*, edited by G. Beale and D. Carson. Grand Rapids: Baker, 2007.

Kuhlwilm, M., et al. 'Ancient Gene Flow From Early Modern Humans into Eastern Neanderthals'. *Nature* 530 (2016): 429–33.

Lambert, W. G. 'A New Look at the Babylonian Background of Genesis'. *The Journal of Theological Studies* 16 (1965): 287–300.
Lamoureux, Denis. 'Lessons from the Heavens: On Scripture, Science, and Inerrancy'. *Perspectives on Science and Christian Faith* 60, no. 1 (2008a): 4–15.
Lamoureux, Denis. *Evolutionary Creation: A Christian Approach to Evolution*. Eugene: Wipf & Stock, 2008b.
Lamoureux, Denis. 'The Erosion of Biblical Inerrancy, or Toward a More Biblical View of the Inerrant Word of God?' *Perspectives on Science and Christian Faith* 62 (2010): 133–8.
Lamoureux, Denis. 'Lamoureux's Response to Montgomery'. *Perspectives on Science and Christian Faith* 63 (2011): 72.
Lamoureux, Denis. 'No Historical Adam'. In *Four Views on the Historical Adam*, edited by Michael Barrett and Ardel Caneday. Grand Rapids: Zondervan, 2013.
Lamoureux, Denis. *Evolution: Scripture and Nature Say Yes*. Grand Rapids: Zondervan, 2016.
Lamoureux, Denis. 'The Bible and Ancient Science: A Reply to Andrew Loke'. *Science & Christian Belief* 31 (2019): 168–93.
Lamoureux, Denis. 'A Reply to Dr Andrew Loke's Letter'. *Science & Christian Belief* 32 (2020): 183–7.
Lennox, John. *Seven Days That Divide the World: The Beginning According to Genesis and Science*. Grand Rapids: Zondervan, 2011.
Levering, Matthew. *Engaging the Doctrine of Creation: Cosmos, Creatures, and the Wise and Good Creator*. Grand Rapids, MI: Baker Academic, 2017.
Lewis, C. S. *Mere Christianity*. New York: Harper Collins, 1980.
Lewis, Geraint and Luke A. Barnes. *A Fortunate Universe: Life in a Finely Tuned Cosmos*. Cambridge: Cambridge University Press, 2016.
Li, Heng and Richard Durbin. 'Inference of Human Population History From Individual Whole-Genome Sequences'. *Nature* 475 (2011): 493–6.
Lilley, Christopher and Daniel Pederson, eds. *Human Origins and the Image of God: Essays in Honor of J. Wentzel van Huyssteen*. Grand Rapids: Eerdmans, 2017.
Livingstone, David N. *Adam's Ancestors: Race, Religion, and the Politics of Human Origins*. Baltimore: The Johns Hopkins University Press, 2008.
Lloyd, Michael. 'Are Animals Fallen?' In *Animals on the Agenda: Questions about Animals for Theology and Ethics*, edited by Andrew Linzey and Dorothy Yamamoto, 149–50. London: SCM Press, 1998.
Lloyd, Michael. 'The Fallenness of Nature: Three Nonhuman Suspects'. In *Finding Ourselves after Darwin: Conversations on the Image of God, Original Sin, and the Problem of Evil*, edited by Stanley Rosenberg. Grand Rapids: Baker Academic, 2018.
Loke, Andrew. 'The Resurrection of the Son of God: A Reduction of the Naturalistic Alternatives'. *Journal of Theological Studies* 60, no. 2 (2009): 570–84.
Loke, Andrew. 'Is the Saving Grace of God Resistible?' *European Journal of Theology* 22 (2013): 28–37.
Loke, Andrew. *A Kryptic Model of the Incarnation*. London: Routledge, 2014.
Loke, Andrew. 'Reconciling Evolution with Biblical Literalism: A Proposed Research Program'. *Theology and Science* 14 (2016): 160–74.
Loke, Andrew. *God and Ultimate Origins: A Novel Cosmological Argument*. Palgrave Frontiers in Philosophy of Religion Series. Cham, Switzerland: Springer Nature, 2017a.
Loke, Andrew. *The Origins of Divine Christology*. Cambridge: Cambridge University Press, 2017b.

Loke, Andrew. 'On the Doing-Allowing Distinction and the Problem of Evil: A Reply to Daniel Lim'. *International Journal for Philosophy of Religion*, 2018: 137–43.

Loke, Andrew. 'Does the Bible Affirm Scientific Errors? A Reply to Denis Lamoureux'. *Science and Christian Belief* 30 (2018a): 116–33.

Loke, Andrew. 'The Doctrine of Predestination and a Modified Hylomorphic Theory of Human Souls'. In *Being Saved: Explorations in Soteriology and Human Ontology*, edited by Mark Hamilton, Joshua Farris and Marc Cortez. London: SCM Press, 2018b.

Loke, Andrew. 'Theological Critiques of Natural Theology: A Reply to Andrew Moore'. *Neue Zeitschrift für Systematische Theologie und Religionsphilosophie* 61 (2019): 207–22.

Loke, Andrew. *Investigating the Resurrection of Jesus Christ: A New Transdisciplinary Approach*. Routledge New Critical Thinking in Religion, Theology and Biblical Studies Series. London: Routledge, 2020a.

Loke, Andrew. 'Joshua Swamidass's The Genealogical Adam and Eve'. *Sapientia*, 2020b. Available at https://henrycenter.tiu.edu/2020/08/is-adam-gods-first-image-bearer/

Loke, Andrew. 'A Response to Lamoureux's Reply'. *Science and Christian Belief* 32 (2020c): 175–82.

Loke, Andrew. *Reply to Reviews of Investigating the Resurrection of Jesus Christ*. 2021a. https://www.academia.edu/45588286/Reply_to_reviews_of_Investigating_the_Resurrection_of_Jesus_Christ_Routledge_2020_.

Loke, Andrew. *A Reply to Lamoureux's Second Reply*. 2021b. https://www.academia.edu/59104928/A_reply_to_Lamoureuxs_second_reply.

Loke, Andrew. 'Creatio ex nihilo'. In *T&T Clark Companion to Analytic Theology*, edited by J. T. Turner and James Arcadi. London: T&T Clark, 2021c.

Loke, Andrew. *The Teleological and Kalam Cosmological Arguments Revisited*. Palgrave Frontiers in Philosophy of Religion Series. Cham, Switzerland: Springer Nature, 2022a.

Loke, Andrew. *Evil, Sin, and Christian Theism*. London: Routledge, 2022b.

Loke, Andrew. 'An Exploration of the Possibility of the Recent Genealogical Adam View'. In *Perspectives on the Historical Adam*, edited by Kenneth Keathley. Nashville: B&H Publishing, Forthcoming.

Longman, Tremper. 'Adam and Eve in the Old Testament'. In *Dictionary of Christianity and Science: The Definitive Reference for the Intersection of Christian Faith and Contemporary Science*, edited by Paul Copan and Tremper Longman. Grand Rapids: Zondervan, 2017.

Longman, Tremper and Raymond Dillard. *An Introduction to the Old Testament*. 2nd edn. Grand Rapids: Zondervan, 2006.

Longman, Tremper and John H. Walton. *The Lost World of the Flood: Mythology, Theology, and the Deluge Debate*. Downers Grove: IVP Academy, 2018.

Loose, Jonathan, Angus Menuge and J. P. Moreland. *The Blackwell Companion to Substance Dualism*. Oxford: Wiley Blackwell, 2018.

Madueme, Hans. *Evolution and Historical Adam? A Provocative But Unconvincing Attempt*. 2020. https://www.thegospelcoalition.org/reviews/genealogical-adam-eve-swamidass/.

Mahlmann, Theodor. 'Articulus Stantis et (Vel) Cadentis Ecclesiae'. In *Religion Past & Present: Encyclopedia of Theology and Religion*, edited by Hans Dieter Betz, et al. Boston: Brill, 2007.

Manson, T. W. *The Sayings of Jesus as Recorded in Gospels According to S. Matthew and S. Luke*. Grand Rapids: Eerdmans, 1979.

May, Gerhard. *Creatio ex nihilo: The Doctrine of 'Creation Out of Nothing' in Early Christian Thought*. London: T&T Clark, 2004.

Mayr, Ernst. *What Evolution Is*. London: Phoenix, 2002.
McBrearty, Sally and Alison S. Brooks. 'The Revolution that Wasn't: A New Interpretation of the Origin of Modern Human Behavior'. *Journal of Human Evolution* 39, no. 5 (2000): 453–563.
McFarland, Ian. *Adam's Fall: A Meditation on the Christian Doctrine of Original Sin*. Oxford: Wiley-Blackwell, 2010.
McFarland, Ian, et al. *The Cambridge Dictionary of Christian Theology*. Cambridge: Cambridge University Press, 2011.
McGrath, Alister. *A Scientific Theology*. Vol. 2. Grand Rapids: Eerdmans, 2003.
McGrath, Alister. *Dawkins' God*. Malden, MA: Wiley-Blackwell, 2004.
McGrath, Alister. 'Augustine's Origin of Species'. 2009. Available at http://www.christianitytoday.com/ct/2009/may/22.39.html (Accessed 7 Febuary 2018).
McGrath, Alister. *Science and Religion: An Introduction*. Malden, MA: Wiley-Blackwell, 2010.
McGrath, Alister. *Darwinism and the Divine: Evolutionary Thought and Natural Theology*. Chichester: Wiley Blackwell, 2011.
McGrath, Alister. *Enriching Our Vision of Reality: Theology and the Natural Science in Dialogue*. London: Society for Promoting Christian Knowledge, 2016.
McGrath, Gavin Basil. 'Soteriology: Adam and the Fall'. *Perspectives on Science and Christian Faith* 49 (1997): 252–63. Available at http://www.asa3.org/ASA/PSCF/1997/PSCF12-97McGrath.html (Accessed 18 January 2014).
McGrew, T. and L. McGrew. 'The Argument from *Miracles*: The Cumulative Case for the Resurrection of Jesus of Nazareth'. In *The Blackwell Companion to Natural Theology*, edited by W. L. Craig and J. P. Moreland. Chichester: Wiley-Blackwell, 2009.
McGrew, T. 'Miracles'. In *The Stanford Encyclopedia of Philosophy (Spring 2013 Edition)*, edited by Edward N. Zalta, 2013. Available at http://plato.stanford.edu/archives/spr2013/entries/miracles/.
McKnight, Scot. 'Adam and the Genome: Some Thoughts from Scot McKnight'. 2017. Available at http://biologos.org/blogs/jim-stump-faith-and-science-seeking-understanding/adam-and-the-genome-some-thoughts-from-scot-mcknight (Accessed 17 August 2017).
Mellars, P. A., K. Boyle, O. Bar-Yosef and C. Stringer, eds. *Rethinking the Human Revolution: New Behavioural and Biological Perspectives on the Origin and Dispersal of Modern Humans*. Cambridge: McDonald Institute for Archaeological Research, 2007.
Merrick, J. and Stephen Garrett, ed. *Five Views on Biblical Inerrancy*. Grand Rapids: Zondervan, 2013.
Meyer, Stephen. *The Signature of the Cell*. New York: HarperOne, 2010.
Meyer, Stephen. *Darwin's Doubt*. New York: HarperOne, 2013.
Meyer, Stephen. 'Intelligent Design'. In *Four Views on Creation, Evolution, and Intelligent Design*, edited by Jim Stump. Grand Rapids: Zondervan, 2017a.
Meyer, Stephen. 'Defining Theistic Evolution'. In *Theistic Evolution: A Scientific, Philosophical, and Theological Critique*, edited by J. P. Moreland, et al. Wheaton, IL: Crossway, 2017b.
Middleton, Richard. *The Liberating Image: The Imago Dei in Genesis 1*. Grand Rapids: Brazos, 2006.
Miller, Johnny and John Soden. *In the Beginning We Misunderstood: Genesis 1 in Its Original Context*. Grand Rapids: Kregel, 2012.

Minton, Ron. 'Apostolic Witness to Genesis Creation and the Flood'. In *Coming to Grips with Genesis*, edited by Terry Mortenson and Thane H. Ury. Green Forest, AR: Masters Books, 2008.

Mitchell, R. W. 'Kinesthetic Visual Matching, Imitation, and Self-Recognition'. In *The Cognitive Animal*, edited by M. Bekoff, C. Allen and G. Burghardt, 345–51. Cambridge, MA: MIT Press, 2002.

Moberly, Walter. 'How Should One Read the Early Chapters of Genesis?' In *Reading Genesis after Darwin*, edited by Stephen Barton and David Wilkinson. Oxford: Oxford University Press, 2009.

Montgomery, John Warwick. 'A Reply to Lamoureux's Review of Beale's "The Erosion of Inerrancy in Evangelicalism"'. *Perspectives on Science and Christian Faith* 62 (2010): 302–3.

Mook, James. 'The Church Fathers on Genesis, the Flood, and the Age of the Earth'. In *Coming to Grips with Genesis*, edited by Terry Mortenson and Thane H. Ury. Green Forest, AR: Masters Books, 2008.

Moreland, J. P. 'The Circumstantial Evidence'. In *The Case for Christ*, edited by Lee Strobel. Grand Rapids: Zondervan, 1998.

Moreland, J. P. 'The Argument From Consciousness'. In *The Blackwell Companion to Natural Theology*, edited by W. L. Craig and J. P. Moreland. Chichester: Wiley-Blackwell, 2009.

Moreland, J. P. 'Substance Dualism and the Unity of Consciousness'. In *The Blackwell Companion to Substance Dualism*, edited by Jonathan Loose, Angus Menuge and J. P. Moreland. Oxford: Wiley Blackwell, 2018.

Moreland, J. P. and William Lane Craig. *Philosophical Foundations for a Christian Worldview*. Downers Grove: InterVarsity Press, 2003.

Moreland, J. P. and John Mark Reynolds, eds. *Three Views on Creation and Evolution*. Grand Rapids, MI: Zondervan, 1999.

Moreland, J. P. and Scott Rae. *Body and Soul, Human Nature and the Crisis in Ethics*. Downers Grove, Ill.: IVP, 2000.

Moreland, J. P., et al., eds. *Theistic Evolution: A Scientific, Philosophical, and Theological Critique*. Wheaton, IL: Crossway, 2017.

Moritz, Joshua. 'Evolutionary Evil and Dawkins' Black Box'. In *The Evolution of Evil*, edited by Gaymon Bennett, Martinez J. Hewlett, Ted Peters and Robert John Russell. Göttingen: Vandenhoeck & Ruprecht, 2008.

Moritz, Joshua. 'The Search for Adam Revisited: Evolution, Biblical Literalism, and the Question of Human Uniqueness'. *Theology and Science* 9 (2011a): 370–1.

Moritz, Joshua. 'Evolution, the End of Human Uniqueness, and the Election of the Imago Dei'. *Theology and Science* 9 (2011b): 307–39.

Moritz, Joshua. 'God's Creation through Evolution and the Language of Scripture'. *Theology and Science* 11 (2013): 1–7.

Moritz, Joshua. 'Animal Suffering, Evolution, and the Origins of Evil: Toward a "Free Creatures' Defense"'. *Zygon* 49, no. 2 (2014): 348–80.

Morledge, Clarke. 'The Groaning of Creation in Romans 8:19–23'. 2015. Available at https://sharedveracity.net/2015/04/18/the-groaning-of-creation-in-romans-819-23/ (Accessed 7 Febuary 2018).

Morris, Henry. *Biblical Creationism*. Colorado Springs: Master Books, 2005.

Morris, Thomas. *The Logic of God Incarnate*. Ithaca, NY: Cornell University Press, 1986.

Mortenson, Terry. 'Jesus' View of the Age of the Earth'. In *Coming to Grips with Genesis*, edited by Terry Mortenson and Thane H. Ury. Green Forest, AR: Masters Books, 2008.

Mortenson, Terry. 'The Fall and the Problem of Millions of Years of Natural Evil'. *The Journal of Ministry and Theology* 16 (2012): 122–58. Available at https://answersingenesis.org/theory-of-evolution/millions-of-years/the-fall-and-the-problem-of-millions-of-years-of-natural-evil/ (Accessed 1 Febuary 2018).

Mortenson, Terry. 'When Was Adam Created?'. In *Searching for Adam: Genesis and the Truth About Man's Origin*, edited by Terry Mortenson. Green Forest, AR: Masters Books, 2016.

Mortenson, Terry, ed. *Searching for Adam: Genesis and the Truth about Man's Origin*. Green Forest, AR: Masters Books, 2016.

Mortenson, Terry and Ury Thane, eds. *Coming to Grips with Genesis*. Green Forest, AR: Masters Books, 2008.

Murphy, Nancey. *Bodies and Souls, or Spirited Bodies?* New York: Cambridge University Press, 2006.

Murray, John. *The Collected Writings of John Murray*. Vol. 2. Edinburgh: Banner of Truth, 1982.

Murray, Michael. *Nature Red in Tooth and Claw: Theism and the Problem of Animal Suffering*. Oxford: Oxford University Press, 2008.

National Academy of Sciences. 'Is Evolution a Theory or a Fact?'. 2008. Available at http://www.nas.edu/evolution/TheoryOrFact.html (Accessed 19 January 2017).

Nelson, Paul. 'Life in the Big Tent: Traditional Creationism and the Intelligent Design Community'. *Christian Research Journal* 24 (2002): 4.

Newman, John Henry. 'Letter to J. Walker of Scarborough, May 22, 1868'. In *The Letters and Diaries of John Henry Newman*, edited by Charles Stephen Dessain. Oxford: Clarendon Press, 1973.

Nicozisin, George. 'Creationism versus Evolution'. 2017. Available at http://www.orthodoxresearchinstitute.org/articles/dogmatics/nicozisin_creationism.htm

Numbers, Ronald. *The Creationists: From Scientific Creationism to Intelligent Design*. Cambridge, MA: Harvard University Press, 2006.

O'Collins, Gerald. *Revelation: Towards a Christian Interpretation of God's Self-Revelation in Jesus Christ*. Oxford: Oxford University Press, 2016.

O'Halloran, Nathan. 'Cosmic Alienation and the Origin of Evil: Rejecting the "Only Way" Option'. *Theology and Science* 13, no. 1 (2015): 43–63.

Olson, Eric. *What Are We? A Study in Personal Ontology*. Oxford: Oxford University Press, 2007.

Osborn, E. *Irenaeus of Lyons*. Cambridge: Cambridge University Press, 2001.

O'Sullivan, James. 'Catholics Re-examining Original Sin in Light of Evolutionary Science: The State of the Question'. *New Blackfriars*, 2016. Available at http://dx.doi.org/10.1111/nbfr.12234 .

Pannenberg, Wolfhart. *Systematic Theology*. Vol. 2. Translated by Goeffrey W. Bromiley. Grand Rapids, MI: Wm. B. Eerdmans, 1994.

Parry, Robin. *The Biblical Cosmos*. Eugene: Cascade, 2014.

Paul, Shalom. 'Creation and Cosmogony in the Bible'. In *Encyclopaedia Judaica Second Edition Vol.5*. Detroit: Macmillan Reference USA, 2007.

Peels, Rick. 'Does Evolution Conflict with God's Character?' *Modern Theology*, 2018. Available at https://doi.org/10.1111/moth.12435

Pigliucci, M. *Evolution, the Extended Synthesis*. Cambridge, MA: MIT Press, 2010.

Plantinga, Alvin. *God, Freedom and Evil*. New York: Harper & Row, 1974.

Plantinga, Alvin. *Where the Conflict Really Lies: Science, Religion, and Naturalism*. Oxford: Oxford University Press, 2011.

Plotkin, Henry. *Evolution in Mind: An Introduction to Evolutionary Psychology*. London: Penguin, 1997.
Polkinghorne, John. 'Christianity and Science'. In *The Oxford Handbook of Religion and Science*, edited by Philip Clayton and Zachary Simpson. Oxford: Oxford University Press, 2006.
Polkinghorne, John. *Science and Religion in Quest of Truth*. New Haven: Yale University Press, 2011.
Pope Pius XII. *Humani Generis*. 1950. https://www.vatican.va/content/pius-xii/en/encyclicals/documents/hf_p-xii_enc_12081950_humani-generis.html.
Provan, Iain. *Seriously Dangerous Religion: What the Old Testament Really Says and Why It Matters*. Waco, TX: Baylor University Press, 2014.
Provan, Iain. *Discovering Genesis*. Grand Rapids: Eerdmans, 2016.
Provan, Iain. *The Reformation and the Right Reading of Scripture*. Waco, TX: Baylor University Press, 2017.
Rana, Fazale and Hugh Ross. *Who Was Adam?* Colorado Springs: Navpress, 2005.
Ratzsch, Del. *Nature, Design and Science*. Albany: SUNY Press, 2001.
Rea, Michael. 'The Metaphysics of Original Sin'. In *Persons: Human and Divine*, edited by Peter Van Inwagen and Dean Zimmerman. Oxford: Oxford University Press, 2007.
Rees, Martin. *Just Six Numbers: The Deep Forces that Shape the Universe*. London: Weidenfeld & Nicolson, 1999.
Reich, David. *Who We Are and How We Got Here. Ancient DNA and the New Science of the Human Past*. Oxford: Oxford University Press, 2018.
Riches, Aaron. 'The Mystery of Adam: A Poetic Apology for the Traditional Doctrine'. In *Evolution and the Fall*, edited by William Cavanaugh and James Smith. Grand Rapids: Eerdmans, 2017.
Rilling, James. 'Comparative Primate Neuroimaging: Insights Into Human Brain Evolution'. *Trends in Cognitive Science* 18 (2014): 46–55.
Roberts, Alexander and James Donaldson, eds. *Ante-Nicene Fathers: Volume III. Latin Christianity: Its Founder, Tertullian*. Grand Rapids: Eerdmans.
Robinson, Marilynne. *The Death of Adam: Essays on Modern Thought*. Boston: Houghton Mifflin, 1988.
Rochat, P. and D. Zahavi. 'The Uncanny Mirror: A Re-framing of Mirror Self-Experience'. *Consciousness and Cognition* 2 (2011): 204–13.
Rohde, Douglas, Steve Olson and Joseph T. Chang. 'Modelling the Recent Common Ancestry of All Living Humans'. *Nature* 431, no. 7008 (2004): 562–6.
Rosenhouse, Jason. *Among the Creationists*. Oxford: Oxford University Press, 2012.
Rosenberg, Alex. *The Atheist's Guide to Reality: Enjoying Life without Illusions*. New York: Norton, 2011.
Rosenberg, Stanley, ed. *Finding Ourselves after Darwin: Conversations on the Image of God, Original Sin, and the Problem of Evil*. Grand Rapids: Baker Academic, 2018.
Ross, Hugh. *The Genesis Question*. Colorado Springs: Navpress, 1998.
Ross, Hugh. *The Creator and the Cosmos: How the Latest Scientific Discoveries of the Century Reveal God*. Colorado Springs: Navpress, 2001.
Ross, Hugh. *A Matter of Days*. Colorado Springs: Navpress, 2004.
Ross, Hugh. *Creation as Science*. Colorado Springs: Navpress, 2006.
Ross, Hugh. 'Additional Explanations on Concordism: A Response to Paul Seely's Critique'. *Perspectives on Science and Christian Faith* 59 (2007): 46–50.
Ross, Hugh. *Hidden Treasures in the Book of Job: How the Oldest Book in the Bible Answers Today's Scientific Questions*. Grand Rapids: Baker, 2011.

Ross, Hugh. 'Defending Concordism: Response to The Lost World of Genesis One'. 2012. Available at http://www.reasons.org/articles/defending-concordism-response-to-the-lost-world-of-genesis-one (Accessed 17 August 2017).
Ross, Hugh. *Navigating Genesis*. Colorado Springs: Navpress, 2014.
Ross, Hugh. 'Old Earth (Progressive) Creationism'. In *Four Views on Creation, Evolution, and Intelligent Design*, edited by Jim Stump. Grand Rapids: Zondervan, 2017.
Ross, Marcus. 'Hedges Around His Garden'. 2020. Available at https://henrycenter.tiu.edu/2020/08/hedges-around-his-garden/
Rusbult, Craig. 'Age of the Earth and Universe'. 2006. Available at https://www.asa3.org/ASA/education/origins/agescience2.htm (Accessed 14 April 2018).
Rusbult, Craig. 'Human Evolution and the Bible'. 2008. Available at http://www.asa3.org/ASA/education/origins/humans.htm (Accessed 17 August 2017).
Rusbult, Craig. 'Noah's Flood in Genesis – Theology & Science'. 2010. Available at http://www.asa3.org/ASA/education/origins/flood.htm (Accessed 17 August 2017).
Ruse, Michael. 'Human Evolution: Some Tough Questions for the Christian'. In *Human Origins and the Image of God: Essays in Honor of J. Wentzel van Huyssteen*, edited by Christopher Lilley and Daniel Pederson. Grand Rapids: Eerdmans, 2017.
Russell, Robert. 'The Groaning of Creation: Does God Suffer with All Life?' In *The Evolution of Evil*, edited by Gaymon Bennett, Martinez J. Hewlett, Ted Peters and Robert John Russell, 129. Göttingen: Vandenhoeck & Ruprecht, 2008.
Russman, H. 'Correspondence'. *Science and Christian Belief* 12 (2000): 165–71.
Sanders, John, ed. *What About Those Who Have Never Heard?* Downer's Grove: Intervarsity Press, 1995.
Sarna, Nahum. *Genesis: The Traditional Hebrew Text with the New JPS translation*. Philadelphia: Jewish Publication Society, 1989.
Scarre, Chris. 'Religion'. In *The Oxford Companion to Archaeology*, edited by Brian M. Fagan. Oxford: Oxford University Press, 1996.
Scerri, Eleanor, et al. 'Did Our Species Evolve in Subdivided Populations across Africa, and Why Does It Matter?' *Trends in Ecology & Evolution* 33 (2018): 582–94.
Schaffner, S. 'Adam, Eve, and the evolution of humankind *In Quest of the Historical Adam: A Biblical and Scientific Exploration* William Lane Craig, Eerdmans, 2021'. 439 pp. *Science* 374, no. 6564 (2021): 162.
Schloss, Jeffrey P. 'Evolutionary Theory and Religion'. In *The Oxford Handbook of Religion and Science*, edited by Philip Clayton and Zachary Simpson. Oxford: Oxford University Press, 2006.
Scott, James W. 'The Inspiration and Interpretation of God's Word with Special Reference to Peter Enns'. *Westminster Theological Journal* 71 (2009): 129–83.
Seely, Paul. 'Concordism and a Biblical Alternative: An Examination of Hugh Ross's Perspective'. *Perspectives on Science and Christian Faith* 59 (2007): 37–45.
Sexton, Jeremy. 'Who Was Born When Enosh Was 90? A Semantic Reevaluation of William Henry Green's Chronological Gaps'. *Westminster Theological Journal* 77 (2015): 193–218.
Simmons, Geoffrey. *Billions of Missing Links*. Eugene: Harvest House, 2007.
Smith, Henry Jr. 'Cosmic and Universal Death from Adam's Fall: An Exegesis of Romans 8:19–23a'. *Journal of Creation* 21 (2007): 75–85.
Smith, Mark. *The Origins of Biblical Monotheism: Israel's Polytheistic Background and the Ugaritic Texts*. Oxford: Oxford University Press, 2001.
Sollereder, Bethany. 'Evolution, Suffering, and the Creative Love of God'. *Perspectives on Science and Christian Faith* 68, no. 2 (2016): 99–109.

Sollereder, Bethany. 'Challenging C. S. Lewis on Evil and Evolution'. 2017. Available at https://biologos.org/blogs/jim-stump-faith-and-science-seeking-understanding/challenging-cs-lewis-on-evil-and-evolution (Accessed 2 Febuary 2018).

Sollereder, Bethany. *God, Evolution, and Animal Suffering: Theodicy without a Fall*. London: Routledge, 2018.

Southgate, Christopher. *The Groaning of Creation: God, Evolution, and the Problem of Evil*. Louisville, KY: Westminster John Knox Press, 2008.

Sparks, Kenton. *God's Words in Human Words*. Grand Rapids: Baker, 2008.

Staubwasser, Michael, et al. 'Impact of Climate Change on the Transition of Neanderthals to Modern Humans in Europe'. *Proceedings of the National Academy of Sciences* 115 (2018): 9116–21.

Steinmann, Andrew. 'Gaps in the Genealogies in Genesis 5 and 11?' *Bibliotheca Sacra* 174 (2017): 141–58.

Stenmark, Mikael. 'What Is Scientism?' *Religious Studies* 33 (1997): 15–32.

Stenmark, Mikael. 'Scientism'. In *Encyclopedia of Science and Religion*, edited by van Huyssteen, J. Wentzel Vrede, 2nd edn. New York: Macmillan Reference, 2003.

Stevenson, L. and D. Haberman. *Ten Theories of Human Nature*. New York: Oxford University Press, 2009.

Stoeger, William. 'God, Physics and the Big Bang'. In *The Cambridge Companion to Science and Religion*, edited by Peter Harrison. Cambridge: Cambridge University Press, 2010.

Stott, John. *Understanding the Bible*. Exp. edn. London: Scripture Union, 1984.

Stringer, Chris. *The Origin of Our Species*. London: Allen Lane, 2011.

Stringer, Chris. 'The Origin and Evolution of Homo Sapiens'. *Philosophical Transactions of the Royal Society B* 371 (2016): 20150237.

Stump, Jim. *Science and Christianity: An Introduction to the Issues*. Oxford: Wiley Blackwell, 2016.

Stump, Jim, ed. *Four Views on Creation, Evolution, and Intelligent Design*. Grand Rapids: Zondervan, 2017.

Suarez, Antoine. 'Can We Give Up the Origin of Humanity from a Primal Couple Without Giving Up the Teaching of Original Sin and Atonement?' *Science and Christian Belief* 27 (2015): 59–83.

Sutikna, T., et al. 'Revised Stratigraphy and Chronology for Homo floresiensis at Liang Bua in Indonesia'. *Nature* 532 (2016): 366–9.

Swamidass, S. Joshua. 'The Overlooked Science of Genealogical Ancestry'. *Perspectives on Science and the Christian Faith* 70 (2018): 19–35.

Swamidass, S. Joshua. *The Genealogical Adam and Eve: The Surprising Science of Universal Ancestry*. Downers Grove: Intervarsity, 2019.

Sweetman, Brendan. *Evolution, Chance, and God: Understanding the Relationship Between Evolution and Religion*. London: Bloomsbury, 2015.

Swinburne, Richard. *The Evolution of the Soul*. Rev. edn. Oxford: Clarendon Press, 1997.

Swinburne, Richard. *The Existence of God*. 2nd edn. Oxford: Oxford University Press, 2004.

Swinburne, Richard. 'The Value and Christian Roots of Analytical Philosophy of Religion'. In *Faith and Philosophical Analysis*, edited by H. A. Harris and C. J. Insole. Aldershot: Ashgate, 2005.

Swinburne, Richard. *Is There a God?* Rev. edn. Oxford: Oxford University Press, 2010.

Swinburne, Richard. 'An Irenaean Approach to Evil'. In *Finding Ourselves after Darwin: Conversations on the Image of God, Original Sin, and the Problem of Evil*, edited by Stanley Rosenberg. Grand Rapids: Baker Academic, 2018.

Tiessen, Terrance. *Who Can Be Saved?* Downers Grove: Intervarsity, 2004.
Thiselton, Anthony C. *Thiselton on Hermeneutics: The Collected Works and New Essays of Anthony Thiselton*. Grand Rapids: Eerdmans, 2006.
Thomson, Keith. 'The Meanings of Evolution'. *American Scientist* 70 (1982): 521–39.
Twelftree, Graham. 'The Message of Jesus I: Miracles, Continuing Controversies'. In *Handbook for the Study of the Historical Jesus*, edited by Tom Holmén and Stanley Porter. Leiden: Brill, 2011.
van Baaren, Theodorus. 'Monotheism'. *Encyclopedia Britannica*, 2018. Available at https://www.britannica.com/topic/monotheism (Accessed 7 Febuary 2018).
van den Toren, Benno. 'Distinguishing Doctrine and Theological Theory'. In *Finding Ourselves after Darwin: Conversations on the Image of God, Original Sin, and the Problem of Evil*, edited by Stanley Rosenberg. Grand Rapids: Baker Academic, 2018.
Van Huyssteen, J. Wentzel. *Alone in the World: Human Uniqueness in Science and Theology*. Grand Rapids: Eerdmans, 2005.
van Inwagen, Peter. 'A Materialist Ontology of the Human Person'. In *Persons: Human and Divine*, edited by Peter van Inwagen and Dean Zimmerman, 199–215. New York: Oxford University Press, 2007.
Van Kuiken, Jerome. 'John Walton's Lost Worlds and God's Loosed Word: Implications For Inerrancy, Canon, And Creation'. *Journal of the Evangelical Theological Society* 58 (2015): 679–91.
Van Seters, J. *Prologue to History: The Yahwist as Historian in Genesis*. Westminster John Knox, 1992.
Varghese, R., ed. *The Missing Link*. Lanham, MD: University Press of America, 2012.
Venema, Dennis. 'Evolution Basics: Becoming Human, Part 1: Mitochondrial Eve and Y Chromosome Adam'. 2014. Available at http://biologos.org/blogs/dennis-venema-letters-to-the-duchess/evolution-basics-becoming-human-part-1-mitochondrial-eve-and-y-chromosome-adam (Accessed 17 August 2017).
Venema, Dennis and Darrel Falk. 'Does Genetics Point to a Single Primal Couple?' 2010. Available at http://biologos.org/blogs/dennis-venema-letters-to-the-duchess/does-genetics-point-to-a-single-primal-couple (Accessed 17 August 2017).
Venema, Dennis and Scot McKnight. *Adam and the Genome: Reading Scripture After Genetic Science*. Grand Rapids: Brazos, 2017.
Visala, A. 'Imago Dei, Dualism and Evolution: A Philosophical Defence of the Structural Image of God'. *Zygon* 49 (2014): 101–20.
Visala, A. 'Human Cognition and the Image of God'. In *The Christian Doctrine of Humanity: Explorations in Constructive Dogmatics*, edited by Oliver Crisp and Fred Sanders. Grand Rapids: Zondervan, 2018.
von Balthasar, Hans Urs. *Theo-Drama, Vol. 4: The Action*, translated by Graham Harrison. San Francisco: Ignatius Press, 1994.
Walls, Jerry. *Purgatory: The Logic of Total Transformation*. New York: Oxford University Press, 2012.
Waltke, Bruce. *Genesis: A Commentary*. Grand Rapids: Zondervan, 2001.
Walton, John. *Genesis (NIVAC)*. Grand Rapids, MI: Zondervan, 2001.
Walton, John. 'Genesis Flood'. In *Dictionary of the Old Testament: Pentateuch*, edited by T. Desmond Alexander and David W. Baker. Downers Grove: Intervarsity, 2003.
Walton, John. 'Genealogies'. In *Dictionary of Old Testament: Historical Books*, edited by Bill T. Arnold and Hugh G. M. Williamson. Downers Grove, IL: InterVarsity Press, 2005.
Walton, John. *Ancient Near Eastern Thought and the Old Testament: Introducing the Conceptual World of the Hebrew Bible*. Grand Rapids: Baker Academic, 2006.

Walton, John. *The Lost World of Genesis One: Ancient Cosmology and the Origins Debate*. Downers Grove: IVP Academy, 2009.

Walton, John. *Genesis 1 as Ancient Cosmology*. Winona Lake, IN: Eisenbrauns, 2011.

Walton, John. *Job: The NIV Application Commentary*. Grand Rapids: Zondervan, 2012.

Walton, John. 'Reading Genesis 1 as Ancient Cosmology'. In *Reading Genesis 1-2: An Evangelical Conversation*, edited by J. Daryl Charles. Peabody, MA: Hendrickson Publishers, 2013.

Walton, John. *The Lost World of Adam and Eve: Genesis 2-3 and the Human Origins Debate*. Downers Grove, IL: IVP Academy, 2015.

Walton, John. 'The Lost Worlds of Genesis: Scripture's Ancient Context and the Modern Origins'. *Biologos Conference 2017*, 2017.

Walton, John and Brent Sandy. *The Lost World of Scripture*. Downers Grove, IL: IVP Acad, 2013.

Warren, Matthew. 'Biggest Denisovan Fossil Yet Spills Ancient Human's Secrets'. *Nature* 569 (2019): 16–17.

Waters, Guy. 'Theistic Evolution Is Incompatible with the Teachings of the New Testament'. In *Theistic Evolution: A Scientific, Philosophical, and Theological Critique*, edited by J. P. Moreland, et al. Wheaton, IL: Crossway, 2017.

Weinfeld, Moshe. *The Place of the Law in the Religion of Ancient Israel*. Leiden: Brill, 2004.

Wenham, Gordon. *Genesis 1-15 (WBC)*. Waco, TX: Word Books, 1987.

Wenham, Gordon. 'Genesis 1-11 as Proto-History'. In *Genesis: History, Fiction, or Neither?: Three Views on the Bible's Earliest Chapters*, edited by Charles Halton. Grand Rapids: Zondervan, 2015.

Wenham, John. *Easter Enigma: Are the Resurrection Accounts in Conflict?* 2nd edn. Grand Rapids: Baker Books, 1992.

Wesley, John. 'The General Deliverance'. In *The Works of John Wesley*, 3rd edn, vol. 6. Grand Rapids, MI: Baker Books, 1998.

Westermann, C. *Genesis 1-11: A Commentary*. Minneapolis: Augsburg Pub. House, 1984.

Whitcomb, John C. Jun. and Morris, Henry. *The Genesis Flood: The Biblical Record and Its Scientific Implications*. Philadelphia: Presbyterian and Reformed Publishing Co, 1961.

Wielandt, Rotraud. 'Exegesis of the Qur'ān: Early Modern and Contemporary'. In *Encyclopaedia of the Qur'ān*, edited by Jane Dammen McAuliffe, vol. 2, 124. Leiden: Brill, 2002.

Wilkinson, David. 'Reading Genesis 1-3 in the Light of Modern Science'. In *Reading Genesis after Darwin*, edited by Stephen Barton and David Wilkinson. Oxford: Oxford University Press, 2009.

Williams, Rowan. 'Interview'. 2006. Available at https://www.theguardian.com/world/2006/mar/21/religion.uk (Accessed 7 Febuary 2018).

Williams, Rowan. 'Archbishop Rowan on Adam and Eve and Evolution'. 2012. Available at s://www.youtube.com/watch?time_continue=28&v=m-6pM-1iyLc (Accessed 16 October 2019).

Wood, T. C. 'Who were Adam and Eve? Scientific Reflections on Collins's *Did Adam and Eve Really Exist?*' *Journal of Creation Theology and Science Series B: Life Sciences* 2 (2012): 28–32.

Woodbridge, John. *Biblical Authority: A Critique of the Rogers/McKim Proposal*. Grand Rapids: Zondervan, 1982.

Wright, N. T. *The Resurrection of the Son of God*. Minneapolis: Fortress, 2003.

Wright, N. T. 'Paul's Use of Adam'. In *The Lost World of Adam and Eve: Genesis 2-3 and the Human Origins Debate*. Downers Grove, IL: IVP Acad, 2015.

Yang, Z. H. 'Likelihood and Bayes Estimation of Ancestral Population Sizes in Hominoids Using Data from Multiple Loci'. *Genetics* 162 (2002): 1811–23.

Young, Davis. *Christianity and the Age of the Earth*. Grand Rapids, MI: Zondervan, 1982.

Zhao, Z., L. Jin and Y. Fu, et al. 'Worldwide DNA Sequence Variation in a 10-kilobase Noncoding Region on Human Chromosome 22'. *Proceedings of the National Academy of Sciences of the USA* 97 (2000): 11354–8.

SCRIPTURE INDEX

OLD TESTAMENT

Gen.
1	9, 10, 28, 41, 45, 45 n.11, 51, 54, 57, 58, 61, 63–5, 69, 73, 75, 135 n.6	1.14-19	58	2.7	49, 54, 65, 90, 109, 119, 120–3
		1.16	58		
		1.20	60, 119		
		1.20-21	59	2.8	90
		1.20-22	73	2.8, 9, 19	75
		1.20-23	49	2.10-14	74
		1.20-24	119	2.11	24
		1.20-25	60, 74	2.15	90, 124
		1.21	59, 123	2.16	90
1–2	17, 33, 46, 52, 53, 65, 132	1.22	55, 59	2.17	76
		1.24	55, 59, 60, 73, 123	2.18	76, 90
1–3	12, 51, 92, 106			2.18-20	118
		1.24-25	60, 73	2.19	49, 90, 119
1–4	14	1.25	49, 55, 59	2.20	88
1–11	27, 28, 47–9	1.26-2	96	2.20; 3.17, 21	90
1.1	54–6, 56 n.24, 57, 59, 61–3	1.26-8	97		
		1.26-27	49, 50, 54, 90	2.21	90
1.1, 21	54	1.26-28	13, 36, 102	2.21-22	49
1.1-2	58, 63	1.26-30	74	2.22	90
1.1–2.3	44 n.10, 49, 50, 65	1.27	59, 76, 90, 106	2.23	90, 124
		1.28	75, 97, 104, 124	2.24	91, 124
1.1-3	55			2.25	90
1.2	55–9, 63, 77	1.29	76	3	48, 75, 76
1.2-31	56	1.29-30	58	3.8	90
1.3	11, 52, 55, 56, 59, 61, 63	1.30	74–6, 119, 123	3.9	90
				3.12	90
1.3-5	57	2	48, 49, 57, 64, 65, 75	3.17	77
1.5	52, 54, 59, 62			3.19	120
1.6-8	52, 57	2–8	44	3.19-23	121
1.8	28	2.1-2	69	3.20	90
1.9-13	57, 58	2.1-3	56, 64	3.22	90
1.10	58, 60	2.3	54	3.22a	126
1.11	58	2.4	47, 49, 56	3.24	90
1.11, 20	83	2.4-7	49	4	141, 143
1.11-12, 20-22	73	2.4-25	49, 50	4.1, 25	90
		2.4b–2.25	44 n.10, 49, 65	4.14	118
1.11-13	49			4.17	141, 150
1.12	55	2.5	90, 94	4.17-22	148
1.14	28, 46	2.5-6	75	4.19-22	147
1.14-18	58, 59	2.5-6, 9	49	4.22	140

4.25	118	20.12	118	27.21	118
4.26	103	23.15	24	32	134
5	38, 91, 93, 133	25.12, 19	47	32.8-9	134
		25.23	109		
5.1	47, 56, 90	36.1, 9	47	Josh.	
5.1, 3-5	90	37.2	47	2.22	50
5.1-3	96	41.57	131	10.12-13	21
5.1-5	90	47.30	123		
5.2	90	111	143	2 Sam.	
5.3	109			22.7-15	22
5.4	118	Exod.		22.16	23
5.9	38	4.12	50 n.14		
6.1-2	117	4.18	50 n.14	1 Kgs	
6.1-4	117	4.19	50 n.14	8	23
6.4	132	12.40	38	8.27	23
6.9	47, 56	14.21	70 n.6	9.13	149
6.9–7.24	131	17.1	50 n.14		
6.12	131, 138	19.1	50 n.14	2 Kgs	
6.17	119	19.2	50 n.14	8–15	38
6.20	73	20.8-10	61		
7.19	130–2	20.8-11	61	1 Chr	
7.20	131	20.11	61	1	133
7.21	131	22.19	118	1.1	90
7.22	119	31.17	64		
8–9	131, 132	31.6	99	Neh.	
8.1	131			9.6	96
8.3-5	131	Lev.			
8.15	131	5.3	106	Job	
9.4	119	11	73	7.12	59
9.5	119	11.14	73	8.7	55
9.6	96, 109, 139	11.42	49	36.27-29	24
9.10	119	11.29 RV	22	37	28
9.15	119, 132	18.23	118	37.18	28
9.18-19	148	20.15-16	118	38–42	75
9.19	131			38.7	117
9.20	140	Num.		38.8-11	132
10	131, 143 n.16, 149	13.33	132	38.9	57, 59
		14.7	76	38.34	131
10.1	47	22	48		
10.24	38	22.28	48	Ps.	
10.32	134	33.52	96	8	61, 109, 132
11	38, 93, 143 n.16			8.3-5	66
		Deut.		8.6-8	97
11.2, 4	140	2.25	131	18.16	23
11.3	140, 141	4	134	19.1	26
11.4	140	4.19	134	19.4-5	23
11.10, 27	47	4.32	134	19.5-6	20
11.31	24	4.17	28	33.7-9	132
12.5	119	14	73	51.20	55

72.9	49	23.14	96	10.34-35	26
74.13	59	32.2	59	10.34-36	25
96.10	22			20.30-31	25
103.14	121	Dan.			
104	61, 132	10.12-14	66	Acts	
104.2	22			4.15-31	134
104.2-3	23	Mic.		16–17,	
104.3	22, 23	7.17	49	37–39	134
104.5	22			16.31	158
104.9	22	Zech.		17.16-31	134
104.21, 24	75	12.1	109, 122	17.25	96, 124
111.2	13			17.26	98, 133, 134
139.13	65, 74	Mal.		17.26b	134
139.13-16	121	2.13	131	17.28	96, 134
				17.31	134, 157

Prov.
3.13-18	126
8.23-29	132

NEW TESTAMENT

Rom.
1.20	40
5.10	158
5.12	78, 120
5.12-19	29
5.12-21	75, 89, 127
5.14	117
8.19-22	79
8.19-23	77
8.22	77
8.23	98
8.29	104, 109
11.26	11
11.36	53

Eccl
1.14	81
12.7	109
12.13	81

Matt.
1.8	38
1.17	38
4.8	24
5.18	25, 26
13.24-30	80
19.4-6	135
19.8	91
22.30	117
24.29	23
24.35	25, 26
24.37-39	129

Isa.
11.6, 7	76
11.6-7	79
11.7	76
11.9	76
27.1	59
34.4	23
35.8	79 n.16
35.9	79 n.16
41.8-9	24
43.1	55
44.2	121
44.24	121
49.23	49
49.5	121
54.16	55

1 Cor.
8.6	11, 53
11.8	124, 135
11.9	89
15.22	89
15.45	89, 111, 116, 135

Mark
10	39
10.6	39, 40
13.19	39
13.31	39

Luke
3.35-36	38
3.38	89, 90, 133
11.50-51	39, 40
24.46-47	157

2 Cor.
3.18	109
4.4	104
12.2	108

Jer.
4.23	77
4.23-31	77
28.1	55
46.8	131

John
1.1-3	11, 54, 62
1.3	10
3.19-20	139
4.24	19, 96, 122
8.44	48

Eph.
4.22-24	109

Phil.
2.5	104
2.10	24

Ezek.
7.20	96

Col.		11.1-3	62	Rev.	
1.15	104			4.11	11
1.16	10, 53	Jam.		5.10	98, 105
1.16-17	53	3.9	109	6.12-14	23
1.20	79, 139			12.9, 202	48
3.9-10	109	2 Pet.			
		2.4	117	**OLD TESTAMENT**	
2 Thess.		2.5	131	**APOCRYPHA**	
2.10	139	3.6	131		
		3.8	65	Tob.	
1 Tim.				8.6	134
2.14	89	1 John			
		2.7	39	Wis.	
2 Tim.				1.13, 2.24	48
3.15-17	25	Jude		7.1	134, 134 n.4
		1.7	118		
Heb.		6	117	10.1	134, 134 n.4
4.4-9	64 n.28	14	89		
7.10	109				

SUBJECT INDEX

Page numbers followed with 'n' refer to footnotes.

Abel   39, 40, 118, 141
  descendants of   145, 146
Adam   1–3, 12–14, 17, 20, 24, 29–30, 36, 38–41, 44, 47, 49, 50, 60, 65, 75–7, 80, 85–129, 133–48, 150, 151, 154–6
  as anatomical *Homo sapiens*   60 n.26, 95, 106, 112
  Ancient   88–9, 133, 135, 140–8, 150, 151, 151 n.20
  biblical account of   20
  as common ancestor   2, 17, 111, 113, 114, 117, 136, 138, 150, 155
  creation of   44, 75, 106, 121, 123, 124, 127
  descendants of   93, 98, 109, 111, 111 n.17, 112, 116, 117, 120, 127–9, 136, 137, 155
  as first God's-image-Bearer   3, 17, 95, 113, 117, 128, 135
  formed of dust   121, 123
  as historical person   17, 89–92, 126, 127
  as *Homo divinus*   94
  as human beings   65, 75, 90, 95, 105, 106, 113, 123, 125, 129, 134, 135, 156
  literal interpretation of   126
  offspring   93, 112, 115, 120, 120 n.29, 137
  population genetics   92–3, 115
  Recent   39, 88, 133–40, 145, 146, 150, 151, 151 n.20
  sin of   75–7, 109, 125
  Symbolic   89
Against Heresies (Irenaeus)   81
agriculture   143–6
Alexander, Denis   7–12, 15, 67, 76, 79 n.16, 82, 88, 147, 155

'already existing body'   122, 123
anatomical *Homo sapiens*   3, 12, 60, 85–8, 92, 94, 94 n.9, 95, 100, 103, 106, 112, 114, 116–18, 120, 122–4, 128, 130, 133, 135–9, 145, 149–51
'anatomically modern humans'   100
Ancient Adam   88–9, 133, 135, 136, 140–8, 150, 151
Ancient Near Eastern (ANE) texts   10, 12, 17, 27, 28, 43–5, 53, 54 n.20, 59, 61, 74, 90, 91, 96, 126, 127, 147, 149
ancient science   22
ANE texts. *See* Ancient Near Eastern (ANE) texts
animalism   95, 95 n.10, 107
animals
  creation of   59–61, 121
  domestication of   146
  human beings and   104, 119, 137–8
anthropology   28
archaeological evidences   87, 143–6
Ardipithecus ramidus ramidus   85
Aristotle   22, 54 n.16, 95, 156
asah   121
asphalt for mortar   141, 142
atheistic evolution   69, 70
Atran, Scott   103, 104
Augustine of Hippo   26, 27, 41, 73–5, 108
Australopithecines   85
Averbeck, Richard   45, 52, 54, 105

baked brick   140, 142
bārā'   54–6, 59, 62, 63
Barrett, Justin   102, 104, 146
Beale, Greg   23, 57
Bealer, George   108

belief   6–7, 10, 25, 26, 35, 42, 67 n.1,
    97 n.11, 103, 155, 157
bestiality   117–20, 139
Bible   4, 4 n.4, 6–8, 10–17, 21, 24–8,
    35–7, 42, 45, 47, 53, 70, 73–82,
    91, 91 n.5, 93, 95, 129, 141, 149,
    150, 154, 156
  dates in the   91 n.5
  Divine Inspiration of   27, 42, 43, 45
  erroneous science   27
  evolution and   3, 12–14, 16, 95, 122,
    154
  evolutionary Adam model   13, 14
  inerrancy   24–7, 29
  passages, interpretation of   16, 73–82
  science and   7–12, 15, 21, 24, 26, 42,
    156
  truth   26
  YEC interpretation of   35, 36, 39, 78
biblical account   3, 12, 16, 17, 20, 29, 33,
    36, 45, 95, 127, 129, 143, 149,
    151, 154
  of Adam   20
  historicity of   127
  of human origins   29
biblical genealogies, interpretation and
    calculation of   37–40
biblical interpretation of creation
  alternative interpretations   36–7
  biblical phrases   39–40
  calculation of biblical
    genealogies   37–9
  Collins, C. John   51–2, 56, 61, 63–4
  of Genesis 1   9, 10, 45, 45 n.11, 46, 51
  of Genesis 1-2   46, 50
  of Genesis 1-3   51–65
  of Genesis 1-11   47–9
  of Genesis 2   49, 50
  non-literal   27, 41
  of opening chapters of Genesis   40–65
  plants in Genesis   49
  six days of creation   40, 41
  snake in Genesis 3   48
  Walton, John
    Functional Creation   51–65
    Seven Days of Genesis 1-2   17, 33,
      52, 57–65
  Young Earth Creationists (YEC)
    36–65

Big Bang theory   8, 8 n.7, 15
bipedalism   85, 102
Bird, Phyllis   98
Blocher, Henri   89, 127, 133, 142, 144,
    145, 150
Bronze Age   147
bronze use   140, 142, 147
Brooks, Alison S.   125, 137, 144
Brown, Andrew   40, 41, 46
Brown, William   8 n.7, 11
Brown-Driver-Briggs Hebrew
    lexicon   141

Cain   118–20, 141
  descendants of   145, 146
Calvin, John   20, 74, 79, 123
Chang, Joseph T.   3, 128, 135, 136, 150,
    155
Chardin, Pierre Teilhard de   3, 29, 92
Christian, David   3, 6, 68 n.4, 70, 72–4,
    85–8, 102, 103, 106, 140, 141,
    143–5
Christian physicalism   107, 111
Christian Theism   111, 125, 157, 158
Christian theology   96, 98, 137
climate and population densities   144, 147
Cohen, Mark   145
Collins, C. John   3, 17, 21, 22, 37, 38, 40,
    43, 48, 49, 51, 52, 56, 61, 63–4,
    80, 91, 97, 117 n.27, 121, 133,
    147, 148, 150
  Functional Creation   56, 61
  and traditional Gap Theory   63
Collins, Francis   6, 67, 69
Collins, Robin   43, 80
common ancestors   2, 2 n.2, 3, 17, 68,
    69, 71, 72, 95, 111–14, 116, 117,
    122, 123, 128–51
  Adam as   113, 114, 136, 138, 150, 155
  Noah as   136, 150
common humanity   134
Concordism   7–15, 51, 64, 132, 154
constitutionalism   95, 95 n.10, 107, 110
Copan, Paul   53, 55, 56
cosmology   7, 28, 54, 103
Coyne, Jerry   2, 3, 7, 124, 155
Craig, William Lane   2 n.3, 14, 22 n.3, 25,
    47 n.13, 49, 51, 53, 55, 56, 67,
    71, 138, 155

creation   6, 11, 14, 17, 26, 28, 30, 31,
    33–83, 153, 154, 156
  of Adam   88, 106, 121, 123, 124
  of animals   59–61, 121
  Biblical interpretation of (see Biblical
    interpretation of creation)
  of dry land   58, 73
  of Eve   44, 120–4, 135 n.6
  and evolution   67, 71, 80, 82, 122,
    124, 153
  in Genesis   46 n.11, 131
  of heaven and earth   39, 40, 55–6, 61
  of human beings   65, 74, 120–4
  material   52, 53, 55, 56
  of period of light   57
  reasons for taking billions of years
    for   65–6
  of sea   59
  six days of   40, 41, 54, 54 n.20
  of space between heaven and earth
    57–8
  of species   73, 83
  of spiritual properties   125
  of sun, moon and stars   58–9
  of universe   36, 40, 70, 82
creation ex nihilo   53, 53 n.19, 57, 62, 64
Creationism   11, 67–83, 85, 108–10,
    108 n.16, 111, 116, 154, 156

Darwin, Charles   70, 71, 78, 80–1, 99,
    101
  evolution   82, 107
  human-animal continuity   99
  natural selection   81
  survival of the fittest   81, 82
dating of Adam to Noah   133–48
dating stars   34
Davis, Ted   7, 8
Dawkins, Richard   3, 7, 67, 72
Day, John   3, 58, 61
death   13, 44, 45 n.11, 47, 75–9, 81,
    92, 108, 120 n.30, 122, 125,
    157
defence   1–4, 47, 71, 78, 153
degeneration   119, 142, 145, 146
deistic evolution   69
Denisovans   87, 100
De Principiis IV (Origen)   41, 89

descendants of Adam   75, 80, 98, 109,
    111, 111 n.17, 112, 116, 117,
    120, 127–9, 137, 143, 155
Dillard, Raymond   29, 44, 45, 45 n.11, 46,
    47, 148
Divine Accommodation   16, 19–31, 36,
    154
  arguments for   22
  two views   20–30
Divine Inspiration of Bible   42, 43, 45
Divine Inspiration of Scripture, doctrine
    of   13, 154
Divino Afflante Spiritu (Pius XII)   9
division of labour   102, 141
DNA   11, 13, 35, 72, 87, 93 n.7, 100, 110,
    111, 115
domestication of animals   146
Drummond, Celia Deane   68 n.3
dualism   53, 96, 107–8, 110, 111, 114,
    114 n.22, 116, 118
Durbin, Richard   93

Earth   5–7, 12, 13, 20–5, 21 n.2, 29, 33,
    34 n.1, 34 n.3, 35–7, 39–41, 46,
    49, 52–63, 65, 69, 73–7, 79, 88,
    94, 96–9, 102, 104, 106, 116,
    120, 121, 124, 127, 131–4, 138,
    140, 141, 143, 148, 156, 157
Ellis, George   5
Enki   44
Enns, Peter   12, 13, 20, 30, 36, 92, 138
Enuma Elish   43, 45–6, 57
'Evangelical Christians'   3, 4, 4 n.4, 67,
    153
Eve   1, 2, 39, 40, 44, 50, 74, 76–7, 89, 93,
    95–110, 112–15, 120, 123–7,
    133, 134, 136, 139
  creation and Genesis 2.7   49, 54, 65,
    90, 109, 120–3
  sin of   76, 125–7
evolution   2–5, 7–17, 29, 30, 66–83,
    85–128
  and Bible   3, 12–14, 16, 122, 154
  creation and   67, 71, 80, 82, 122, 124,
    153
  defined   2 n.2, 68
  evidences for   17, 71–2, 85
  of human (see human evolution)

and interpretation of Bible
    passages   73–82
  undirected   69–71
Evolutionary Creationism   39, 67–83, 85,
    88, 89, 122, 141
evolutionary evils   17, 78, 80, 83
evolutionary population genetics   1–3,
    17, 92–5, 111, 112, 115, 116,
    127–30, 148–51, 155, 156
evolutionary process   10, 17, 29, 70, 71,
    78, 80, 114, 121, 122, 125, 153,
    155
experimental science   35
Ezra, Ibn   54, 62

Falk, Darrel   93 n.7
Flood   17, 18, 28, 34, 38, 47, 73, 91, 93,
    117, 129–33, 138, 140, 146–51
  extent of   130–3
  Neolithic dating of   140, 146–7
  Noah   17, 34 n.3, 93, 129, 130, 132,
    140, 148, 150–1
Franke, John   27
Functional Creation   17, 40, 41, 51–65

GAE model. *See* Genealogical Adam and
    Eve (GAE) model
Galileo   14, 21, 36, 37, 156
Garden of Eden   44, 47, 53, 57, 60, 74–6,
    94, 121, 126, 138, 147, 155
Garraghan, Gilbert   50
Genealogical Adam and Eve (GAE)
    model   2, 14, 111–16, 145, 155
genealogical ancestry   112–14, 116,
    135–6, 155
generation of humans after Adam and
    Eve   107–10
Genesis narratives   89
Genesis Rabbah   62
geocentricism   37
'Gilgamesh Epic'   44, 147, 148, 150
Gingerich, Owen   67, 69–71
'God forbid'   137
God's Image-Bearer model   94–5, 98,
    100, 101, 106, 117–18, 120, 122,
    128, 130–3, 136, 139, 149
  Genealogical Adam and Eve (GAE)
    model   2, 14, 111–16, 145, 155

Gordon, B. L.   34
Gospel of Matthew   129
Gould, Stephen Jay   6, 10
gradual evolution of humans   124–5, 155
Gray, Asa   69, 78
Green, William   38
Greenway, Tyler   99, 102, 104, 146
Grudem, Wayne   26, 69, 71, 106, 109,
    118, 121, 123, 124

Haarsma, Deborah   35, 71, 72, 133
Ham, Ken   13, 34 n.4, 35, 61, 72 n.10, 76,
    77, 148, 149
Hamilton, Victor   49, 53, 138
Hanson, Anthony   26
Hanson, Richard   26
Harari, Yuval Noah   3, 103–4, 157
Harlow, Daniel   3, 44, 44 n.10, 49, 147
Harris, Mark   23, 62, 81, 89, 91 n.5, 92,
    96, 156
Hart, David Bentley   3, 89, 107
Hawking, Stephen   7
heaven   20–3, 25, 27, 28, 39–41, 46, 50,
    53, 55–9, 61, 62, 66, 77, 80, 97,
    99, 130, 131, 140
hermeneutical principles   9, 10, 15, 16,
    37, 43, 64, 89, 126, 154, 156
Hess, Richard   28, 73, 83, 97
historical science   35–6
Hoekema, Anthony   96, 104, 109, 139
hominids   79, 92, 94, 99, 101, 103, 105,
    117, 123, 125
hominins   85, 88, 93, 100
Homo divinus   12, 13, 94
Homo erectus   86, 99, 100, 101
Homo floresiensis   86–7, 100, 101
Homo habilis   85–6
Homo heidelbergensis   86
Homo luzonensis   87
Homo naledi   86–7
Homo neanderthalensis   86, 99, 100, 101
Homo sapiens   1, 3, 12, 33, 60, 85–8,
    92–5, 94 n.9, 99, 100, 103,
    106, 112, 115–18, 120, 122–4,
    127, 128, 130, 133, 135–9, 145,
    149–51, 155
  populations   1, 86, 92–3, 115, 127
Houck, Daniel   2, 117

human/human beings   139
  and animals   104, 118, 119, 122, 137–8
  behaviour   144
    characteristics of   137
  capacity for religious thought   103
  Christian theology   137
  creation of   30, 33, 40, 50, 59, 65, 74, 120–4
  defined   95
  evolution   3, 17, 85–128, 145, 153, 154
    Christian responses to   88–92
    gradual   124–5
    religion as a by-product of   103
    scientific data   85–7
    symbolic language   102
  formed of dust   54, 121
  as God's representatives and agents   96
  language   86, 102, 119, 143–4, 143 n.16
  origins   1–20, 24, 29, 31, 47, 92, 125, 134, 155, 156
  revolution   144
  rights   104
  unique capacities   69, 82, 97–9, 101, 102, 104, 109, 111, 112, 114, 115, 119, 123, 139
Humani Generis (Pius XII)   4, 29, 122
humanity   1, 3, 18, 24, 30, 39, 40, 49, 51, 58, 66, 74, 76, 80, 83, 87, 91, 96–7, 102, 122, 134, 137, 153, 156–8
humanness   124–5
Hurtado, L.   62

image of God   3, 6, 13, 29, 40, 60, 65, 79, 82, 94–106, 109, 111–19, 121–5, 127, 128, 130, 137, 138, 150, 154, 155, 157
  Adam as possession of   112–13
  anatomical *Homo* to possessing the   3, 105, 106, 116–17, 127, 128, 138
  command to human beings   75, 76, 97
  functional aspect   59, 104–5, 109
  generation of souls   111
  giving the unique capacities to human beings   98–9
  human beings
    and animals   104, 118, 119, 122, 137–8
    capacity for religious thought   103
    as God's representatives and agents   96–8, 101, 105, 106, 116, 125, 127, 138
    unique capacities   69, 82, 97–9, 101, 102, 104, 109, 111, 112, 114, 115, 119, 123, 139
  qualities   111, 114, 115, 119
  representative view   96–7
  resemblance in capacities   96–7
  structural aspect   47, 104–5
incarnation   99, 108, 111, 118
interdisciplinarity   2
Irenaeus   26, 41, 81
iron use   140, 142, 147

Jesus Christ   13, 24, 25, 25 nn.4–5, 25 n.8, 26, 27, 39, 53, 81, 89, 90, 92, 98, 104–6, 111 n.17, 117, 117 n.27, 119, 127, 129, 130 n.1, 134, 138, 139, 157
John's Gospel, author of   62

Kant, Immanuel   97
Keener, Craig   108, 134
Keil, C. F.   141
Kemp, K. W.   113 n.20
Kepler, Johannes   20–1, 21 n.2
Kidner, Derek   23
Kingsley, Charles   71
Kitchen, Kenneth   45, 49, 50 n.14
Koons, Robert   108
Korsgaard, Christine   97

Lambert, W. G.   44
Lamoureux, Denis   4, 20, 23–4, 27, 28, 30, 36, 58, 121–2
laws of Mendelian inheritance   115
Lennox, John   9–10, 42, 51
Letter of Aristeas   21–2
Leviticus   21–2, 73
Lewis, C. S.   126
Li, Heng   93
Lilith   135 n.6

The Literal Meaning of Genesis
    (Augustine)   74, 75
living creature   59, 60, 73, 82, 119, 120,
    122, 123, 132
Loke, Andrew   1–18, 22 n.3, 24, 28, 37,
    47, 49, 51–3, 57, 58, 66, 70, 78,
    81, 104, 108, 108 n.16, 110,
    111 n.17, 117, 122, 125, 135 n.7,
    138, 139 n.12, 140, 153, 156, 157
Lombard, Peter   41, 108
Longman III, Tremper   29, 44–7, 126,
    148, 150
Loose, Jonathan   3, 95 n.10, 107, 110

McBrearty, Sally   125, 137, 144
McFarland, Ian   3, 92, 106, 108, 109, 114
McGrath, Alister   14, 73
McGrath, Gavin Basil   74–6, 94, 142
McKnight, Scot   1, 4 n.4, 8, 12–13, 30, 89
Madueme, Hans   113
material creation   52–3, 55–6, 61
Matthean Jesus   129
May, Gerhard   53 n.19
merism, Semitic   55, 55 n.23
Mesopotamian mythology   44
methodological naturalistic evolution   70
Middleton, Richard   96, 97, 143 n.16
migration   3, 35, 135, 136, 144, 146, 150
Minton, Ron   40
'Mitochondrial Eve'   93, 112, 114
mitochondrial inheritance   115
Moberly, Walter   40
modern human brain   103
Monism   95, 107, 110, 114–16
monotheism   53, 103
morality   6, 104, 157
Moreland, J. P.   47 n.13, 66 n.29, 67, 71,
    80 n.18, 107, 110, 111
Moritz, Joshua   3, 80, 96, 98–101, 119,
    121
Morris, Henry   130
Morris, Simon Conway   70 n.5
Morris, Thomas   65
Mortenson, Terry   38–40, 77
Mosaic Law   120
Most Recent Common Ancestor
    (MRCA)   39, 116, 128, 135,
    136, 150
multidisciplinarity   2

Murray, John   123
Murray, Michael   78–9

naturalistic world view   47
natural selection   2, 68, 81
Neanderthals   86–7, 100, 106, 117
Neolithic Adam. *See* Ancient Adam
'the Nephilim'   132
Newman, John Henry   71
Ninhursag   44
Noah   17, 18, 47, 73, 93, 129–35, 140,
    148–9
  as common ancestor   136, 150
  descendants   18, 148–50
  Flood   17, 34, 93, 129, 132, 148,
    150–1
  sons of   148, 149
non-human anatomical *Homo*   94, 95,
    111, 117–21, 128, 130, 139, 149,
    150
non-human animals   80, 99, 101, 137,
    138

offspring   68, 93, 111, 112, 115, 117, 120,
    123, 134, 137
Old Earth   35, 39, 88, 141
Olson, Steve   3, 96, 128, 135, 136, 150,
    155
Origen   19, 27, 41, 51, 88, 89
Original Guilt   110
Original Sin   29, 110, 139
  doctrine of   89, 109, 110, 156, 157
origins
  human   1–4, 6, 7, 16, 17, 19, 20, 24,
    29, 31, 47, 92, 125, 134, 155, 156
  of sin and the fall   125–7
Osborn, E.   53 n.19

Palaeolithic   35, 103, 140, 142
Paul   92, 134–5
Peels, Rick   66, 80, 81
personal responsibility   97, 98
personhood   97, 98, 138, 151 n.20
Philo of Alexandria   41, 49, 51
philosophy
  science and   5–7
  theology and   7
physicalism   107, 107 n.15, 110, 111
physical neurological processes   114

physics   6, 7, 11, 108, 157
Pius XII, Pope   3, 4, 9, 29, 69, 122
Plantinga, Alvin   67, 71, 78, 139 n.12
Plotkin, Henry   143
population
　genetics   1–3, 17, 92–3, 95, 111, 112, 115, 116, 127–30, 148–51, 155, 156
　isolation   136
　subdivision   3, 135
post-Mosaic glosses   45, 45 n.11
pre-existence   107, 108
Provan, Iain   39, 74, 76

Quran   8, 30

radiometric dating of rocks   34
Rae, Scott   110, 111
Ramm, Bernard   7
rationality   138
rationalization   36
Recent Adam   39, 88, 133–40, 145, 146, 150, 151. *See also* Ancient Adam
Reich, David   87, 100
religion   1, 7, 13, 15, 78, 81, 83, 103, 141, 157, 158
　science and   1, 6–7, 10, 15, 18, 153, 155, 157, 158
Retractationes (Augustine)   108
revelatory insights   62, 63
rib   44, 124
Robinson, Marilynne   42
Rohde, Douglas   3, 128, 135, 136, 150, 155
Rosenhouse, Jason   3, 94, 139, 140
Ross, Hugh   8, 14, 34 n.4, 40, 51, 57, 59, 61, 77, 89, 131–3, 141, 142, 147 n.19
Rusbult, Craig   36, 37, 93 n.6, 143
Ruse, Michael   1, 3, 4, 71, 93, 114
Russman, H.   12

salvation   25, 27, 99, 139 n.13, 157
Sandy, Brent   10
Sarna, Nahum   3, 54, 55, 57, 132
Schloss, Jeffrey P.   80, 138
science   1–16, 5 n.6, 18, 19, 21, 22, 26, 27, 29, 31, 33, 35, 36, 41–3, 46, 69, 70, 72, 74, 90, 92, 93, 95, 113, 114, 116, 123, 125, 128, 142, 143, 153–8
　and Bible   4, 7–12, 15, 21, 24, 26, 42, 95
　and philosophy   5–7
　and religion   1, 6–7, 10, 15, 18, 153, 155, 157, 158
　and theology   7, 10
scientific errors   4 n.4, 16, 20, 21, 24, 30, 31, 154, 156
scientific evidences   10, 17, 33–7, 95, 119, 132, 145, 149
scientific theory, criteria for   5
scientism   4, 5, 5 n.6
Seely, Paul   36, 130, 131, 140–2, 142 n.15
Semitic merism   55, 55 n.24
Sentences (Lombard)   41
serpent   48, 125
Seven Days of Genesis 1   51, 57, 64, 75
Sexton, Jeremy   38, 39
sin   12, 29, 79, 80, 92, 110, 117, 120 n.31, 125, 127, 139, 156, 157
　of Adam   75–7, 109, 125–7
　of Eve   125
　origin and the fall   125–7
small-group religions   103
Sollereder, Bethany   12 n.7, 79–82, 101, 139
Solomon's prayer   23
soul   3, 29, 69, 82, 89, 95, 96, 98, 107–12, 114–16, 118, 119, 122, 123, 139
　and body   108
spiritual mechanism   111, 112, 115
starlight from faraway galaxies   34
Stenmark, Mikael   4 n.5, 5
Stoeger, William   7
Stott, John   38, 67, 94
Stringer, Chris   87, 133, 144, 147
strong naturalistic evolution   69
Stump, Jim   7, 51, 67, 76
Suarez, Antoine   113 n.20, 133
substance dualism   107–8, 110–12, 114–16, 118
suffering   65, 76, 78, 79, 81, 82, 101, 125, 139, 157
Sumerian myth   44
survival of the fittest   81, 82
Swamidass, S. Joshua   2, 113, 113 n.20, 121, 123, 136
Symbolic Adam   89
symbolic human language   102

theistic evolution   2, 67, 69, 70
theodicy   78, 156
theology   2, 6, 7, 10, 15, 28, 36, 44, 57, 78, 83, 96, 98, 108, 109, 122, 137–8
theory of evolution   2, 14, 30, 74
Thomson, Keith   68
tōhû wābōhû   57, 63, 77
Tower of Babel   140, 142, 143
traditional Gap theory   63
Traducianism   107–10, 108 n.16, 111, 115, 116, 153
transdisciplinary approach   15, 153
   for human origins   1–4
   use of   4–7
Tree of Knowledge of Good and Evil   125–7
Tree of Life   120 n.31, 126, 127
tselem   96, 96 n.11
Turretin, Francis   109

universe   6, 7, 9, 10, 17, 20, 23, 24, 33–5, 42, 53, 54, 61, 63, 64, 66, 68–70, 81, 82, 104, 125, 153, 157
   creation of   36, 40
Ussher, James   38

van Baaren, Theodorus   103
Van Huyssteen, J. Wentzel   3, 96, 99, 102, 103, 105
Van Kuiken, Jerome   118, 134
Venema, Dennis   1, 4, 8, 30, 89, 93 n.7, 112, 136–7

Waltke, Bruce   51, 74
Walton, John   3, 10, 17, 28, 37, 39 n.9, 40, 43, 44, 48, 51, 54 n.21, 60 n.27, 67, 75, 76, 88, 89, 92, 106, 117, 120, 120 n.31, 121, 124, 126, 127, 131–4, 143, 143 n.16, 149, 150, 154
   different uses of the word 'ādām   90 n.4
   Functional Creation   51–65
   Seven Days of Genesis 1-2   52, 57–65
Waters, Guy   90, 91, 156
Waw-Consecutive-Imperfective   50 n.15
wayyiqtol   56, 63
weak naturalistic evolution   68
weaving and pottery   144
Wenham, Gordon   27, 28, 30, 47–8, 58, 117, 132, 138
Wenham, John   50
Wesley, John   79
Westermann, C.   3, 45, 46, 51, 54 n.20, 55, 62
Whitcomb, John   130
Wielandt, Rotraud   9
Wilkinson, David   41, 51
Williams, Rowan   3, 42, 43, 89, 90
Woodbridge, John   25, 26
Wright, N. T.   50–1

yatsar   121, 122
'Y-chromosome Adam'   93, 112, 114
Y-chromosome inheritance   115
YEC. See Young Earth Creationists (YEC)
'young earth'   36
Young Earth Creationists (YEC)   7, 34 n.4, 35–40, 42, 51, 52, 61, 62, 75, 76, 78, 80, 88, 130, 132, 137
   interpretation of the Bible   36–65

ziggurat   140

www.ingramcontent.com/pod-product-compliance
Lightning Source LLC
Chambersburg PA
CBHW061833300426
44115CB00013B/2366